HUMAN AND
DIVINE AGENCY

Anglican, Catholic, and
Lutheran Perspectives

F. Michael McLain
W. Mark Richardson

University Press of America,® Inc.
Lanham • New York • Oxford

Copyright © 1999 by
University Press of America,® Inc.
4720 Boston Way
Lanham, Maryland 20706

12 Hid's Copse Rd.
Cumnor Hill, Oxford OX2 9JJ

ISBN 0-7618-1470-1 (cloth: alk. ppr.)
ISBN 0-7618-1471-X (pbk: alk. ppr.)

Contents

Acknowledgments

All but two of these papers were presented at a conference entitled, Freedom of the Will and Its Significance for Theology, held at the Center for Theology and the Natural Sciences in Berkeley, California, January 4–7, 1992. The conference was made possible in part by the generous contribution of V. Glenn and Nancy Crosby. The Center's staff facilitated a memorable occasion. Some of the papers were subsequently published as noted below.

The editors are indebted to Kevin Barré, Kirk Bingaman, and Karen Winterton for superb manuscript preparation. We thank the editors at UPA for their encouragement and patience.

Resources for the preparation and publication of the volume were contributed by the Rhodes College Department of Religious Studies and its office of the Academic Dean, as well as funds associated with the R.A. Webb Chair of Religious Studies.

Several of the essays reflect the inspiration and influence of Austin Farrer's philosophical theology. We hope the publication of this volume will contribute to continuing interest in Farrer's work.

Parts of chapter 1 appeared in section 4 of "Freedom and Good in the Thomistic Tradition," in *Faith and Philosophy* (July 1994): 414-435.

Chapter 3 appeared as "Predestination as a Condition of Freedom," in *Lutheran Quarterly* 12 (1998): 57-78.

Chapter 10 appeared as "Aquinas on the Sufferings of Job," in *Reasoned Faith*, ed. Eleonore Stump. (c) 1975 by Cornell University Press.

Chapter 11 appeared as "Must Job Live Forever? :A Reply to Aquinas on Providence," in *The Thomist* 62 (1998): 1-39. (c) 1998 by The Thomist Press.

Introduction
F. Michael McLain

The renaissance of philosophical attention to religion has tended to focus on the justification of religious belief and fine-grained analyses of a small group of issues central to classical theism. The commendable rigor of much of this work has the unfortunate consequence of restricting readership to a relatively small group of professionals. More problematic still is a tendency noted by Thomas Tracy in his essay on evil in this volume. Tracy observes that much recent "philosophical discussion has tended to abstract the problem of evil from its religious and theological context. The resulting debate, while sometimes exquisitely clever, is often of dubious relevance to the religious traditions which spawned the problem in the first place."

This volume seeks to avoid these tendencies by locating a fundamental metaphysical issue, freedom of the will, in the context of those theological topics for which free will is of central concern: the nature of the person and God, salvation, and the reality of evil in the world. Without sacrifice of rigor, the essayists write for a wide audience interested in contemporary discussion of matters central to the Western theological tradition.

The essays were presented first at a conference entitled "Freedom of the Will and Its Significance for Theology." This was the fifth conference to give attention to themes basic to the work of the noted English philosophical theologian and interpreter of scripture, Austin Farrer. Farrer combined a remarkably full and rich grasp of theological traditions with an equally remarkable ability to imaginatively present traditional concerns to a wide contemporary audience. Written in something of the same spirit, a number of the conference essays display an indebtedness to Farrer, as well as an extension of insights he first contributed.

A range of theological concerns, the most important of which the essays address, involves the theme of free will. Yet "free will" invites the obvious and basic questions: What is it? and Do we have it? Since the work of Gilbert Ryle and Ludwig Wittgenstein, a philosophical consensus has emerged that any attempt to answer such questions must recognize that there are yet prior ones to be considered. It is *actions* which are free (or not) and *agents* who perform them freely (or not). Austin Farrer, whose Gifford Lectures bear the title *Freedom of the Will*, recognized the importance of these questions and offered his proposal about action and agency in his Giffords. In lucid, summary terms, Mark Richardson locates, describes, and assesses Farrer's contribution in the context of the Anglo-Saxon discussion of action and agency.

Richardson finds noteworthy Farrer's account of the person as a unified being with the distinctive power of intentional action freely undertaken. Although he is not entirely sanguine about Farrer's success in defending freedom within this unified account of the self, he focuses our attention on the use Farrer made of agency in his account of the formation and sustaining of theistic belief. The shape of thought about God required by religious practice, Farrer believed, is that of a perfect agent with whom the believer interacts. Thus, unlike much Western thought, Farrer departs from a mind-body, dualistic view of the human person as the appropriate model for conceiving God.

Brian Hebblethwaite and Edward Henderson explain Farrer's idea of God in relation to classical theism and situate it in the context of current debate about the nature of God. Hebblethwaite's reflection draws on Farrer and Hans Urs von Balthasar to compare finite and infinite freedom. He deftly navigates the shoals between assimilating divine freedom to a libertarian model and a disjunctive account of divine action as necessitated. The narrow channel between these alternatives is negotiated with the aid of a model of artistic creativity. The practical upshot of Hebblethwaite's analysis is a glimpse of how finite human freedom is fulfilled through participation in God's infinite, creative freedom. Henderson's contribution serves as an excellent introduction to Farrer's philosophical theology. In *The Supremely Free Agent*, he argues that Farrer used the analogy of the self as personal agent to unite the transcendence of God in traditional thought with a process emphasis on God's real relatedness to the world. From our lived experience as free agents, we can form the idea of a perfect, unconditioned will, free to limit itself in relation to, and dependence upon, the world's constituents. In his later thought, Farrer attempted to bring the lived belief of religious practitioners in a God with whom they interact into line with philosophical reflection on the divine being. In Henderson's judgment he succeeds by conceiving God as the supremely free agent.

Farrer believed that human agents as he understood them possess libertarian freedom. To the question, Do we have free will?, he gave a resounding Yes. Furthermore, he was convinced that the adequate treatment of the range of theological topics considered in this volume requires this response. Steven Duncan agrees. Arguing along lines congenial to Farrer, Duncan addresses the reality of free will from the experience of the agent herself, resisting efforts to assimilate this perspective to that of an external observer, the perspective which dominates the academy and culture of the modern scientific world. A libertarian construal of free action as intentionally performed by the agent and not causally determined by the circumstances in which she acts, evaporates, notes Duncan, when the objective point of view replaces the agent's inside account of her action. His judicious defense of the truth of the agent's account takes the form of an attempt to establish a presumption in its favor.

Libertarian free agency, as discussed by Richardson and defended by Duncan, is the theological focus of most of the remaining essays. It is a matter of controversy, both historically and in contemporary discussion, as to whether such freedom is crucial in our relationship with God. Divine initiative for our salvation, God's grace, and the ordering of ongoing events, divine providence, raise obvious and contested issues when placed in relation to human freedom. If the exercise of free choice is a condition of our salvation, the necessity of grace is unclear and the omnipotence of divine providence is called into question.

The volume first locates such theological concerns in the historical contexts which gave lasting shape to subsequent discussion. The Protestant Reformers, notably Martin Luther, were less concerned with the metaphysical question of freedom than the role of free will in the economy of divine salvation. Luther boldly denied the significance of free will for salvation in the light of his reading of the Christian gospel. While agreeing on this point, Kyle Pasewark and Elizabeth Galbraith give interestingly divergent accounts of Luther's wisdom in doing so. For Luther, claims Pasewark, the irrelevance of human freedom for our salvation is the necessary condition of turning in disinterested service to the neighbor. True liberty is freedom *from* the need to establish fundamental meaning in human life through decisions we must make, and, argues Pasewark, the idea of meaning secured independent of autonomous human action is the enduring legacy of Luther.

On Pasewark's interpretation, Galbraith seems correct in her contention that scholarly views of Luther as the precursor of Kantian autonomy are misplaced. She claims that Kant's true kindred spirit was Luther's opponent, Erasmus, who found it imperative to give human freedom a place in the economy of salvation if our dignity is to be preserved. So Kant, whose primary concern was to save human autonomy and responsibility from every form of necessitation, whether by nature or God, stood in an important *religious* tradition when he insisted upon the importance of free human cooperation with divine grace in achieving salvation.

A second historically rich theological issue is taken up by John Wright and Thomas Loughran. If the sovereignty of divine grace imperils the autonomy of human subjects, so at first glance, does the imperative of divine providence. Few are the theologians, ancient or modern, who have addressed this recondite issue with the care of Thomas Aquinas. Wright, the noted Jesuit scholar, summarizes in straightforward terms his considered view that Aquinas sought to reconcile libertarian freedom with providential control of human affairs. He does not convince Loughran who offers a compatibilist account of Aquinas' reflections on free choice and providence. On a compatibilist view our free actions may, or even must, be causally determined, even if free. There is no incompatibility in claiming, on such views, that an action is determined by God or nature, yet the result of the agent's free choice. Such actions are ones for which we are responsible and which may be known by providential omniscience.

Interestingly, Galbraith ends her essay with the thought that Kant (and Farrer) cannot escape a compatibilist account of human freedom. However, it is the contention of numerous writers that no successful account of divine existence in the face of evil can survive the erosion of libertarian freedom. If God determines our free and responsible actions, there should be manifestly fewer and less extreme instances of humanly perpetrated evil, if any at all.

This point sets the stage for all of the essays in the final section. Thomas Tracy is persuaded initially that libertarian freedom is vital to a plausible response to evil in a providentially governed world. However, after reflection on the conditioning of freedom by the circumstances in which an agent acts, Tracy opines that the imperative of grace requires a nod in the direction of the compatibilist's basic point. At the end of the day, Tracy suggests, divine grace may be irresistible after all, if God's purpose shall triumph. Echoes of Luther can be heard in his interesting proposal to resolve the seeming requirements of grace, freedom and providence.

Strategies to defend God in the face of evil, the so-called free will defense, in particular, betray a distinctly modern preoccupation with apparently undeserved human suffering. If we assume that human fulfillment is to be found in this life, as moderns typically do, the question of such suffering haunts the imagination. Aquinas sees it differently, and Eleonore Stump invites us to join him in looking at evil while holding the belief that happiness occurs in relation to God in a life after death. For Aquinas, evil does not so much call into question God's goodness (or existence) as it require us to reflect on the nature and operations of divine providence. Stump's eloquent account of Aquinas attempts to loosen the hold of modernity's prejudice while softening the strangeness of his medieval worldview.

In his critique of Aquinas, Timothy Jackson finds much to admire in Stump's effort to rehabilitate Aquinas for serious modern consideration. Jackson's minimalist reading of theology's contemporary prospects, however, requires him in the last analysis to disconsole it of the dogmatic certitude Aquinas' view requires. On the contrary, it is Jackson's contention that those who can and will "put agape first" have no need for an afterlife to avoid meaninglessness or malice. Minimal belief in charity as participation in the life of God is its own reward and, perhaps, a sufficient justification for God's creation of a world rife with evil. In a curious way, Luther's updated voice is audible once again.

In the concluding essay of the volume, Margaret Falls-Corbitt mines the theological tradition to clarify the issues surrounding the agent's choice of evil. She displays considerable sympathy, however paradoxical it may sound, for the Pauline-Augustinian view that we are capable of and, alas, responsible for doing wrong knowingly. While following her argument, the reader will want to keep focused the issue of libertarian freedom. Whatever the merits of compatibilism, the thought that God might necessitate the knowing choice of moral evil will surely cause the reader to ponder. Falls-Corbitt's essay and the others intersect and overlap in ways provocative enough to keep the serious reader engaged for a very long time indeed.

Section I:
A Historical Look at the Problem:
Aquinas and Luther

Chapter 1

Aquinas, Compatibilist

Thomas J. Loughran

What possible reason could there be for God who is good and almighty to permit the sin, suffering, and even ultimate failure of creatures He loves? Without supposing that St. Thomas posed the question in quite this way, it is fair to say that interpreters of St. Thomas in the 20th century have been intensely interested in this question, and have been driven by it to explore what seem to be tensions in and among Aquinas' accounts of human freedom, divine providence, and the goodness of God. The works of three such interpreters have been made widely available, and a brief overview of each of their approaches will serve as an introduction to the perceived tensions in Aquinas' thought.

One interpretive direction for resolving those tensions, a self-styled traditional Thomist view popularized in this century by Reginald Garrigou-Lagrange, has anchored itself firmly in the causal certitude of providence.[1] While it insists that no sum of natural causal antecedents to choice determine how or whether the will chooses, the Thomist view (following in the tradition of Dominic Bañez) holds that God moves the will through an internal physical premotion, applying it to determinate acts without violating its freedom. Although they are adamant that God does not will that sin occur, these interpreters hold that whether or not a creature freely sins follows inevitably from the sort of help which God (logically prior to any foreknowledge of merit) chooses to give to that creature; sin follows inevitably when merely sufficient rather than efficacious help is given as the creature's will is determinately applied to its act. God determines of Himself for mysterious purposes which human beings will be saved and which permitted to remain lost. Hence the Thomist reading of the relation of providence to creaturely freedom seems in tension with the claim that God desires the salvation of all, and thus with the doctrine of divine goodness.

Rejecting this perceived assault on "the absolute innocence of God," Jacques Maritain proposed after more than six centuries an apparently fresh reading of Aquinas which far more fully assuages libertarian intuitions about freedom.[2] Moored in the very deep waters of a two-tiered metaphysic, Maritain generally accommodates what Aquinas says about causation by referring it to the line of being, even while he distances God from causal responsibility for sin by interjecting between divine causal stimulus and creaturely sinful response free initiatives in a newly discovered line of nonbeing. By thus inserting the metaphysic of nothingness, Maritain seems to accommodate libertarian intuitions about freedom while championing divine innocence. But Maritain's view affords a remarkably different purchase on the causal certitude of providence and specifically on the doctrine of predestination than do traditional Thomist readings. Sympathetic modern readers of Aquinas may be glad to have the teaching of the angelic doctor cut free of such devilish entanglements. But such freedom comes at a price: Maritain's view seems to require a being who is pure act to react either to what He somehow knows free creatures would do, or to what He sees them actually do. Either way, Aquinas' account of God's knowledge does not seem to provide the resources needed to sustain such a reading.[3]

Bernard Lonergan offered a third significantly different interpretation of Aquinas on these matters, arguing forcefully against the account of God's operation which both Garrigou-Lagrange and Maritain accepted.[4] Lonergan proposed an account on which God operates through creatures by creating beings with causal powers and sustaining their existence in the context of a complex causal network intended to produce whatever of being and act follows from it. God controls the activity of each creature not by an immediate determining activation of its causal powers–the Bañezian reading of activation adopted by both Garrigou-Lagrange and Maritain–but rather by placing a complete set of mutually ordered created causes from which the acts of each created being follow determinately. Only the acts of free creatures have a measure of independence from this causal order. Insofar as they cooperate with Him, God moves free creatures, too, by situating them in a complete set of causal circumstances, but free creatures are capable of voluntary refusal to cooperate with that order and thus with its Author. This refusal is unintelligible, absolute objective falsity. It is the source of a third category of relations between the will of God and created effects: in addition to those effects which occur because God wills, and those which do not occur because God wills that they do not, there are effects which are permitted to occur. Sinful acts of free creatures alone make up the latter category of created effects. Whether a free creature's actions fall into the first or the third category is determined by the creature, not by God; Lonergan adopts Dom

Odon Lottin's thesis that Aquinas' thought about the nature of creaturely freedom underwent a fundamental change some time prior to the writing of the *De Malo*, a change away from intellectual determinism to a
new-found freedom of the will. That theory of change turns out to have
far less evidence in its favor than its advocates initially hoped.[5]

Lonergan's treatment of Aquinas' theory of operation poses a significant challenge to the readings of Maritain and Garrigou-Lagrange; the
criticism of the theory that Thomas's teaching on the will underwent fundamental change places Lonergan's reading in question, as well. These
weaknesses leave the three interpretive vessels listing but not yet cap-
sized. No interpretive account can be overturned in the absence of a more
promising rival account. As I read the texts of Aquinas and the state of
the discussion among his interpreters, an alternative interpretation suggests itself. My impression is that traditional interpreters left Aquinas'
account of the relationships among human freedom, providence, and
divine goodness inadequately defended, while Maritain and Lonergan
with fair intention subverted it, because their readings were hampered by
libertarian intuitions about human freedom which Aquinas did not share.

Understanding Aquinas' account of freedom in compatibilist terms
reveals greater coherence in his account of the nature of human freedom
and the role our freedom plays in the created order than do accounts
infected with libertarian notions of freedom. Once the compatibilist
conception of freedom is comprehended, it functions like a lens of superior clarity through which other aspects of Aquinas' thought concerning
the created order can be seen afresh. Accordingly, our first task is to
craft the lens itself: a compatibilist conception of freedom will be
ground from the material available in Aquinas' writing on the will, its
acts, and their causes in a way unclouded by the apparent tensions
between causality and freedom which libertarian intuitions introduce.
Then grasping the compatibilist lens, we will see through it a coherent
account of the high purpose in the plan of providence for free creatures.
Finally, we will observe coherence in Aquinas' account of the permission of sin and even the ultimate failure of free creatures through the
perspective afforded by compatibilist freedom.

The Human Will, Its Acts, and Their Causes: A Compatibilist Rendering

A compatibilist understanding of freedom reveals an account of the
will, its acts, and their causes unclouded by perceived tensions between
the freedom of the will and its determination by the universal causal
order in which the will is moved to act. Libertarian readers find tensions

between the apparent determinism of the causal order within which the will and intellect operate, and the clear rejection of necessitation of the will's acts found consistently throughout Aquinas' writings on the will. To avoid what seems to libertarians to be a contradiction, they make distinctions: Garrigou-Lagrange, between natural and supernatural causal antecedents to choice (no sum of the former but only the latter determine the will *ad unum*); Maritain, between the line of being (which operates causally) and the line of nonbeing (in which intelligent creatures can freely and culpably resist cooperating with any and all natural and supernatural causal antecedents to choice); Lonergan, between earlier (deterministic) and later (nondeterministic) accounts of the will. All these interpreters have looked past a clear alternative for resolving this apparent tension between determinism and freedom in Aquinas: reading the texts on freedom along compatibilist lines. One reason for looking past the compatibilist alternative is the recognition that Aquinas clearly rejected the necessitation of the will's acts, coupled with the supposition that this rejection amounts to a rejection of causal determinism. A second reason for ignoring the compatibilist alternative is the recognition that it is an account of *freedom* that is needed, coupled with the supposition that compatibilist freedom is no real freedom at all. Both of these suppositions are false. To show this, I will present an overview of Aquinas' teaching on the will, its acts, and their proximate causes along compatibilist lines. The free acts of the will, on that account, will be shown to be causally determined but not necessitated. Aquinas' own remedy for recognizing the reality of the compatibilist freedom which emerges from that account will be presented. The account of the nature and modality of creaturely free acts which emerges from this discussion will plainly cohere with the determinism of the Aristotelian causal order embraced by Aquinas, and will be available for investigation into the coherence of his accounts of providence and the permission of sin.

Intellect, Will, and Freedom

"The act of the will," St. Thomas wrote in the *Pars Prima*, "is nothing but an inclination which follows on an apprehended form, just as natural appetite is an inclination which follows on a natural form."[6] The capacity for rational apprehension is the capacity to apprehend aspects of reality which are not sensible. Aquinas called the faculty of rational apprehension the intellect, and the faculty of inclination responding to such apprehension, the will. Whatever the intellect can apprehend, the will can take as its object; that is, we can incline toward whatever we can apprehend, since there is always something of being in any apprehended object, and thus something desirable, as useful or for its own sake, under some circumstances or other.[7]

Thought the will *can* incline toward whatever the intellect can apprehend, all finite being can be apprehended insofar as it lacks being. Thus the will *need not* incline toward any created apprehended object, since any such object can be apprehended *as lacking in being*, that is, as lacking some mode of being in virtue of which one might incline toward the apprehended object, were it present instead of lacking.[8] The ability of the intellect to *abstract*–to notice in apprehended objects certain aspects (such as their lacking a given perfection) which are capable of multiple instantiation–is the ground of the nonnecessary character of the will's inclination toward finite apprehended objects. This is part of what St. Thomas meant by his claim that the root of freedom is in the intellect: given simply the fact that some finite being is apprehended, no inclination of the will toward it follows with necessity, since the intellect can apprehend that object insofar as it lacks being.[9]

Freedom from necessity is one of the three conditions which St. Thomas consistently designated as belonging to creaturely freedom; the other two–self-movement and control–will be introduced shortly.[10] First, though, we should note that the freedom from necessity on the level at which we have so far considered it is of a passive sort: the will is not moved of necessity by any given apprehended object because of something which *can happen to* the intellect, namely, its apprehending a given created object as good, or as lacking in being in some respect. But there is a second dimension of the power of the intellect which transforms the passivity of the will's nonnecessitation. Among the aspects of created being which the intellect can apprehend are its own acts (we can notice that we are thinking, for example), and those of the will (we can notice that we intend something or other.[11]) This capacity to apprehend its own acts and those of the will is the intellect's capacity for *reflection*.[12] The will, in turn, can have inclinations corresponding to these reflective apprehendings, and these inclinations in turn can be apprehended. A fuller description of the interplay between intellect and will would reveal even more complexity.

Since human beings can apprehend their own apprehendings and willings, can incline toward these in various ways, and can apprehend the causes of these of their states, they can incline to change what they apprehend, what they will, whether they apprehend, and whether they will. As rational animals, human beings move themselves, like nonrational animals, in the sense that their principle of motion for each act - the apprehended object–is internal to them. Yet nonrational animals are passive with respect to what that internal principle of motion, that apprehended object, will be. With rational creatures things are otherwise. Because of their capacity for reflection–for apprehending the acts of the intellect and will–the source of the specification of their internal principle of motion is also in a way internal to rational creatures. For the intellect can apprehend its own acts, and the will can incline or not toward any of these apprehended acts of the intellect.

Rational creatures are in this sense active with respect to their internal principle of motion, the apprehended good, and so can be said to move themselves in a richer sense than can nonrational animals. The intellect moves the will, in the primary sense that the will's inclination just is a response to the intellect's apprehension of an object. But the will also moves the intellect to act, because the intellect can apprehend its own acts, and the will can incline accordingly.[13] The will moves the will, as well, since it is in virtue of its inclination toward an end that the will inclines toward an object apprehended as a means to that end.[14] In this way, the will moves itself to act, as well as moving the intellect and, in various ways and to various degrees, the senses, the passions, and the executive powers–like speech–to act.[15]

We have seen how the will is both not necessitated by any finite apprehended object, and that it can play a role in specifying which objects it will apprehend, and in what way. Rational creatures have the full range of created being as possible objects of inclination, and they can move themselves to apprehend whichever objects they will in fact incline toward. Nonnecessitation coupled with self-movement amounts to control. Rational creatures not only have control over how they will fulfill their desires (as nonrational animals do), but over what their desires will be, whether or not they will yield to them, and under what conditions. This control which rational creatures have over their own acts is as indefinitely deep as is the intellect's capacity for reflection. The control which rational creatures have over *what* they incline toward has been called *freedom of specification*, and their control over *whether* they will incline toward a given apprehended object, *freedom of exercise*.[16] Aquinas clearly distinguished between these dimensions of nonnecessitation of the will's act, and located the roots of both in the capacity of the intellect to reflect on its own acts, as well as on those of the other faculties, including acts of the will.[17]

It is particularly the will's control over the judgment of the intellect which marks the choices of rational creatures as free. St. Thomas is explicit in his claim that human free choice comes from our power over our own judgments in the *Summa Contra Gentiles* and the *De Veritate*, and he cites the intellect's capacity to consider an apprehended object from a different point of view–a capacity over the exercise of which the will has power–as the grounds for the freedom and nonnecessitation of the will's acts in the *Prima Secundae* and the *De Malo*.[18] We have seen that the will both is moved by the intellect and can move the intellect. Because the will can exercise control over the acts of the intellect, the free agent can be said to move the judgment of the intellect freely. (The resulting free judgment, *liberum arbitrium*, is the act from which the power is named.[19]) But insofar as the will is moved to exercise its control over the judgment of the intellect, that control is dependent on the causes of the will's acts. To understand the nature of that control, then, the variety of causes operating on the will, and the extent of the will's control over those causes, must be examined.

The Causes of the Will's Acts

The will is a self-mover, moving itself from willing the end to willing an apprehended means, and because particular acts of the intellect can be among these suitable apprehended means, the will is able to play a role in forming the intellect and the will, the wellsprings of human action. According to St. Thomas the will is not only a self-mover, though, but is a moved mover as well. St. Thomas understood being a moved mover and a self-mover as fully compatible.[20] Having examined the sense in which the will is a mover, we need next to explore the senses in which it is moved.

There are five important dimensions to the will's being moved which we should briefly consider. First, the intellect moves the will, as we have said: the will is nothing but an inclination responding to a form understood. These apprehended objects do not necessitate the will's acts, again, since the intellect can consider any finite apprehended object under different aspects, so that it seems good under one and not good under another. The will can incline toward a wide range of apprehended objects, but none of these moves the will with necessity insofar as they can be apprehended as lacking in being (and thus as not good) in some respect. Hence, all that we can say about the will's nature is that it inclines toward *whatever* the intellect apprehends as good, which is to say toward the good in general. This is what St. Thomas meant by identifying the universal good as the will's proper object: by its nature, the will inclines toward whatever is apprehended as good.[21]

Since the intellect can apprehend its *own* act of considering any object under any given aspect, the will can incline toward such apprehended acts of apprehension and can thus move the intellect from considering an object under one aspect to consider it under another. Thus, while the will is moved by any object apprehended as good and suitable, the will has control over whether a given apprehended object is apprehended as good and suitable, and thus over which apprehended objects move the will; this control is freedom of specification.

In a second and related sense, God moves the will in virtue of His providence over the causes of the intellect's apprehending as it does.[22] God has given to all beings in the created order their natures with the attendant causal powers which flow from those natures, both at their moment of coming into being–this is *creation*–and at every subsequent moment of their existence (*conservation*). He has placed those beings in various causal orders which are themselves mutually ordered and inter-acting according to the plan of providence. (This placement is *applica-tion*.) He thus operates through all created being, accomplishing His purposes, proximate and ultimate, for each being, for each order, and for the whole created order by means of the interactions of the beings with-in and among these causal orders; no created being acts without there-by accomplishing God's purposes. (Being thus employed all created being exhibits *instrumentality*.)[23]

God exercises this control without in any way necessitating the will's acts, for the nature of the will remains open to being moved or not moved by any particular apprehended object.[24] Neither does God's con-trol over the intellect's apprehending as it does obviate the will's con-trol over how the intellect apprehends; primary causality operates through secondary causality, as the woodsman's intention to remove the tree in no way obviates but rather is the cause of the ax's role in felling it.[25] Thus, neither the proximate nor ultimate (nor, *a fortiori*, any inter-mediate) causes on the side of the object of the will's act are opposed to the will's freedom of specification.

The next two senses in which the will is moved concern the exercise of the will's act. In a third sense, the will moves itself, from willing the end, to inclining toward the means. (The precise form of the will's incli-nation toward the means can vary: from consent, to choice, to use.) We touched on the way in which the will moves itself when considering the various sorts of control the will exercises; here we need to focus on the moved side of the will's relationship to itself. The will is moved in virtue of its inclination toward the end to choose the means: it is in virtue of my willing to be healthy, a state of affairs apprehended as a universal, that I choose to take the medicine I apprehend as productive of health (and finally see as this particular tablet: action concerns par-ticulars.) But the intellect can apprehend various means to the same end, or apprehend a given means as useful for one end though useless for or even impeding others, i.e., as not suitable. Therefore, even while will-ing the end, the will is under no necessity to move itself to choose an apprehended means.

The reduction from willing the end to willing the means takes place only insofar as the means is considered as suitable to the end. But that act of consideration can itself be apprehended by the intellect as good, or as not, and the will can accordingly incline or not incline toward that apprehended act of consideration, moving the intellect to continue that consideration or to cease from doing so. Thus, the will has control over whether or not it will reduce itself from willing an end to willing a certain means, even given the apprehension of that means as suitable[26]; this control is freedom of exercise.

The fourth dimension of the will's being moved is related to the third as the second was to the first: In creating the will with the nature that it has and in sustaining that nature in existence, God moves the will to the universal good, that is, in accord with its nature.[27] St. Thomas' reasoning runs as follows: since no particular end has been perpetually actually willed by any given human will, the will must have come to will that end. But if the will had moved itself to will that end, that end would have had to have functioned also as a means to some further end: moving itself from willing the end to willing the means is the only kind of self-movement St. Thomas allows for the will, for nothing can reduce itself from potency to act in the same respect. If the will moved itself to will the end, deliberation would have had to have taken place for the will to move itself, from willing some further end to willing what with respect to that act of will is the means, and with respect to our original act is the end. No infinite regress of deliberation is possible, though, and so at some point the will must be moved–in the order of exercise, and not only of specification–by something else.[28] That something else must be God, who alone is capable of moving the will by sustaining it in existence with an active inclination toward its natural object, which is the universal good, the good-in-general.[29] Since God's movement of the will in this fourth sense is toward whatever is good, the will's act of choice is not necessitated by this divine motion, any more than by the divine control over the objects of the intellect's apprehension, the second sense.[30] Nor does God's moving the will to the universal good obviate the will's control over whether it moves itself from willing the end to willing the means, for it does not destroy the intellect's ability to apprehend its own acts of apprehending either a given end or any given means to that end, and these acts can be apprehended as other than good and suitable. So neither the proximate nor highest (the only) causes moving the will to the exercise of its act are opposed to the will's freedom of exercise.

The fifth and final sense in which the will is moved by another is not only distinct but also different from the others, since those four all apply to every conceivable act of the will. St. Thomas thought, however, that sometimes[31] God moves the will beyond His control on the side of the object through the providential arrangement of the causes of apprehension (sense two), and on the side of the exercise of the act by sustaining the will in existence with an inclination toward whatever is apprehended as good (sense four). God also moves the will (in the fifth sense) by bestowing upon it a higher power than it has from its own nature[32]; that power is grace, a participation in God's nature.[33] Grace is not always present in every human will: the will is capable of acting to achieve the goods within the reach of its natural powers–to toil in fields, to take nourishment, and to have friends, for example[34]–without grace in this sense. But to achieve goods which exceed their natural capacity–to inherit eternal life, say–human beings require the help of a higher force.

This higher power–present in the soul as a habit[35]–is to the soul as form is to matter, and all matter must be properly disposed to receive any form. But were this proper disposition itself the work of a higher power present in the soul, a new proper disposition would be required for the second higher power to effect disposition toward the first. The impending regress is avoidable; no higher power need be present in the soul to properly dispose the soul to receive grace.[36] Still, divine help is needed to properly prepare to receive this higher power as habitual grace. God effects proper disposition in the soul in two ways: by moving its act immediately toward the highest good, and toward proximate goods through subordinate movers.[37] This divine assistance is the kind of help every creature needs to achieve its good[38]; it is the same twofold help which rational creatures need to know those truths or achieve those goods which require only their natural powers[39]: this divine assistance is providence, the second and fourth senses (above) in which God moves the will, insofar as ordered to the higher end of creaturely participation in the divine nature.[40]

Thus the proper disposition toward grace is the effect of providence insofar as God directs men to Himself as to a special end.[41] God creates and conserves beings, places them in a causal nexus, and thereby creates disposing conditions for his operating immediately with and through the lives of free creatures to whose natures he conjoins his own. Aquinas compares the reception of this higher power to illumination by a divine light, who is God Himself.[42] In the *De Malo* Aquinas asserts that the divine light is everywhere accessible to beings insofar as they are properly prepared to receive it:

> God as He is in Himself communicates Himself to all according to their capacity; hence if a thing has some deficiency in the participation of this goodness, this is because there is to be found in the thing itself some impediment to this divine participation. In this way, then, if some grace is not given, the cause is not from God, but from this, that the man himself, to whom the grace is given, presents an impediment to grace, in as much as he turns away from a light which does not itself turn away...[43]

So grace is always present *to* the will, but not always present *in* or operating *through* the will.

God's moving the will to prepare for grace is compatible with human freedom, since providence does not destroy the contingency of effects, and specifically not the freedom of human choice, as shown above in the discussions of the second and fourth senses in which the will is moved. Neither does the higher power, once present as habitual grace in the properly disposed soul, obviate free choice. Its effect is the proper ordering (justification) of the soul consisting of an inclination of the will toward God and away from sin, enabling the will to freely choose in ways which merit eternal life. Neither God's motion to justice nor to merit takes place without a movement of the created will.[44] Thus neither God's movement of the will to prepare the soul for grace (in senses two and four considered as ordered toward participation in the divine nature), nor His movement of the soul in virtue of its participation in his divine nature (sense five) diminishes the capacities of the intellect and the will, nor thus the freedom of the will's acts.

These are the causes of the will's acts. None of them remove the radical proximate contingency of the will. More specifically, none of them remove the intellect's capacity to apprehend finite goods, including those goods which are its own acts and the acts of the will, as limited goods and hence as not good in some respect. Hence none of these causes removes the will's control over the practical judgments of the intellect; *liberum arbitrium* is preserved through the operation of these causes. So in answer to our inquiry about the extent of the will's control over the judgment of the intellect and thus over its own acts, we may reply that the will retains control over whether and to what it is moved given any of these causes of its acts.

But included in these five senses in which the will is moved are all the causes of the will's act; beyond these, there is nothing with respect to which the will stands in potency. Thus both whether the will chooses any particular object, and how the will chooses it, follow determinately from the exercise of the causality of the first cause, God himself. Hence any particular act of the will "may fall outside the order of any particular active cause, but not outside the order of the universal cause, under which all particular causes are included."[45] This order of universal causality is the order of providence. God's providential control over the acts of the will is certain; all its effects–including the free choices of rational creatures–follow inevitably. Thus the control which the will has over its own acts is control from a certain point of view, a conditioned control: the will has control over its own acts, those of the intellect, and over some of the causes of these acts, from perspectives embracing fewer than all the orders of created causes acting on the intellect and will. But the created will does not have control over the order embracing all the causes with respect to which it stands in potency; it does not have control over the order of providence.

Causation without Necessitation

Let us summarize the nature of freedom associated with this conditioned control. According to the interpretation presented, the will may be moved by any object it apprehends as good–which is to say, by any object which when apprehended may move the will–as by a sufficient cause.[46] Such apprehended objects are sufficient in St. Thomas's sense: when the cause is posited, the effect follows always, unless some obstacle impedes the cause.[47] Many things can impede the will's being moved by a rationally apprehended good, and the will itself is among these. Because of the indefinitely deep capacity of the intellect to abstract and reflect, the intellect can apprehend any created object, including its own acts and those of the will, as good, or as not. Thus, even when the intellect apprehends an object which is sufficient to move the will, the will can impede that movement. Because the intellect can apprehend its own acts, the will can move the intellect to consider that sufficient cause of the will's movement as lacking in being in some respect. So considered, that object which is sufficient to move the will under some considerations will not in fact move the will. The cause impeding the sufficient causality of that apprehended object is the will itself, having moved the intellect to consider that sufficient cause differently. So the will has control over which apprehended objects it will incline toward: this is freedom of specification. Nor need the will act even toward an object which is being considered as good–this is freedom of exercise–since the intellect can apprehend many other goods whose pursuit entails cessation of its act of consideration of such an object, thus moving the will to move the intellect to cease consideration of that object.[48] This wondrous depth of the intellect's capacities for abstraction and reflection is the ground of the substantial control which free creatures can exercise over their own lives.

Yet the will can move the intellect toward or away from any particular apprehended object only in response to some additional act of apprehension.[49] This additional act of apprehension is either moved by the will (commanded), or not. If by the will, then the will is being moved by the intellect's judgment of that additional act of apprehension as good. This deliberative chain must ultimately terminate in acts of apprehension which are not commanded by the will. The causes involved in the production of any such chain, however complex, must extend beyond the will, if we are to understand the will as the rational appetite, the faculty of response to rational apprehension.[50]

On this view, the sum of the causal influences on the faculty of rational apprehension which are causally prior to any act of the created will are sufficient causal conditions for bringing about that particular act of the will.[51] Given the placement of such a full set of causal antecedents, it is impossible for the will to exercise its very real causal power over its own acts and those of the intellect otherwise than it in fact does, for there is no element of potency left in the will which is not being determinately moved to act. Acts of the created will–as do all creaturely acts–follow inevitably from the placement of the full range of causes in the order of universal causality, the order of providence. That inevitability seems, on the face of it, to imply necessitation of the sort we have already seen Aquinas reject as incompatible with free will; here lies the apparent inconsistency between Aquinas' accounts of created freedom and causally certain providence.

That apparent tension in Aquinas' thought dissolves, in part, once we grasp his account of the modality of created effects. On Aquinas' understanding of causation and modality, effects are called necessary precisely when they are the proper effects of *per se* causes which cannot be impeded in the production of their proper effects; contingent effects are those brought about through the operation of *per se* causes which can fail in the production of their proper effects. In order to fail, a contingent cause must be impeded by some cause from another independent causal order. The conjunction of such independent causal orders is an accidental union. This union, insofar as it is not the proper effect of some higher *per se* cause, has no higher cause: "accidental being has no cause and is not generated."[52] What follows from the accidental intersection of causal orders is determined *ad unum* through the placement of those causal orders, even while is not necessitated (i.e., produced by an unimpedible *per se* cause) by such placement.

Some conjunctions have a certain unity, a certain being, such as intentional unions (like a meeting of servants in the market, planned by the master who sent them) or natural ones (like a family.)[53] Insofar as there is an intentional ordering of the otherwise accidentally ordered causes of an event, then *from the point of view of the orderer* (the master, or God) the event is not a product of chance, but of causation. Divine providence orders all events insofar as they have being and act; accordingly, Aquinas held that considered as falling under the order of providence–the only higher cause governing the conjunction of all of the causes of the will's acts–all created effects are found to be necessary.[54] Yet effects are called necessary or contingent after their proximate causes, not their higher causes.[55] And so God determines not only which effects occur, but also their modality (contingent, or necessary) in assigning to some effects causes which can, and others causes which cannot fail in the production of their proper effects.[56]

From the point of view of providence, the effects of causes which can be impeded follow no less inevitably than the effects of causes which cannot be:

> Although contingent causes left to themselves can fail to produce an effect, the wisdom of the divine economy brings it about that the effect will inevitably follow when certain supplementary measures are employed, which do not take away the contingency of that effect. Evidently, therefore, contingency in things does not exclude the certainty of divine providence.[57]

The contingency of effects produced through *liberum arbitrium* is accounted for explicitly in terms of this same model of the modality of created effects. For predestination, that part of providence though which God secures merit and glory for those He has chosen, produces its effects inevitably, but imposes no necessity because it does not destroy the contingency of the proximate cause, *liberum arbitrium*.[58] Aquinas had only just explicitly discussed creaturely freedom when he asserted that "the effect of every cause is found to be necessary insofar as it comes under the control of Providence."[59]

So on Aquinas' account of the modality of created effects, no assemblage of causal orders which is sufficient for determining a given effect *ad unum* destroys the contingency of that effect unless that assemblage includes the unimpedible *per se* cause of that effect, or unless that assemblage itself has a kind of unity. But the will is not an unimpedible *per se* cause. Nor is fate, considered in itself apart from providence, a unified order; it is an accidental assemblage of independent causal orders.[60] So the acts of the intellect and will would retain their contingency, were they subject to fate, on the same grounds as do any accidental effects in nature.

But the intellect and the will are not subject to fate in the way the acts of nonrational beings are. Acts of the intellect and will are at a further remove from necessitation than are the acts of nonrational animals. That the sheep sees a bolt of lightning is accidental, but that having seen it the sheep flees, is not. Human beings are not led by natural instinct to their actions, as are other animals whose powers are affixed to corporeal organs.[61] When a man sees and fears, he might well remember and decide not to flee. Human memory and human acquired habit bring the experiences of the past to the present, impacting the way a human being will respond to the placement of even a full set of accidentally ordered present circumstances. Of course, nonrational animals also learn from experience, naturally or in response to training. But none of them notice that they so learn, nor participate actively in coming to learn. So human beings have control over the first principles of their own reactions in any full set of present causal circumstances. They thus exhibit a degree of independence from natural causal circumstances which nonrational beings do not. Present circumstances do not determine human acts. And the full sum of causal antecedents to choice, linked together–abstracting from the order of providence–only in their impact on the human memory and will, are an accidental union neither having nor constituting a *per se* cause, for "what does not exist together cannot be the cause of anything."[62]

Thus acts of human intellect and will, though determined by the placement of a full set of causal antecedents to choice, are contingent effects; they are products of accidentally ordered unions of causes. Their claim to contingency in this sense is based upon no special property of free creatures; the blooming of a flower is contingent in this same sense. But the blooming follows inevitably from the specification of a relatively narrow range of causal circumstances. The inevitability of acts of nonrational animals follows from a somewhat broader set; that of acts of animals which can learn from experience, from a set broader still. The inevitability of acts of the human intellect and will follow from the most broad range of causal antecedents: anything we rationally apprehend (past or present) can impact the acts of these powers. This range of causal antecedents which must be placed in order to produce a determinate act of the intellect or will is larger than the mind of an individual human being can altogether grasp.[63] So human beings experience independence from any measure of the causal antecedents to choice which they can comprehend.

This independence–this ground of compatibilist freedom–is real, but it is not the whole causal story. We can reason to the existence of a full set of causal antecedents to choice, which is the universal order of causality. Should that order be comprehended and intentionally placed (by an intellect and will which must be far greater than our own), that intelligent agent would be a necessary *per se* cause of all the effects of that order. Aquinas reasoned to the existence of such an order, the order of providence, which is an order precisely because it is intentionally placed by such an orderer. In placing just the order He does, God at once causally determines each created effect and assures the contingency of those effects which follow inevitably from however complex an assembly of independent causal orders–an assembly accidental in every respect save from the point of view of providence–that suffices to produce them. In just this way, God determines the acts of free creatures without necessitating them; ours is a compatibilist freedom.

Compatibilist Freedom?

Thus part of the apparent tension between Aquinas' accounts of freedom and providence dissolves, once we see that his account of the modality of created effects enables a rejection of necessitation of acts which follow inevitably on placement of the full order of providence. It remains open to the libertarian interpreter, however, to insist that the sort of freedom which escapes necessitation only in *that* sense is no real freedom at all.

To those to whom it seems that divine determination rules out the possibility of real creaturely freedom, the compatibility of such providence with the causal efficacy of intercessory prayer is likely to fare no less well. For if God, prior (in nature, if not in time) to taking account of any actions of created beings, determines exactly, efficaciously, and unchangeably which events will occur and which will not, what could be the use asking Him to do anything at all? St. Thomas affirmed both the efficacy of prayer and the immutability of providence, however:

> It is apparent, then, from the foregoing that the cause of some things that are done by God is prayers and holy desires. But we showed above that divine providence does not exclude other causes; rather, it orders them so that the order which providence has determined within itself may be imposed on things. And thus, secondary causes are not incompatible with providence; instead, they carry out the effect of providence. In this way, then, prayers are efficacious before God, yet they do not destroy the immutable order of divine providence, because this individual request that is granted to a certain petitioner falls under the order of divine providence. So, it is the same thing to say that we should not pray in order to obtain something from God, because the order of His providence is immutable, as to say that we should not walk in order to get to a place, or eat in order to be nourished; all of which are clearly absurd.[64]

Few among the many physical determinists in the world have taken the determinism of the whole physical order to cast doubt on the efficacy of attempts to walk, or eat; that would be absurd, in the way St. Thomas meant. But prayer is asking God to do something different than would otherwise happen, and many are intimidated away from prayer by the thought that all events are determined by the order of divine providence. While the absurdity of such a position seems less clear, the mistake is no less real, according to Aquinas:

> Now, if a person carefully considers these statements, he will find that every error that occurs on these points arises from the fact that thought is not given to the difference between universal and particular order. For, since all effects are mutually ordered, in the sense that they come together in one cause, it must be that, the more universal the cause is, the more general is the order. Hence, the order stemming from the universal cause

which is God must embrace all things. So, nothing prevents some particular order from being changed, either by prayer, or by some other means,
for there is something outside that order which could change it...

But, outside the order that embraces all things, it is not possible for anything to be indicated by means of which the order depending on a universal cause might be changed. That is why the Stoics, who considered
the reduction of the order of things to God to be to a universal cause of
all things, claimed that the order established by God could not be
changed for any reason. But again on this point, they departed from the
consideration of a universal order, because they claimed that prayers
were of no use, as if they thought that the wills of men and their desires,
from which prayers arise, are not included under that universal order. For,
when they say that, whether prayers are offered or not, in any case the
same effect in things follows from the universal order of things, they
clearly isolate from that universal order the wishes of those who pray.
For, if these prayers be included under that order, then certain effects will
result by divine ordination by means of these prayers, just as they do by
means of other causes...Therefore, prayers retain their power; not that
they can change the order of eternal control, but rather as they themselves
exist under such order.[65]

Aquinas included free choice under precisely the same solution as he
did intercessory prayer.[66] The solution which he spells out explicitly
regarding the efficacy of prayer is the same general solution he offers
for the modality of all created effects: that God determines not only
which effects will occur, but also their modality. For all effects occur
necessarily, from the point of view of providence, and necessarily with
the modality God intended them to derive from their proximate causes.
    Even those with libertarian intuitions about human freedom can
imagine, now, that God *had* created a world inhabited by creatures with
the rational and appetitive faculties I described above, under the compatibilist interpretation. Surely divine providence would no more rule
out the efficacy of those creatures' deliberations, in such a world, than it
would the efficacy of prayer in our own. That imaginary world would
contain pretty impressive rational creatures, but without libertarian freedom, and in their deliberations and choices they would exercise substantial control over their own lives. Their wills would be open to opposite
courses of action and they would exercise control over their own apprehendings and choosings, insofar as they can comprehend the proximate
causes of these states. Considered, however, from the perspective of that
order embracing all created and uncreated causal influences with respect
to which the created intellect and will stand in potency–i. e., considered
under the order of providence–the acts of their intellects and wills would
be determined *ad unum*, since there is nothing outside that highest order

with respect to which they stand in potency. As I read St. Thomas, ours is a world inhabited by rational creatures operating in such a causal order. His was a compatibilist account of creaturely freedom.

Hence the tension between causal determination and human freedom can be avoided; on the compatibilist model, it is only determination at proximate causal levels which must be rejected, and this can be done without rejecting determinism *simpliciter*. The compatibilist model leaves human beings with exactly the measure of independence from proximate causal orders which reflection on human experience reveals, a measure of independence which elicits ever more wonder as that reflection deepens. But that independence from proximate causal orders, freedom from necessity in that sense, in no way implies independence from the entire order of created causality. There is scarcely a trace of evidence to the contrary to be found in the writings of Aquinas, and plenty of evidence on behalf of this thesis of causal dependence.[67]

To interpreters who sympathetically grasp only libertarian intuitions concerning freedom, or who are captivated by the agenda of others who grasp only such intuitions, freedom from necessity of the sort which follows from this compatibilist analysis will seem plainly insufficient to preserve freedom; worse, it seems irrelevant. For libertarians, causal determinism of any sort, even of the suave Bañezian variety allowed by Garrigou-Lagrange and others, does not merely weaken freedom; it destroys it entirely.[68] Rather than ascribe to Aquinas–and Augustine, too[69]–what seems to them to be such a significant mistake, interpreters with libertarian sympathies comb the texts of Aquinas to find resources for resolving a tension which was never present in his thought.

Predictably, the pickings are slim. There is little support in the texts for Maritain's discovery of separate metaphysical line of nonbeing. There is little support for Lonergan's claim that Aquinas' thought in his later writings underwent a profound change away from "momentary aberration(s)" in the *De Veritate*, the *De Potentia*, and in the *Prima Pars* in which Thomas asserted that freedom from coercion makes necessary acts free. There is little support for the traditional Thomist view that the will stands causally aloof from the entire sum of natural causal antecedents to choice. Bringing a compatibilist intuition about freedom to the texts of Aquinas enables them to be taken as a whole, meeting the criterion which Aristotle laid out for wholeness in the *Poetics*: its parts "so closely connected that the withdrawal of any one of them will disjoin and dislocate the whole. For that which makes no perceptible difference by its absence is no real part of the whole."[70] Libertarian readings require resources to extirpate created freedom from a deterministic causal order, resources not found in the texts; thus they treat the thought these texts embody as disjointed, as less than whole. But throughout his writings Aquinas did not seem to notice his omission of what to libertarians seems the obvious.

Yet there is a coherence in Aquinas' writing on freedom which emerges once the texts are read through a compatibilist lens. If one gives up the search for libertarian freedom, one finds in the texts of Aquinas a rich compatibilist analysis–presented above only in overview–of the psychology of human deliberation and freedom of choice. That analysis, for all its richness, has been overlooked by libertarian interpreters of Aquinas since it implies that human beings operate entirely in a deterministic causal order. Some of the reason, at least, for rejecting determinism and thus compatibilist analyses of freedom lies in what are feared to be its unseemly implications for the problem of evil.[71] If only in a preliminary way, then, we must turn the compatibilist lens toward the heavens, considering the entire order of creation and the salvation of free creatures within that order. It will turn out, I think, that the prospects for compatibilism are considerably brighter than libertarians have supposed.

The Role of the Free Creature in the Plan of Providence

To adequately consider the plan of providence insofar as it is ordered to the final outcome of the lives of free creatures, it is necessary first to consider their origin. Why are there free creatures, anyway? This question seems especially pressing insofar as free creatures are part of the same causal order as the rest of creation; if free creatures have some special status or worth on the compatibilist model, it is not in virtue of any degree of ultimate independence of their will from that causal order. Yet we can see from the compatibilist perspective a coherent account of the high purpose of free creatures in the plan of providence. A first look at the heavens though the compatibilist lens will not result in the careful collection of data through which initial observations are confirmed and analyzed; it is necessary to begin by getting a broad view. And while it is right to recognize that even the most careful efforts will produce tentative and only partial results, the grandeur of the objects of this inquiry should not deter us from asking the difficult questions which will drive our inquiry as far as it might profitably go. We will need to inquire into the end of God's creative activity, and into the means by which He directs the created order toward that end.

In the beginning, God created the heavens and the earth. Why? Aquinas' answer is to reflect God's glory, to make His nature manifest. In order to accomplish that end, God the first cause of all else confers the dignity of causality to created effects: providence operates *through* created causes to manifest His wisdom, His power, and His love. To manifest His wisdom, He created creatures capable of achieving a measure of wisdom, rational creatures, who immediately on account of their rationality partake in a measure of God's freedom. In the real causal power communicated to free and all creatures, God makes manifest His own power. By His participating in the nature of rational and free creatures–first, though the Incarnation–He invites them to participate in the divine nature, sharing His own divine life with them in a manifestation of His love.

It is of the nature of wisdom to order, and thus God in His wisdom orders all created effects by operating through rational creatures in their wisdom. Since God has chosen to direct created effects through rational intermediaries, it is only insofar as God directs the activity of rational creatures that He directs the activities of the rest of the created order–on this point, Aquinas insists:

> All corporal beings are governed through spiritual beings...But spiritual beings act on the corporal through the will. Therefore, if choices and movements of the wills of intellectual substances do not belong to God's providence, it follows that even corporal beings are withdrawn from His providence. And thus there will be no providence at all.[72]

Thus questions of the manner and the extent to which God directs the free activities of rational creatures are central to understanding the manner and the extent of His direction of the whole created order. Let us consider first the manner, and then the extent.

To grasp the manner in which God operates in created effects, it will be necessary to recall first the general account of divine operation in created effects, and then–both to show that the general account is complete, and to focus on God's operation in free creatures in particular–the dimension of divine operation which is specific to His interaction with free creatures: His ordering them toward participation in His own life.

God operates in all effects in the following manner: He gives all created beings the natures, and thus the causal powers they have from the first moment of their existence and at every moment thereafter. God has created and conserves these beings in the context of a complex dynamic network of causal orders; placement in that network determines the causal conditions in which the causal powers of each being will be moved to act and in turn move other beings to act. Placing them in this dynamic set of causal relations constitutes applying them to act, in the Aristotelian, not Bañezian sense[73]: this placement of the causal conditions sufficient to move each creature to determinate exercise of its causal powers occurs temporally prior to its coming to act; and that placement may involve a change in the being whose causal powers will be activated, or in the being who will be acted upon. In bringing into existence this dynamic causal order God intends a set of proximate and ultimate ends, and He operates in the actions of all creatures who are thus instruments through which and through whom God accomplishes whatever He intends.

Yet the order God established in creation is knowable to us only to an extent; God intends to bring about effects in creation whose nature and causal requirements outstrip the ability of our intellect to comprehend them.[74] Central among these higher intentions is God's plan to enter his creation and dwell therein through cooperation with free creatures who have been disposed as matter for participation in the divine nature. The order in created effects insofar as intended to accomplish these higher purposes is the order of grace.

What are to us two orders–the one we can comprehend in principle, and the one we cannot–are a single order in themselves (i.e., to God), and through that single order God operates to accomplish his ultimate intention and proximate intentions, the whole plan of providence. God works in and through the activity of the whole created order, much as a general who commands a flagman to signal the start of a planned invasion works in and through the flagman as an instrument. The flagman has the power to start the invasion, a power of which he may or may not be aware. That power is present in him nonetheless, in virtue of his being situated in an order of properly disposed causes, the extent and the efficacy of which he cannot know, but only suppose. The general, more so than the flagman, signals the invasion when the latter acts as instructed. And at a higher level still than the general's ordering of causes is the whole plan of providence, which God alone can fully understand and intend. God's intention to implement the order of providence works through the flagman more surely than the general's intention: since God's order extends to all contingencies, the divine plan is executed in the flagman with certainty, whereas the general's plan may fail.

The flagman is thus an instrument of God, even more so but in the same way in which he is an instrument of the general. Suppose for a moment that both the readiness to obey orders which his training produced and his subsequent faithfulness in executing those orders were arranged by God in the flagman for salvific purposes and were transformed in the flagman by the presence of a genuine love for God. In such a case, the flagman's readiness and faithfulness in execution would be (roughly speaking) grace in the flagman.[75] (Both would be something like habitual grace, operative in the training which imparted the habit, cooperative in the steadfastness with which he acted as trained.) The instruction of the general to signal *now* would be actual operative grace: not a habit, but an operation ordered to a salvific end. The flagman's intention to signal at the right moment would be an effect which could be produced in him by God only through the flagman's will: this is cooperative actual grace. All these would be effects in the flagman ordered to God's salvific purpose, just as analogous effects in the flagman–including a readiness to obey for love of country, say–might be ordered by a single general for the accomplishment of his own purposes. The flagman would be both an instrument of the general and an instrument of God: powers ordered by the general toward the lower end of victory, and by God to the higher end of salvation, would both be present in the flagman. The former power is a natural power; the latter flows from grace, and is thus a supernatural power. This notion of supernature adds to the notion of nature–to the idea of beings with causal powers flowing from their natures situated in a complex and dynamic causal order–no new thing other than the notion of an end whose nature and causal requirements surpass in principle our ability to fully comprehend and thus to effect them.

There is an elegant simplicity to Aquinas' account of providence and grace, nature and supernature which was lost to the tradition of interpretation which succeeded him. This account–my repackaging of Lonergan's reading, if I understand his–adds no new motions to those we observe, as did the tradition of Bañezian premotion, but only a new frame of reference for what is already familiar to us.[76] The accompanying account of grace is a special case of the general theory of universal instrumentality;[77] the very same causal order involved in ordinary providence receives a new level of being which is precisely the presence of an intention coordinating ordinary causal powers to higher ends, as the power of the general's intention is present in the properly situated flagman.[78] This (Lonergan's) alternative to the traditional Bañezian account of application[79] poses a challenge to the interpretations of the standard Thomist positions as well as to that of Maritain. In what follows I will presume (as I did in the discussion of the nature of the will and its freedom, above) that Lonergan's account is essentially correct. I will not pause to consider the prospects for adjustment of standard Thomistic or Maritain's accounts in light of Lonergan's unseating of their approach to the manner in which God directs the created order.[80] Instead, let us consider differences which can arise concerning the extent of that direction, given the manner of that direction described just above.

Given this account of providence on which God directs the activity of lower effects through rational intermediaries, the central interpretive question regarding the extent of God's direction of created effects is this: does the complete set of circumstances, including whatever proper disposition toward participation in the divine nature God has ordered those circumstances to produce, fully determine the activity of free creatures[81]? Interpreters with libertarian intuitions about created freedom will insist that the act of the will remains undetermined even given the placement of that complete set of causal antecedents. Plainly, Lonergan himself falls in this category: according to him, "God exercises control [over the will's acts] through the created antecedents...but that is not...infallible...."[82]

The interpretive difficulties which face this libertarian rejection of divine determinism are formidable. First, divine providence seems weakened, since God is left to work with whatever cooperation free creatures are willing to give Him. Second, either a) God's knowledge is not the cause of each thing known (when joined to His will), since He must conform His intellect to objects whose form He does not entirely determine[83], or b) He does not know a great deal of what occurs in His creation. Third, the cause of the distinction between creatures who cooperate with God and those who do not lies in the creatures themselves, on libertarian views. But St. Thomas ascribes the distinction to predestination, which involves

> the choice by which he who is directed to the end infallibly is separated from others who are not ordained to it in the same manner. This separation, however, is not on account of any difference found in the predestined...[84]

These difficulties are well known in Thomist interpretive tradition, and need not be treated in depth here.[85] But mentioning them here serves to highlight the clarity, simplicity, and close fit with the Thomistic texts of the fully deterministic model which the lens of compatibilist freedom brings sharply into focus.

Thomists have traditionally recognized that on Aquinas' account God determines all created effects, but they secured that determination through an account of application which Lonergan has unseated. Thus there is a void in the interpretive conversation, one which the compatibilist reading can fill. Aquinas held that God determines created effects through created intermediaries.[86] Since free creatures are included among (and indeed at the apex of) those intermediaries, God determinately directs the acts of free creatures (especially). Since the acts of free creatures are themselves created effects, God must direct those free acts through the placement of the full order of the causal antecedents to those free acts (detailed in the first part of this essay); beyond this full set of causal antecedents, there is nothing with respect to which the created will stands in potency. That the created will both determines and is determined is characteristic of all causal interaction in the created order. But the created will, at the apex of the order of causal intermediaries, determines much, and is itself determined only by so complex a set of causal arrangements that only divine intention makes their coincidence other than fortuitous. Here is an orderly account of the causal certitude of providence which embraces the elegant simplicity of Lonergan's reading of Aquinas' account of God's operation in created effects (consisting of creation, conservation, application, and instrumentality) while preserving the divine determinism which traditional interpreters have recognized. Of course, this simple and orderly account can be embraced only at the cost of libertarian freedom. But creaturely freedom is not an expendable part of the Thomistic system. Thus it is the compatibilist conception of freedom which enables this simple and deterministic account of providence to be seriously entertained, explored, and sharpened.

In the first part of this essay I gave an overview of that compatibilist conception of freedom, an account of human action situating the deliberation and choice of rational creatures in a deterministic causal order, an account which stays near to the texts of St. Thomas. And in this second section, we have had a quick look at how creatures with compatibilist freedom function in the order of causally certain providence. But those who would reject a compatibilist reading of Aquinas out of hand are most likely to do so not on account of its lack of support in what Aquinas wrote about human action, or for any alleged inability of a compatibilist account to secure the causal certitude of providence. Rather, concerns about compatibilist freedom center on what a deterministic order seems to imply about the goodness of God. But it turns out that safeguarding the doctrine of divine goodness seems a principle strength, and no weakness, of a compatibilist reading of Aquinas on freedom and providence. Let us turn, finally, to explore God's permission of sin from a compatibilist perspective.

The Permission of Sin and Ultimate Failure in Free Creatures

To those inclined toward a libertarian conception of freedom, determinism seems repugnant to the goodness of God, since it seems opposed to the freedom and dignity of rational creatures. But as an interpretation of Aquinas, the determinist/compatibilist reading seems to secure the goodness of God better than traditional Thomist and more fully libertarian readings. For their attempts to graft libertarian intuitions into Aquinas' account of the permission of sin have rendered his account incoherent.

A coherent account of God's permission of evil must include the specification of a state of affairs the existence of which constitutes a *greater good* than would the nonexistence of all the evil which actually exists, and it must include an account of why the permission of all that evil is *necessary* for that greater good to obtain. Traditional Thomistic accounts, cast as they are in terms of Bañezian premotion, fail to specify a state of affairs which cannot be achieved without the permission of sin. Libertarians can point to a state of affairs–the existence of creatures with libertarian freedom–which indeed cannot be achieved without the permission of sin, but to make that account sound like one Aquinas might have held, the language used to describe it must be misshapen to the point where coherence is lost. (There may be coherent alternatives to Aquinas' position, but they are not included among the legitimate readings of Aquinas' position.) But the compatibilist reading can provide a state of affairs which quite plausibly cannot be achieved without permission of sin, and it can describe this state of affairs without importing concepts which Aquinas did not himself employ. Again, while this material deserves fuller treatment, the aim here is to employ the compatibilist lens for a preliminary set of observations. But prior to taking up that perspective, let us first take a brief look at the troubles afflicting traditional Thomist and more fully libertarian readings to remind ourselves of the view without the compatibilist optic, that the differences between libertarian and compatibilist perspectives may stand out more sharply.

Put plainly, traditional Thomists have been unable to clearly specify a state of affairs which cannot be obtained without the permission of sin.[87] They talk about God's maintaining an order of justice, but with all libertarians they insist that the placement of all causal antecedents to choice in the order of nature–the only order of which we have any clear idea–is compatible both with the occurrence and nonoccurrence of sin. Justice involves the preservation of order[88]: exactly what sort of order is preserved when God gives less help than he might without violating the natural order to free creatures who are failing? Why would God demonstrate the possibility and consequences of failure? What is He showing to whom? Such an order of justice seems "obscurissima"[89] at best; "an insult to the absolute innocence of God,"[90] at worst.

Maritain, Lonergan, and other full-blown libertarians can extricate the doctrine of divine goodness from this morass. God cannot determine the free acts of creatures; the nature of freedom, as libertarians conceive of it, logically precludes determination of any sort. The very existence of free creatures is thus the greater good for which the permission of sin is logically necessary. This may be a very sensible thing to think about

God and freedom, but as an interpretation of Aquinas–concerning what he actually held, not what he should have held–it faces severe difficulty. Some of that difficulty was mentioned in the previous section: the resulting notion of providence is weakened; Aquinas' account of God's knowledge is rendered incomplete; the distinction between the righteous and the reprobate is rooted in the free creatures themselves.

Especially regarding this last point, the difference in impressions one gets from reading the texts of Aquinas and those of his libertarian interpreters is striking. It seems that Aquinas is bent on denying the very heart of the position his interpreters are striving so desperately to preserve. In fact, the more careful and precise Aquinas' treatment, the worse he sounds to libertarian ears.[91] Accordingly, Maritain sought to preserve the language of Aquinas to the fullest extent possible. It is only in the line of nonbeing, about which Aquinas virtually never wrote[92], that free creatures have the first initiative; in the line of being and act, God is the first and full cause of all that is good, of being and act, in the creature. If the creature cooperates with grace (conceived of in Bañezian terms), that cooperation is an act moved by God, and to God goes all the credit. If the creature resists (not actually resists–that would be an act–but rather nihilates, impedes God's grace by a free initiative in the line of nonbeing), the creature alone is the cause.

Perhaps there is nothing incoherent in the idea of a causal order which is not fully deterministic. There is no contradiction, perhaps, even in the notion of a two-tiered metaphysic, with free creatures being first causes only of a strange sort, having in virtue of their freedom only the capacity (even if because of its limited domain we refuse to call it a power or an ability) to negate causal influence, whether from grace or from nature. What is incoherent is ascribing this nihilating initiative to the creature, while ascribing all to God and nothing to the creature when the creature refrains from nihilating.[93] One cannot refrain from doing nothing, perhaps. But as nihilating gets close enough to doing nothing so as to warrant ascribing everything in cooperative activity to God, just so close does nihilating come to a simple failure to be moved.[94] But insofar as nihilating is doing something, refraining from nihilating also seems to be doing something. One cannot have power over only one of a pair of contrary alternatives; if nihilating is in the creature's power in any sense of power, then not nihilating is also in the creature's power in that same sense of power. In its attempt to graft a libertarian notion of freedom onto the Thomistic account of God as the first and full cause of all that is of being and goodness, Maritain's account has so twisted the Thomistic conception of moral evil as to render what is in some respect incomprehensible, instead incoherent.

So neither traditional Thomist nor more fully libertarian readings of

Aquinas can employ Aquinas' own concepts to give a coherent account of a sufficiently greater state of affairs for the sake of whose attainment the permission of sin is necessary. But the compatibilist account can.

The existence of a complex causal order entailing a series of interactions of finite creatures on whom has been bestowed the dignity of causality and through the interactions of whom the entire order is brought into wondrous order and wholeness: the existence of such an order requires that some of these creatures fail. For "...the large number and variety of causes stem from the order of divine providence and control. But granted this variety of causes, one of them must at times run into another cause and be impeded...."[95] Aquinas asserted that it is contrary to the rational character of the divine regime to refuse permission for created things to act in accord with their nature. A consequence of their acting in accord with their nature will be that they impede one another at times, due to the incompatibility of the proximate ends to which they are directed (the lion to eat, the lamb to continue in existence, for example.) Hence corruption and evil result inevitably from the placement of such an order.[96]

When the strong who eats the weak is a human being who has not yet properly interacted with a culture sufficient to produce in him a lasting recognition that weaker human beings deserve special care and not special targeting, the evil which results is moral evil. This and every other sort of evil which results—indeed, every instance of evil which results in the playing out of a deterministic order—is necessary given the existence of that order, since it follows inevitably from the placement of that order. If there is some greater good for the sake of which this order's existence is permitted, then all the evil which actually results is necessary for the achievement of that good. A lion would cease to live if there were no slaying of animals; there would be no patience of martyrs if there were no tyrannical persecution.[97] Both kinds of evil occur in a deterministic order, and thus both are necessary for, because they are entailed by, the existence of whatever deterministic order produces them. The compatibilist model of freedom enables us to take seriously the possibility that Aquinas thought of the created order as deterministic, and when we take that possibility seriously, the necessary connection between evil and the greater good of the entire order of creation brought to fulfillment in Christ comes sharply into focus.

If the compatibilist lens makes plain the necessary connection between the existence of evil (and thus the permission of sin) and whatever good results from the placement of the deterministic created order, it may seem to provide less clarity with regard to the goodness of the resulting order. The good of preventing the evil which exists must be clearly outweighed by—consider St. Paul's "not worth comparing to"[98]–the good for which permitting that evil is necessary. Doubts about the good of any state of affairs in which free creatures inevitably fall into sin and failure leap right to the fore of the libertarian mind. It seems morally perverse even to permit, if (supposing there's a difference) not directly intend the inevitable sin, suffering, and death of free creatures (supposing that compatibilist freedom is enough to make them free.) So no deterministic system which entails the occurrence of sin or at least of ultimate failure can outweigh the good of avoiding that evil. So the libertarian objection might proceed. How might the compatibilist respond?

Arguing for the goodness of the created order is an imposing task. But *of course* the universe–our universe–is good, whether or not it is deterministic. The universe is fuel for the fire of divine love. The love of God is enkindling that wood as it seasons, consuming and consummating, like the fire of the burning bush from which the Lord spoke to Moses. The love of God is real, intensely attractive, and as it consumes us it turns our hearts toward others, bringing us into the life of Christ through whom the invisible God is made known. As confidence in the love of God increases, doubts about the goodness of whatever He does decrease.

But is precisely the love of God called into question by the inevitability of ultimate failure of rational creatures, the objection continues? Yet the compatibilist account need only accept whatever degree of failure is necessary for the existence of a created order which is good, an order of which human beings are essentially a part. A universe in which the wills of some rational creatures are inevitably malformed so as to resist the outstretched hand of God's saving love is the price of our own existence, an existence which is a great good. The libertarian objector does not accept such a universe. But such a universe is essential (if actual) to his objecting; this is an objection which reflects a desire for the good of each intelligent creature, a desire which is in fact found more perfectly in God. But the goodness of that desire can only be made manifest in human beings if human beings exist. And if the created order of which human beings are essentially a part is both deterministic and productive of sin and ultimate failure, then the goodness of that expressed concern can only exist if such sin and failure is permitted by God. Both human existence and the loving concern for others in which is the fruit of that existence are in fact good things; practically wise human beings are in fact inclined to preserve them both.

Thus God's loving presence can be understood as transforming creation as it is made ready through the unfolding implications of a causally deterministic order. That order exists precisely to receive God's wise and loving rule through the participation of rational creatures in God's own nature. But those creatures are essentially part of an order which does not immediately prepare the way for the Lord, but rather only in the fullness of time. The creation is subject to futility in this respect, as it groans while awaiting the revealing of the children of God. The failure of rational and thus free creatures–perhaps even the ultimate failure of some[99]–follows inevitably from the interplay of causes in the created order. That failure produces groaning in us which is both a proper response to and part of the remedy for the fearsome. But that failure need not extinguish hope which drives us to heal the wound of sin. Sin is inevitable, but it is not permanent.

The compatibilist lens reveals a world in which the horror of sin is not diminished, yet is made intelligible and in principle able to be endured and overcome. By accepting the compatibilist perspective, sin is seen as inevitable, but also as necessary for a greater good which includes–more, ensures–the overcoming of sin. Once sin and our freedom from it are viewed as inevitable, the greater good of the whole created order moves to center stage in the drama of creation. The unfolding of the full plan of God in and through the created order is the real wonder. The existence of the very created order we see, and not any obscure order of justice, is the greater good for which the permission of sin is necessary. Aquinas' teaching concerning the goodness of God and the permission of sin shows new promise of coherence once his doctrine of freedom is understood in a compatibilist light.

Conclusion

Understanding Aquinas' account of freedom in compatibilist terms thus indeed reveals greater coherence in his account of the nature of human freedom and the role our freedom plays in the created order than do accounts infected with libertarian notions of freedom. The compatibilist understanding of freedom opens our eyes to a real and impressive level of control over their own actions which rational creatures exhibit, a level of control which is every bit as impressive as human experience reveals, even while it operates in a deterministic causal order. The compatibilist understanding of freedom reveals the possibility that the created order is fully causally deterministic, thus grounding a causally certain providence working though secondary causes, but without having recourse to immediate Bañezian intervention through which God steers the whole order through endless manipulation of its parts. The compatibilist understanding of freedom makes manifest the unfolding of the whole plan of God for creation as the proper context within which to view God's permission of sin; God's flooding the universe with his own wise and loving rule by drawing a properly disposed humanity into cooperative participation in His own nature is the greater good for which the permission of sin is necessary.

There seems to be a compatibilist alternative to traditional and more fully libertarian readings of Aquinas on freedom, providence, and the goodness of God.

Notes

1. See R. Garrigou-Lagrange, *God: His Existence and His Nature*, and *Predestination*, both tr. Dom Bede Rose, (St. Louis: B. Herder Book. Co.) 1936, 1939, and *Grace*, tr. Dominican Nuns (St. Louis: B. Herder Book. Co.) 1952. There are of course a number of distinguished writers with varying positions which–in part for lack of competence, in part for lack of space–I am grouping together under the "traditional Thomist" label. Some justification for this categorization lies in the fact that Maritain, Garrigou-Lagrange, and many others with greater competency and more space did the same: see *God and the Permission of Evil*, p. 18-19; *Grace*, p. 202-203; see also Msgr. Joseph Pohle's *Grace: Actual and Habitual*, ed. A. Preuss (St. Louis: B. Herder Book Co.) 1945, p. 232-248; Mark Pontifex, *Freedom and Providence* (New York: Hawthorn Books) 1960, p. 66-68.

2. Jacques Maritain, *God and the Permission of Evil*, tr. Joseph Evans, (Milwaukee: Bruce Pub. Co.) 1966; *St. Thomas and the Problem of Evil* (Milwaukee: Marquette University Press, 1942). By libertarian intuions about freedom I mean the inclination to accept entirely or in some modified form the definition of freedom given by Molina in the *Concordia*: "Free will is the faculty which, given all the requirements for acting, can either act or not."

3. To follow one set of responses to this and other problems facing libertarian readings of St. Thomas, see Fr. John H. Wright, S.J., "The Eternal Plan of Divine Providence," *Theological Studies* Vol. 27, No. 1, March 1966; "Divine Knowledge and Human Freedom: The God Who Dialogues," *Theological Studies* Vol. 38, No. 3, September 1977; and his articles entitled "God," "Providence," and "Predestination" in *The New Dictionary of Theology* (Wilmington, DE: Michael Glazier, Inc.) 1987, pp. 423-436, 815-818, 797-798. My thanks are due to Fr. Wright for his remarks on a draft of this paper. To see one way in which Fr. Wright's views seem to diverge from St. Thomas's, see esp. p. 45 and note 42 of his "The Eternal Plan of Divine Providence;" cf. *Summa Theologiae I* q. 23, a. 7, where both the number and the specific individuals who are certainly predestined is said to be preordained *per se*. Fr. Wright's claim that predestination of specific individuals is accom-

plished through God's consequent will does not seem to provide him with the resources to account for the clear distinction which St. Thomas makes in this article between the prosperity of the particular ox (which must be ordained through God's consequent will) and the salvation of particular rational creatures.

4. Lonergan's work originally appeared as a series of four articles (cited individually below) in *Theological Studies*, Vols. II (1941) and III (1942), reprinted as *Grace and Freedom: Operative Grace in the Thought of St. Thomas Aquinas* (Herder and Herder, 1971). On the implications of Lonergan's work for the interpretations of Maritain and Garrigou-Lagrange, see Fr. David Burrell's "Jacques Maritain and Bernard Lonergan on Divine and Human Freedom" in *The Future of Thomism*, ed. Deal W. Hudson and Dennis W. Moran, University of Notre Dame Press, 1991.

5. For a critical review of Lottin's (and Lonergan's) theory of a radical change in Aquinas' understanding of freedom, see Daniel Westberg, "Did Aquinas Change His Mind about the Will?", *The Thomist* Vol. 58, No. 1 (Jan 1994), p. 41–60. The presentation below of a compatibilist reading of the nature of the will, its acts, and their causes is itself evidence against the thesis that Thomas' thought underwent drastic movement toward the ascending voluntarism of his day.

6. *Summa Theologiae I* (hereafter *I, I-II, II-II, III*) q. 87, a. 4: "...actus voluntatis nihil aliud est quam inclinatio quaedam consequens formam intellectam, sicut appetitus naturalis est inclinatio consequens formam naturalem." And in the *Prima Secundae*: "...the act of the will is nothing else than an inclination proceeding from the interior principle of knowledge, just as the natural appetite is an inclination proceeding from an interior principle without knowledge." ("actus voluntatis nihil est aliud quam inclinatio quedam procedens ab interiori principio cognoscente: sicut appetitus naturalis est quaedam inclinatio ab interiori principio et sine cognitione." *I-II* q. 6, a. 4.) All quotations from Aquinas are from the Marietti edition, save those from the *Summa Contra Gentiles*, which are from the Leonine.

7. *Summa Contra Gentiles* (hereafter *SCG*) II, 47, 48.

8. *De Veritate* q. 22, a. 6; *I* q. 105, a. 4; *I-II* q. 10, a. 2; *De Malo* q. 6, a. 1.

9. *I-II* q. 10, a. 2, and q. 17, a. 1, ad 2m; *De Malo* q. 6, a. 1.

10. On nonnecessitation: *De Veritate* q. 22, a. 6; q. 24, a. 12; *I* q. 82, a. 1; *In III De Anima* L. 3, (621); *De Malo* q. 6, a. 1; On self-movement: *De Veritate* q. 24, a. 1; *SCG* II, 48; *I* q. 83, a. 1c, ad 3m; *Compendium Theologiae* I, c. 76; *De Malo* q. 6, a. 1; On control: *De Veritate* q. 24, a. 1, 2, 4; *SCG* II, 48.

11. *I* q. 87, a. 4; *I-II* q. 17, a. 1.

12. *SCG* II, 48: "...no judging power moves itself to judge unless it reflects on its own action; for it is necessary, if it moves itself to judge, that it know its own judgment." ("Nulla autem potentia iudicans seipsam ad iudicandum movet nisi supra actum suum reflectatur: Oportet enim, si se ad iudicandum agit, quod suum iudicium cognosca.")

13. *I* q. 82, a. 4.

14. *I-II* q. 9, a. 3.

15. I am leaving aside a good many complexities arising from the distinction between commanded and elicited acts: the will can move itself and other faculties either directly, indirectly, or (for some faculties) both. For a discussion of some of the complexities of the complete human act, see Alan Donagan's "Thomas Aquinas on Human Action" in *The Cambridge History of Later Medieval Philosophy*, ed. Kretzmann, et al. (Cambridge University Press, 1982) p. 642-654.

16. The distinction between these dimensions of human freedom is discussed most clearly in *De Malo* q. 6, a. 1; See also *I-II* q. 9, a. 1, and q. 10, a. 2; *De Veritate* q. 22, a. 6.

17. Some interpreters (see Joseph J. Sikora, S.J., "Freedom and Nihilation," *The Modern Schoolman*, XLIII, Nov. 1965, p. 23ff.) have identified freedom of exercise as the root of freedom of specification, and thus as the most basic element of freedom. It seems to me that St. Thomas's position was precisely the reverse. It is because the intellect can apprehend its own acts as particular goods—and thus as good or as not good in some respect—that the will is able to incline or not to incline toward the intellect's continuing to consider a given object under the aspect of good and suitable. Hence, particular apprehended objects need not move the will, even if the intellect's assessment of them continues to be that they are both good and suitable, because the intellect can focus on its own continued apprehension under an aspect in which that continued apprehension is not both good and suitable. See *De Malo* q. 6, a. 1; *I-II* q. 10, a. 2; q. 13, a. 6.

18. *De Veritate* q. 24, a. 1, a. 2; *SCG* II, 48; *I-II* q. 17, a. 1, ad 2; *De Malo* q. 6, a. 1.

19. *I* q. 83, a. 2 ad 1. See J. B. Korolec's "Free Will and Free Choice" in *The Cambridge History of Later Medieval Philosophy*, p. 629-641, for a brief discussion of the history of *liberum arbitrium* and its relationship to intellect, will, choice, and freedom.

20. *I* q. 83, a. 1 ad 3; *I-II* q. 9 a. 4 ad 1, 3; *Compendium Theologiae* I, 129; *De Malo* q. 6, a. 1 ad 4.

21. *De Veritate* q. 22, a. 9; *I* q. 82, a. 4, and *I-II* q. 9, a. 6; *De Malo* q. 6. a. 1.

22. *De Veritate* q. 24, a. 14; *I-II* q. 6, a. 1 ad 3: "God moves man to act...by proposing the appetible to the senses, or by affecting a change

in his body..." ("...Deus movet hominem ad agendum...sicut proponens sensui appetibile, vel sicut immutans corpus...")

23. *De Potentia* q. 3, a.7; *SCG* III, 67.

24. *I-II* q. 6, a. 1 ad 3.

25. *SCG* III, 70; *I*, q. 22, a. 2, 3.

26. *I-II* q. 10, a. 1; *De Malo* q. 6, a. 1.

27. *De Veritate* q. 22, a. 9; *I* q. 82, a. 4, and *I-II* q. 9, a. 6; *De Malo* q. 6, a. 1.

28. *I-II* q. 9, a. 4, and *SCG* III, 89; *De Malo* q. 6, a. 1.

29. *I-II* q. 9, a. 6, corpus and ad 3.

30. *I* q. 83, a. 1c, ad 3 and q. 105, a. 4, ad 2; *I-II* q. 6, a. 1, ad 3, and q. 9, a. 4, ad 1, 3; *De Malo* q. 6, a. 1 ad 4.

31. *I-II* q. 9, a. 6 ad 3m.

32. *I-II* q. 109, a. 1, 2.

33. *I-II* q. 110, a. 3.

34. *I-II* q. 109, a. 2, 5.

35. *I-II* q. 109, a. 7: "...requiritur auxilium gratiae ad hoc quod homo a peccato resurgat, et quantum ad habituale donum, et quantum ad interiorem Dei motionem." ("...the help of grace is required in order for a man to rise from sin, both as to a habitual gift, and as to the interior motion of God.")

36. *I-II* q. 109, a. 6c and ad 3, a. 9 ad 3.

37. *I-II* q. 109, a. 6.

38. *I-II* q. 109, a. 9 ad 1.; q. 110, a. 2.

39. *I-II* q. 109, a. 1, 2.

40. The twofold pattern of movement on the side of the exercise of the will's acts and on the side of the specification thereof is repeated throughout Aquinas's discussion of divine help beyond bestowing habitual grace in *I-II*: q. 109 a. 1, a. 2 ad 1 (ex), ad 2 (spec), a. 6, a. 9; q. 110 a. 2; q. 111, a. 2. See also *De Veritate* q. 24, a. 15.

41. *I-II* q. 109, a. 6.

42. *I-II* q. 109, aa. 1, 6, 7.

43. *De Malo* q. 3, a. 1, ad 8.

44. *I-II* q. 113 a. 3c and ad 2 on justice; a. 7 ad 4 on merit.

45. *I* q. 19 a. 6.

46. *De Malo* q. 6, a. 1, ad 15.

47. In *VI Libros Metaphysicorum* L. 3 (1192, 3); *SCG* III, 86; *I-II* q. 75, a. 1, ad 2.

48. These grounds for the will's nonnecessitation are given in *De Malo* q. 6, a. 1.

49. *I* q. 82, a. 5, ad 3; *I-II* q. 113, a. 7 ad 2; *SCG* III, 89; *De Malo* q. 6, a. 1. James F. Keenan stops short of considering this possibility; see his "The Problem with Thomas Aquinas' Concept of Sin," *Heythrop*

Journal XXXV (1994), pp. 401–420, esp . p. 405. Keenan argues that Aquinas overcame his intellectual determinism by introducing the priority of the will's exercise over its specification, and that he carried that revised emphasis on exercise into his treatment of the theological virtues (where the parallel distinction is between charity and prudence), but that Thomas failed to adjust his account of sin accordingly. The compatibilist reading seems committed to turning the perceived failure around, employing it as evidence that the perceived shift toward priority of freedom of exercise is illusory. I think that Westberg's discussion ("Did Aquinas Change His Mind about the Will") and the presentation of a compatibilist reading of freedom unseats Keenan's (and Lonergan's, Lottin's) change thesis. But Keenan is owed a compatibilist reading of Aquinas' account of the virtues.

    50. A position reaffirmed in *I-II* q. 6, a. 4; see note 6, above.

    51. Here as elsewhere I have omitted a discussion of the role of the faculties of sensory apprehension and appetite (the passions.) Including mention of these and the causes operating on them would complexify but not substantially alter the overview of the nature of the intellect, will, and their causes offered here. See *I-II* q. 9, a.2; q. 10, a. 3; and then q. 6, a. 1 ad 3.

    52. In *VI Libros Metaphysicorum*, L. 3, 1201: "ens per accidens non habet causam neque generationem;" also, *De Malo* q. 6, a. 1, ad 21: "Nor again is it true that everything that is done has a natural cause, for those things which are done *per accidens* are not done by any active natural cause, since what is *per accidens* is not being and one." ("Nec iterum verum est quod omne quod fit, habeat causam naturalem; ea enim quae fiunt per accidens, non fiunt ab aliqua causa activa naturali; quia quod est per accidens, non est ens et unum.") See also SCG III, 74; *I* q. 115, a. 6; q. 116, a. 1.

    53. In *I Peri Hermeneias* L. 14; *In I Libros Ethicorum* L. 1, l. 5. Thanks to Al Howsepian for pointing out to me the latter text in his comments on a draft of part of this paper.

    54. In *VI Libros Metaphysicorum*, L. 3, 1220.

    55. *SCG* III, 72; *In VI Libros Metaphysicorum*, L. 3, (1221).

    56. In *VI Libros Metaphysicorum* L. 3, (1201); In *I Peri Hermeneias* L. 14.

    57. *Compendium Theologiae I*, c. 140: "Multo magis hoc ex sapientia divinae dispositionis contingit, ut quamvis causae contingentes deficere possint quantum est de se ab effectu, tamen quibusdam adminiculis adhibitis indeficienter sequatur effectus, quod ejus contingentiam non tollit. Sic ergo patet quod rerum contingentia divinae providentiae certitudinem non excludit." (See Cyril Vollert, S.J., *Compendium of Theology*, B. Herder Book Co., 1947, p. 150.)

58. *I* q. 23, a. 6.

59. *In VI Libros Metaphysicorum* L. 3, (1220): "Invenitur igitur unius cuiusque effectus secundum quod est sub ordine divinae providentiae necessitatem habere."

60. The ordering itself of secondary causes is said not to have the nature of fate, except as dependent on God (*I* q. 116, a. 2 ad 1); but inasmuch as all that happens on earth is subject to divine providence, the existence of fate can be admitted (q. 116, a. 1). See the example in *I* q. 115, a. 6 of a burning object crashing down on particular combustible matter.

61. *I* q. 114, a. 4.

62. *In VIII L. Physicorum* L. XII (1074): "...ea quae non simul sunt, non possunt esse causa alicuius..."

63. Whether these causes can be comprehended through classification of causes in the context of an extended community of shared inquiry is another—and open—question; whether there can be a scientific study of human behavior, that is.

64. *SCG* III, 96 (8), tr. Vernon J. Bourke (NY: Doubleday & Co.), 1956.

65. *SCG* III, 96 (14), tr. Bourke.

66. *SCG* III, 94, esp. (6), (15) of Bourke's translation.

67. The best piece of evidence to the contrary is employed forcefully by Lonergan ("St. Thomas' Thought on Gratia Operans," *Theological Studies* III (1942), p. 549-552.) The suggestion Aquinas makes that moral evil may fall into a special category of absolute objective falsity does, on the face of it, suggest that the will stands outside the order of determinate causality in some respect; why else might one distinguish between the category of intelligible but accidental failure, on one hand, and unintelligible accidental failure, on the other? One direction for a compatibilist reply would note the difference between God's intentions for the good of intelligent species, versus nonintelligent creatures: only with intelligent creatures does God intend the good of each individual member of the species. Failure of an intelligent creature, which necessarily involves voluntary evil, is directly contrary to the antecedent will of God, and stands in need of an explanation. And while an explanation is forthcoming for moral evil in general, there is none for the moral failure of each individual. For the will of that creature is the proximate *per accidens* cause of its sin, and there is no higher cause, since the sin is not intended by God. Nonmoral evil also has only a *per accidens* cause, but no explanation for it is called for, since it is not opposed to the antecedent will of God; hence, the lack of a *per se* cause of nonmoral evil constitutes no lack of intelligibility.

68. See the Pohle-Preuss analysis of the standard Thomist position in

Grace: Actual and Habitual (St. Louis: B. Herder) 1945, p. 232-248.

69. See Portalié's summary in Edmund G. Fortman, S.J., ed., *The Theology and Man and Grace* (Milwaukee: The Bruce Publishing Co.) 1966, p. 139: "In our time, we must admit, a good number of critics on all sides favor the strict interpretation which sees in Augustine a theory of divine determinism fatal to freedom of the will."

70. *Poetics* 1451a30.

71. Consider Maritain's vehement accusation against antecedent permissive decrees as insulting to "the absolute innocence of God." *God and the Permission of Evil*, chapter I, section II.

72. *SCG* III, 90: "Omnia corporalia per spiritualia administrantur...Spiritualia autem agunt in corporalia per voluntatem. Si igitur electiones et motus voluntatem intellectualium substantiarum ad Dei providentiam non pertinent, sequitur quod etiam corporalia ipsius providentae subtrahantur. Et sic totaliter nulla erit providentia."

73. See esp. sections III and IV of Lonergan's "St. Thomas' Theory of Operation," p. 383-391.

74. *De Vertitate* q. 24 a. 15: "non enim potest sciri modus praeparationis ad formam, nisi forma ipsa cognoscatur." See also *SCG* III, q. 149.

75. The love of God itself would be grace, properly speaking; the readiness and steadfastness would be supernatural virtues, effects of that grace. *I-II* q. 110 a. 3.

76. *Theological Studies* III (1942), "St. Thomas' Theory of Operation," p. 399.

77. *Theological Studies* III (1942), "St. Thomas's Thought on Gratia Operans," p. 572.

78. The general's intention is present in the flagman only as the principle of intelligible ordering of the effects the general produced in the flagman precisely in order to accomplish the general's intention. With grace, the analogous effects are present in the soul, but the intention is present there in an additional way, as well; the soul participates in the divine nature, and thus God's intention is present because God is.

79. On the Bañezian account, God's application constitutes an immediate activation directed toward each act of each created agent in addition to whatever activation derives from a being of its nature being placed in determinate causal circumstances. Garrigou-Lagrange objected to the attachment of the Bañezian appellation to standard Thomistic accounts of grace; he thought the Bañezian line was plainly rooted firmly in the texts of Aquinas and the interpretive tradition prior to Bañez. (See *Grace*: the section entitled "The Bañezian Comedy and Contemporary Syncretism," p. 445.) Pohle-Preuss ascribes the Thomist position to Bañez in just the way that troubles Garrigou-Lagrange; see

their *Grace: Actual and Habitual*, p. 232.

80. Fr. Burrell considers these prospects to be bright, along the lines of Maritain's interpretation. See his "Jacques Maritain and Bernard Lonergan on Divine and Human Freedom" in *The Future of Thomism*, ed. Deal W. Hudson and Dennis W. Moran, University of Notre Dame Press, 1991.

81. Here and above I am leaving aside the evident development of Aquinas' thought on the extent of the causal certitude of providence. Plainly the model which Aquinas employed in his discussions of providence in *De Veritate* q. 5 and 6–one of divine government ordered toward the achievement of generalized ends while leaving aside concern for which particular means achieves those ends–gave way by the time of the *Contra Gentiles* (III, 64–98) to the notion of a universal cause including all particular causes within its causal reach. That same doctrine of the universal order is carried over into the *Prima Pars* and beyond. Treating the mature view as Aquinas' view *simpliciter* is a suitable approach, since the later view is not a radical departure from the earlier views, but rather the result of a more careful thinking through of the implications of earlier views. For with respect to the most important matters, providence was certain in its detail even in the *De Veritate*: see the account of predestination in q. 6 a. 3, and compare it with *SCG* III 163, where the notion of predestination has been brought under the notion of providence conceived of as universal cause.

82. Lonergan, "St. Thomas on Gratia Operans," p. 553. Lonergan allows "no end of room for God to work on free choice without violating it," but insists that no created antecedent can rigorously determine choice. Yet he never discusses whether the entire sum of causal antecedents determines choice. He implies that they do not when he insists that whatever is permitted to follow inevitably from a policy of inaction is intelligibly ordered, and thus not irrational, while sin is irrational (p. 552). But he offers little argument for his linking inevitability with intelligible ordering. In his silence he leaves unaddressed the possibility that what is foreseen by God as inevitably occurring but in no way intended requires an explanation insofar as it is a privation, a lack of due perfection and not a mere absence (*I-II* q. 75 a. 1). Sin alone falls into this category, and it has no *per se* cause, but only the created will as *per accidens* cause. But what has only a *per accidens* cause is fortuitous, and from every point of view save that of any intelligence who/ intentionally arranged for such an effect to be brought about through a combination of causes (*SCG* III, 92). But God does not combine causes with the intention of producing sin. Hence, sin which is a privation and requires an explanation has only a *per accidens* cause (the will of the creature), and thus no explanation of the sort required. So it is unintel-

ligible, in that sense, whether or not it follows inevitably from causes which God combined to produce other (nonsinful) effects.

83. These objects are either possible (a), or actual (b). If (a) God knows how free creatures will behave in every possible circumstance, and then chooses to actualize certain circumstances, then His knowledge when joined to His will is the cause of all actual things known in a substantial sense. But it would not be the cause of all possible things known; the ground for the truth values of counterfactual propositions about created free choices would lie outside of God (and apparently in no other being, since He would know these propositions logically prior to having created anything.) The resources necessary to sustain such an account must be drawn from outside the texts of Aquinas; Molinism is not a viable interpretive direction, unless as a corrective supplement to Aquinas' thought. But (b) if God "takes into account" the noncooperation of free creatures logically posterior to His having created them, then the state of these actual creatures is the cause of the likeness in God's knowledge. God's knowledge would seem to depend on His creation. (Sikora claims that "God does not depend on our nihilations in order to constitute His eternal plan; He simply takes them into account in freely decreeing this plan creatively." But God's taking into account a determining factor in created activity which God does not cause is a pretty close unfolding of what we might mean by God's knowledge and plan "depending" on creatures. See his "Freedom and Nihilation," Part II, p. 30.) But this dependence seems incompatible with the claim that God is pure act, standing in potency to nothing whatsoever (*SCG* I, 16). Aquinas insisted "that things that occur in time are the cause of something occurring in God...[is] impossible" (*SCG* III 96), and that God's knowledge is not in potency with respect to anything at all (*SCG* I, 71).

84. *De Veritate* q. 6, a. 1; see also aa. 2–4; *SCG* III, 161–163; *I* q. 23 aa. 1-8.

85. See Garrigou-Lagrange's discussion of the difficulties in his *Grace*, p. 450-464.

86. In *I* q. 22, a. 3, Aquinas affirms an immediate providence. But that immediacy is located in the plan of providence as it exists in the mind of God: He intends all that He causes, down to the detailed effects for which particular causes are assigned and given power. (This power is the natural power that follows from their natures, rather than any immediate divine activation beyond creation, conservation, and application via situation in particular causal circumstances, on Lonergan's account of providence.) But the execution of that plan of providence employs intermediate causes, that the dignity of causality might be imparted even to creatures. Divine determination is mediated in that sense.

87. See Garrigou-Lagrange, *Predestination*, tr. Dom Bede Rose (St. Louis: B. Herder Book Co.), 1939, p. 206-212. The section is entitled "The Motive for Reprobation."

88. *I* q. 21, a. 1.

89. R. Garrigou-Lagrange, *The One God*, p. 701.

90. Jacques Maritain, *God and the Permission of Evil*, chapter I, section II.

91. E.g., "it is impossible that the whole of the effect of predestination in general should have any cause as coming from us, because whatsoever is in man disposing him toward salvation is all included under the effect of predestination, even the preparation for grace" (*I* q. 23, a. 5).

92. Writing in the tradition of Maritain, Joseph Sikora admits that St. Thomas does not discuss initiatives in the line of nonbeing, but Sikora insists that this lack of discussion does not mean that St. Thomas was unaware of these matters. See Sikora's "Freedom and Nihilation: An Essay on the 'Free Existent and the Free Eternal Purposes'," part II, *The Modern Schoolman*, XLIII, Nov. 1965, p. 38.

93. *God and the Permission of Evil*, chapter II, section I.

94. That simple failure to be moved, on account of its own inadequate formation, is just the right description of the relationship between the grace of God and the uncooperative created will, on the compatibilist picture. Grace is always available, but the poorly formed will is inadequately disposed to be moved by it; there is no *per se* cause of that lack of proper formation, but only a *per accidens* cause, which is the will in its own movement toward whatever else besides cooperation with grace the will in fact inclined toward at the moment cooperation with grace was due.

95. *SCG* III, 74.

96. *SCG* III, 71.

97. *I* q. 22 a. 2 ad 2.

98. Romans 8:18.

99. Aquinas' expressed confidence (*I* q. 23, a. 7 ad 3) that those who ultimately fail are in the majority reveals the implications of Aristotelian natural philosophy and then-current approaches to interpreting the New Testament, more so than the inexhaustible hope of the children of God.

Chapter 2

Human Freedom and Divine Action:
Libertarianism in St. Thomas Aquinas

John H. Wright, S.J.

Compatibilists in considering God's providential action and human free choice affirm that God determines how human beings choose, but that these choices are nevertheless free. Human free choice, they say, is compatible with divine determinism. Libertarians, on the other hand, maintain that God's action does not determine the free act of the creature. Human freedom is incompatible with any kind of genuine outside determinism, even from God. The thesis of this paper is that the libertarians are right, and that this, at least implicitly, is the position of St. Thomas Aquinas.

Each position has its own problems. The compatibilists are hard pressed to explain how human acts are free. Libertarians are hard pressed to explain how God can know and cause an act whose specific determination truly comes from another agent.

Compatibilists maintain that all things, including the free acts of the created will, are subject to the order of divine providence in the sense that prior to taking account of any actions of created beings, God determines exactly, efficaciously, and unchangeably which events will occur and which will not. Further, God's providence is causally certain with respect to acts of the will: he determines each act of the will in precisely the way he likes, intending and causing everything of being and act in every act of a created will.

Explanations of how the human will acts freely in this concept of providence vary greatly. They agree in saying that to carry out this plan of providence God determines the free acts of the will to one of several possibilities, but without destroying human freedom. Molinists appeal to "middle knowledge," whereby God knows prior to any divine decree what every free creature will actually choose to do freely in every conceivable set of circumstances. God then arranges the circumstances (especially his own *concursus*, or cooperating motion), and so brings about the human act he wants to happen. The major problem with middle knowledge is that the connection between circumstances and free choice (which God is said to know) has no foundation either in God's essence or will (since this would mean determinism), or in the human will (since it has not acted). Banesians speak of a divine "physical" (i.e., actually real) premotion of the will to one, that moves the will infallibly, not only to its act, but to the mode of its act, viz. freedom. The major problem here is that it seems contradictory to say that the will is infallibly moved to one act and that the will is still free to choose to do another act, as the nature of free choice requires.

Libertarians reject the notion of providence as an exact, efficacious, immutable divine determination of all events that will occur or not occur, made prior to taking account of any actions of created beings. The plan of providence rather opens up possibilities and God then operates within these possibilities by a kind of contingency planning, i.e., he takes into account the various possibilities and determines in advance how to respond to them if they should occur.

We recognize this in human affairs. If I am planning a garden party, I will consider the possibility that it may rain and then make some provision for this possibility in my initial planning with a backup plan. My plan involves a goal with alternative plans for reaching the goal, depending on how contingent factors develop.

Similarly, the plan of providence has three moments[1] (what we describe here is an order of natural priority, not a temporal sequence):

> (1) God first determines the end that he intends in the act of creation: the divine goodness itself as shared in a particular way with created beings. God intends through creation to bring into existence a great community of finite beings sharing his happiness through vision, love and joy. This is eternal salvation, the society of the blessed.
>
> (2) To realize this goal God devises a plan that has two moments: the antecedent plan and the consequent plan of providence.
>
> In the antecedent plan God determines all that will actually be possible in the world throughout the course of time. This determination is made without taking into account any actual created acts or choices. It simply opens up the world of possibilities. Here God makes possible the salvation of all free created persons, and wills them to participate in the society of the blessed. He provides all that is necessary to bring this about. But he also makes it possible for these beings to refuse salvation, since

the community he intends is a community of friends, not of slaves and automata. Thus, this plan contains the possibility of evil without determining that any particular evil actually happens. It also contains how God responds to whatever happens, how he orders to his goal whatever possibilities are chosen.

(3) In the consequent plan, God actualizes those possibilities of the antecedent plan that correspond to the choices made by free creatures, and he orders the acts they have chosen to the end he intends. The consequent plan of providence actually governs the world and brings forth infallibly and efficaciously all that it contains. But it takes into account the choices of creatures.

That Thomas Aquinas himself actually thought in terms of contingency planning is shown, it seems to me, when he asks whether the will of God is always fulfilled. St. Augustine had answered this question in terms of the omnipotence of the divine will. In the *Summa Theologica* (1a p., q. 19, a. 6), Thomas answers it in terms of the universality of the divine will:

> Since therefore the will of God is the universal cause of all things, it is impossible that the divine will will not achieve its effect. Hence what seems to depart from the divine will according to one order falls back into it according to another. Thus, a sinner, who as far as it lies with him, departs from the divine will by sinning, falls into the order of the divine will, while he is punished by God's justice.

I do not agree that anything or anyone outside the free agent itself determines the act of the human will to one. The human being determines his or her own power of acting to one act, freely resolving the contingency of the human acting power, by choosing one out of a number of alternative ways of acting that are perceived as actually possible. In the *Summa Contra Gentiles* (Book 1, ch. 68), Thomas wrote: "The dominion which the will has over its own acts, through which it is in its power to will or not will, excludes the determination of its acting power (*virtus*) to one, and the contrary motion (*violentiam*) of an exterior acting cause; but it does not exclude the influence of a higher cause, from which it has existence and activity. Thus, causality remains in the first cause which is God with respect to the motions of the will: so that God knowing himself can know things of this sort." It is important to note here that Thomas does not suppose that causality itself is always determining.

God's Knowledge of Free Acts

Having taken a resolutely libertarian position I am faced with the fundamental difficulty I noted earlier: How can God know free acts in his causality without himself determining those acts to one?

The old argument between Banesians and Molinists in the late 16th and early 17th centuries, on the matter of grace and free will noted above, centered around how God determines the free will to one act and yet leaves it free. I first learned of this confrontation back in 1940 when I was eighteen years old, reading the life of St. Robert Bellarmine, by James Broderick, S.J. My immediate reaction was: both sides are mistaken. They are trying to explain away an intrinsic contradiction. I have never departed from this conviction.

I got an insight into a new way of viewing the problem in 1944 or 1945, when I was studying philosophy. It took some time to mature, but I eventually published two articles: "The Eternal Plan of Providence," in *Theological Studies* in March 1966, and "Divine Knowledge and Human Freedom: the God Who Dialogues," in the same journal in September 1977.

Over the years I have tried in various ways to express as simply and clearly as I could what seems to me to be the truth about this fundamentally mysterious and profound matter.[2] I offer this as another way of expressing it: Both causality and knowledge are everywhere constituted by *intentional structure*, i.e., by a network of relations or intentions which in one case join cause and effect, and in the other, knower and known. For example, when I freely act as a cause of something, I choose to produce a particular effect. In the intentional structure of causality, my free choice orders my power of making to bring about this effect.

Likewise, in and through the act of human judgment, where I affirm S is P, I know and possess some truth. The intentional structure of this act of knowledge is very clear: a certain intelligible content (the predicate) is referred to, affirmed of, a subject. Note that the act of referring the predicate to the subject does not increase or change the intelligible content of the predicate, but it does give it a kind of order to the subject for the knowing agent, which it does not have apart from this act of referral. Likewise, the choice to make something does not increase or change my power of making, but it does direct it to a particular effect. The actual making no doubt changes my power of making, but that is subsequent to the choice.

In God, knowledge and causality of the created world also involve an intentional structure which, without increasing or changing the divine perfection, orders it to be shared in some way with the created world. We may note three related ways in which Thomas speaks of this intentional structure. First, he says that God's knowledge is a cause of things, inasmuch as his will is joined to it. This is the commonest way for him to speak. It means that God knows and causes the actual world by willing something to exist which he knows can exist (cf. S.T. 1a p., q. 14, a. 8.). Second, he expresses this by saying that the idea of a creature in God is incomplete unless an act of the will gives it an order or respect to the creature. He refers to an analogy with the form of an art object in the mind of an artist: it becomes the idea of an actual object only when the artist wills to execute it (cf. De Pot. q. 1, a. 5, ad 11.). Finally, Thomas distinguishes between the substance of the divine action, which is eternal and necessary, and the order to an effect, which depends on the divine will. He says that although the divine action itself could never cease, the order to the effect could, if God wished it (cf. De Pot., q. 5, a. 3, ad 6m.).

In all of this Thomas is describing the intentional structure which constitutes God's causative knowledge. What God knows to be possible as a created participation in his goodness, he wills to be actual and in this union of knowing and willing he establishes an order to the effect through which he both knows and causes the actual effect.

Furthermore, this intentional structure is not just in our minds as we reflect on God's action; it is also, Thomas says, in God's mind, as known by him (cf. De Pot. q. 3, a. 16, ad 14m; S.T. 1a p., q. 15, a. 2, ad 4m.).

We must note that the intentional structure of knowing and causing in God are identical: he knows the existing world and everything in it in causing it; he causes the world in knowing it. Whatever, then, is required for the intentional structure of causing by that very fact is required for the intentional structure of knowing, and vice versa. Let me anticipate a bit to observe that if God cannot cause a free human act except through a human will acting freely, he cannot know a free human act except through a human will acting freely.

Now, the divine will is related in different ways to what is possible and what is actual. God in willing the possible makes it actual. Then, existing creatures, when they have come to be, are objects of the divine will. In the initial act of creation, when a creature is being first made to exist, only the divine goodness as imitable by the creature is an object of the divine will; but when the creature itself has come into existence, it too is an object of the divine will. As Thomas wrote: "God wills both himself to exist and other things; but himself as end, other things as [ordered] to the end, inasmuch as it is fitting for the divine goodness that other things participate in it" (S.T. 1a p., q. 19, a. 2.).

Now, if God wills creatures as ordered to the divine goodness, then creatures themselves by that very fact enter into the intentional structure by which God causes them to participate in his goodness. This means that they enter into the intentional structure by which God knows and causes them to exist, the intentional structure which is the union of the

divine will with the divine knowledge of what is otherwise merely possible. St Thomas wrote: "Although the divine will cannot be hindered
or changed by something else, still according to the order of wisdom it
bears upon something according to the condition of that thing; and thus
something is attributed to the divine will from our part" (*De Veritate.* q.
23, a. 2, ad 4m).

Likewise, God is the first cause not only of the being but also of all
the activities of which creatures are the secondary and specifying causes. This means that God causes the activities of creatures through these
creatures. They enter into the intentional structure by which God is the
cause of their actions. As God wills the creature to act, God wills the
acting creature as ordered to the divine goodness to participate in it in
this way, and thus through the acting creature the will of God is united
to the divine goodness known as imitable, so that God knows and causes the creature to act according to its own proper nature.

Finally, when God wills a free creature to act freely, he moves it to
act without determining its will to one act, either internally or externally, though he may indeed through grace incline it nonnecessarily to a
particular act. The human will under the impulse of the divine will
freely orders its own power of acting to one of several possibilities. This
ordering to one is not itself a further perfection of its power of acting,
but the determination by which the power of acting is directed toward
one act. God, willing the creature as so determining itself, produces
through the creature the free act that the creature is choosing. The freely
acting creature enters into the intentional structure by which God knows
and causes. That is, it enters into the union of will and knowledge,
which constitutes causative knowledge. God, in this way, both causes
and knows the free act of the creature without determining the free creature to one, but leaving the determination of the act in the power of the
creature.

This raises a further question about the relationship of time and eternity. For we suppose that God's knowledge is eternal and does not wait
upon developments in time. I add here three short paragraphs from a
response I gave in 1989 at a meeting of the Catholic Theological
Society of America:

> It seems to me that in the divine duration there are no successive
> moments, where something truly comes to be that was not there before.
> I can recognize an order of priority, as we say that the Father is before the
> Son, and the Father and the Son are before the Holy Spirit. But there
> never was a time when the Son or the Holy Sprit was not. Similarly,
> though the choice to create is a free choice, and God is intrinsically intel-
> ligibly different for making this choice, there never was a time when he

had not chosen to be Creator. In the very depths of the divine eternity, from the very beginning, God chooses to be Creator, to share the abundance of the divine goodness with others who are not God. This created world may or may not have had a first moment of its existence; but throughout its existence it has always depended on this free choice of God.

This choice of God seems to me to contain the whole divine initiative toward creation. It supposes the total awareness of all that is possible, for God here makes it possible. And God's providence here determines how every possible eventuality may be directed to the goal of his loving purpose. He does not determine in this creative choice what those eventualities will actually be, but he foresees all that can be, and decides how the creatures involved may be led through every situation and occurrence toward the divine goal, if only we are willing.

Time then exists as a genuine but incommensurable reality within the total expanse of eternity. The entire temporal continuum lives within the creative choice of God, distinct from that choice and yet totally dependent on it. In this temporal continuum creatures freely and responsibly choose among the possibilities that are opened to them by the creative love of God. And all of these choices from the beginning to the end without end, are present to the Creator in the eternity of the divine choice. He knows them eternally because he causes them eternally in and through the free, self-determining choices of creatures, who are all present to him, even though they are not all present to one another, but succeed one another in time.[3]

Notes

1. See my "The Eternal Plan of Providence," *Theological Studies* 27 (1966): 27-57.

2. See "Divine Knowledge and Human Freedom: the God Who Dialogues," *Theological Studies* 38 (1977): 450-477, and the articles in *New Dictionary of Theology* (Wilmington, DE: Michael Glazier, Inc., 1987): "God," 423-436; "Providence," 815-818; and "Predestination," 797-798. See also "A Response to 'Not a Sparrow Falls': On Providence and Responsibility in History," *Proceedings of the Forty-Fourth Annual Convention*, Catholic Theological Society of America (1989): 39-42.

3. CTSA *Proceedings* 44 (1989): 40-41.

Chapter 3

Predestination as a Condition of Freedom:
Reconsidering the Reformation

Kyle A. Pasewark

Introduction: Rediscovering the Question of Predestination
There is hardly a more universally despised theological doctrine than that of "predestination." It is nothing short of an embarrassment. Even those theologians who continue to be pleased that Christian thought is "foolishness to the Greeks" shrink from the nonsense of predestination. Foolishness is one thing, absurdity quite another. Is it not clear, after all, that a predestining God renders human freedom and therefore moral responsibility, intellectual discovery, and aesthetic creativity, utterly moot? Is not everything in history, all that is done, thought, or said, for better or worse, made merely an epiphenomenon of a divine board game played purely for a perverse divine pleasure? And is it not obvious that this God who would do little more than toy with us could not be a God of love but only of heartless domination?

Yet it is at least curious that many of the great giants of Western thought, from Augustine to Thomas to Luther and Calvin, found themselves driven to affirm some form of what has come to be called "predestinarianism." It is surprising that despite their differences on other theological and philosophical issues, partial agreement on this most distasteful assertion remained.[1] It is possible, of course, that the nineteenth and twentieth centuries as well as the predestinarians' own opponents are correct. But is it not also possible to question these opponents, to say nothing of ourselves? We may ask whether our usual manner of discussing the doctrine of predestination, to the extent we bother really discussing it at all anymore, has anything at all to do with how its advocates understood it. Moderns believe predestination is but another word for strict determinism, albeit a divine determinism above one operating merely through finite causes and effects. The question between mundane determinism and predestination, it seems, is only whether there is a super-cause above who enslaves us, God, or whether the great tyranny is effected by much lesser causes. If one finds earth-bound determinism unpalatable then certainly divine determinism is incomparably more offensive.

But this equation between predestinarianism and determinism is the point at which twentieth-century thought must be questioned. Does the classic understanding of predestination fit neatly into debates between determinism and free will or has it been miscast by being placed within the scope of these disputes? Is predestination another name for inscrutable and inevitable external causalities or does that interpretation force our own notions upon the history of thought? And if predestination means something other than deterministic causality, does it mean something valuable for the late twentieth century? Our claim is twofold: first, predestination is not principally a claim about divine causality and second, predestinarianism has much to teach us about the conditions and limits of freedom. Far from being the negation of freedom, some notion of predestination is in fact the condition of meaningful freedom. We will demonstrate the thesis by means of a treatment of the strictest and apparently most offensive understanding of predestination, the double predestination of Luther and Calvin, with emphasis upon Luther.[2] The fundamental insight contained in these most belligerent predestinarians is this: freedom cannot establish its own significance; instead, the condition of the meaningfulness of freedom must arise from beyond the realm of any and all particular free choices and even from beyond free choice itself.[3]

The Meaning of Predestination for Luther: Beyond Determinism

We must begin by unlocking predestinarianism from the deterministic cage into which it has been forced. A preliminary indication of the error of our usual understanding of predestinarianism as supernaturally elevated determinism consists in the odd fact that none of the classical champions of predestination, including Augustine and Thomas, can be interpreted as merely wanting to safeguard divine causality against the finite causalities posited by determinism. All believed God operates through finite causes and is omnipotent in relation to them. Certainly, the Reformation understanding of predestination is not primarily a theory of finite causality. This is its principal difference from all forms of determinism, and equally its distinction from direct responses to determinism. The disagreements between determinists and libertarians are largely irrelevant to the Reformers' focus. Although Luther's predestinarianism has been distorted frequently by exclusive concentration on the *Bondage of the Will* while ignoring Luther's broader theology, even a careful reading of *Bondage of the Will* should be enough to give pause to an equation between predestination and determinism. Luther is quite clear that he is not speaking about earthly, finite causes. Erasmus, Luther protests, misunderstands him.[4] To be sure, free choice "does many things, but these are nonetheless 'nothing' in the sight of God."[5] Erasmus "quibbles about temporal bondage, as if this had anything to do with the case."[6] Free choices are possible but are "allowed to man only with respect to what is beneath him and not what is above him;" free choice indeed exists on earth since humans are the greatest of earthly creatures but our choices cannot pertain to matters of God and salvation, those matters above us.[7]

Luther's meaning is simply this: whatever else freedom does, it does not influence one's salvation—it can neither cause it nor cooperate in it. Many have exercised "free choice to the utmost of their powers" but "none of them was able to attain to grace."[8] This is a quite different proposition than an argument about whether I am compelled by certain prior causes to write this article. Its writing is "below" me, a matter for my earthly freedom, for my decision of yes or no. Rather, Luther's assertion is that this writing makes no difference to my final destiny, which is either salvation or damnation. And this destiny is uncontrollable by finite human actors; rather, it is decided by God above us.

Luther's Theology of Grace

It is clear, then, why Luther gave Erasmus credit for attacking the center of his thought. *Predestination is simply another expression of Luther's doctrine of justification by grace alone.*[9] It is a combination of the "alone" and a different geography of grace that gives the Reformation understanding of justification its distinctive cast. No empirical, earthly factor can interfere with or influence God's sovereign decision either to save or allow the devil's domination to take its course to damnation.

The forensic, juridical aspect of Luther's concept of justification by grace is irreducible. Justification is not exhausted by its forensic component but that element cannot be eliminated. Grace is simply God's decision to save, to transfer the sin that we are and which merits our damnation onto Christ.[10] This is Luther's principal difference from the classical Roman understanding of grace. In contrast to the Roman church Luther denies that grace is a quality of the soul that becomes the believer's property. Erasmus among others does not seem to have grasped this point. Grace is not a component of earthly being. Through original sin, sin became our substantial character. Grace, in contrast, is purely at God's discretion and remains always external to its recipient.[11] Therefore,

> although forgiveness has been imputed and thus sin is removed so that it is not imputed, nevertheless, it is not substantially or essentially destroyed except in the conflagration of fire by which the whole world and our bodies will be completely purified on the last day...In the meantime, while we live, original sin also lives...Therefore, sin is only remitted by imputation, but when we die, it is destroyed essentially.[12]

Luther's notion of grace is not psychological; in the end it may have psychological effects but purely as grace it stands outside its beneficiary.

Thus, grace cannot be acted upon by humans under any circumstances because it is not ours as a possession. *Grace is predestining grace by definition.* But since it is utterly external to its beneficiary and to the world it cannot alter or remove freedom in the world. The distance between predestination and a theory of causality is evident from the beginning. It is possible to confuse these two with each other only if grace is made a present possession of the elect, a quality the elect possess in the same way they possess a body, spirit, history, and so on.

The externality of grace implies, in addition, that the decree of grace is a declaration about the entire person and not particular aspects of the person. Grace and wrath are judgments upon the whole person-one cannot be, for Luther, partially saved or condemned, just as the lawbreaker cannot be imprisoned partially. Luther says:

> Now it follows that these two, wrath and grace, are so related-since they are outside us-that they are poured out upon the whole, so that he who is under wrath is wholly under the whole of wrath, while he who is under grace is wholly under the whole of grace, because wrath and grace have to do with persons...[God] does not divide this grace as gifts are divided.[13]

The totality of God's judgment is a clear indication of the expanse between Luther's view of predestination and arguments about worldly determinism. No earthly cause is total and irrevocable. The determinist position relies upon positing a series of partial causes which together bind that which they affect to a certain course. Had one or two of the complex of causes been different the effect would have been altered also. In grace, however, the divine decision is total, admitting of no alteration through whatever partial causes may be brought to bear on the affected person. Conversely, the libertarian alternative to determinism is equally far removed from Luther, for it discerns freedom from gaps in the causal picture but again on a finite, partial level. In the doctrine of predestination we are not, however, in the earthly realm at all but in the heavenly realm, without direct earthly effect. Grace remains external to its recipient; it does not change the being of its beneficiary. The decree of salvation removes sin not in the inner being of the sinner but only insofar as one stands under the mercy of God.

Since predestination does not refer to the range of finite causes and effects, this implies two further differences between the determinist and anti-determinist camps, on the one side, and the Reformers on the other. The first is a difference in temporal reference. Determinism asks whether our present choices are determined by a series of causes pulsating into the present from the past, whether in fact either present or future are open to anything really new at all. The libertarian response to determinism argues for a present in which some field for decision remains so that the truly new can appear in the future by means of choices in this open space. The moral agent seeks a certain good, and moral decision renders more or less likely this good's future appearance, or at least one's future presence to the good being sought. Freedom arises in the present in order to create a future.

The predestinarian alternative of the Reformation has a different temporal impulse. Summarily stated, the heavenly realm above and outside time impacts the historical present. In so doing, it makes freedom possible–not freedom in relation to the eternal itself, but freedom in relation to the temporal future. If eternity is depicted temporally, as Luther was prone to do, then the same point can be put this way: God decreed one's salvation from the foundation of the world, communicates that decree in baptism and Word, and is the assurance that one's final salvation is safe in God's hands. We are told these things by means of the Word externally and by the Spirit present to our hearts inwardly. Past, future, and eternal present are declared as certain and conspire to create the temporal present.

Faith, Works, and World

The thesis requires clarification. In the notion of communication of God's decree of salvation, we have introduced an element beyond the naked grace always external to its recipient. The second of Luther's two realms, the earthly, has entered covertly. At first glance this realm seems superfluous. After all, the ultimate destiny of each person is already determined by God. What possible importance remains for life on earth? This issue was raised not only by Erasmus but also by a great many of Luther's Catholic counterparts.[14] Luther, however, never asks the question in this form. He never considers the possibility that God would have kept the decree of forgiveness of sin a secret from its beneficiary. Indeed, it is the very purpose of the Word to publish God's decision to forgive and the very function of faith to know that the decree of forgiveness applies not just to persons in general but to me. Faith, in short, is the heart's knowledge of standing in God's grace, the knowledge that nothing one does or fails to do can conquer the efficacious decree of forgiveness.[15]

Two points are worth comment. First, we have seen Luther does not deny the existence of "free will" despite his argument that one is predestined. Now we understand why he can hold both positions. Earthly freedom may exist but it is not efficacious for salvation. Free will, whatever else it may do, cannot satisfy the commands of God;[16] it "is nothing and neither does nor can do good in the absence of grace–unless you wish to give 'efficacy' a new meaning."[17] Free choice has no "power"[18] or rather, "has no power while Satan rules over it but to spurn grace."[19] One may be free to choose between things or acts but no choice impacts upon the salvific relationship between God and person. Free acts and their effects are two different things. Freedom to act does not imply ability to control the results of that act. A person born outside the United States can act freely but regardless of what he or she does, will never be eligible to be president. In a similar fashion freedom exercised in order to achieve salvation may do many things–but it cannot have the effect it intends. However, freedom's failure to achieve what it wants is no indication it is illusory–at worst, it is evidence of ignorance or bad planning.

Luther, of course, means more than this. The will is ridden by either God or Satan.[20] If by Satan, then the substance of sin which inheres in us is permitted free reign to the end of one's ultimate destruction. If by God and the gift of Spirit, the will is turned in order to eradicate sin progressively though not totally.[21] It is not that God causes one to do this thing at this time but that whatever is chosen and done is under the inner dominance of God or the devil. This brings us to the second point. It is a tremendous distortion of Luther's notion of predestination if it is interpreted as both the antinomians and many Catholics in Luther's own time did–namely, since I am saved in any event, there is no law, no person, no principle I must heed. Luther's Catholic contemporaries retreated from this implication in horror while the antinomians embraced it with delight. If the notion of predestination is viewed as exclusively a heavenly event, a decree having the whole of its being *and effects* in another world, there can be no answer to this argument. Yet Luther and Calvin, predestinarians both, believed the antinomian understanding of predestination was a sure sign its adherents were not in fact among the elect. Moreover, it really is surprising that there is no question of a concealed decision of salvation. Both the Reformers' opposition to antinomianism and the inevitability of the worldly publication of grace to the believer through Spirit and Word indicate that grace is intended to have worldly effects even though in itself grace is restricted to God's sovereign will in heaven.

Between Legalism and Antinomianism

The explanation for both the Reformers' disgust with libertine antinomianism and their emphasis on the publication of grace through God's gifts is that their predestinarianism makes sense only when understood from within the context of faith, that is, from the *a priori* conviction in earthly life that one is a member of the elect. In Calvin's 1559 *Institutes*, predestination receives sustained treatment beginning only in the last five chapters of the third book. It stands as conclusion to doctrines of faith, sin, and knowledge of God in the Word, and immediately precedes a treatment of the doctrine of the church as an external aid to our "society with Christ." Likewise, Luther's sustained defense of God's ordinance of election and damnation in *Bondage of the Will* is motivated by the need to defend the omnipotence of God. In its turn, the omnipotence of God requires affirmation because only through it can we be certain that God's salvific aim for believers, that is, for me, cannot be frustrated no matter what occurs in the finite, worldly realm. The Reformers' endorsement of predestination is intended in the first instance as a comfort to believers; *it is an existential pronouncement of faith's security before it is an objective affirmation.*

If predestination is understood as proclamation of a personal salvific guarantee it becomes quite clear why the Reformers opposed both a legalism that made personal obedience to the commands of God a *condition* of salvation and an antinomianism that denied all legitimacy and necessity to such obedience. Legalism rocked certainty explicitly; in fact, it was the opposite of certainty. Instead of resting in the certain power of God, legalism reserves a measure of salvation to human effort. It is not just that this robs God of due glory;[22] it is also doomed to final failure because of our original constitution in sin.

Not only is legalism theoretically bankrupt as a way to future salvation, however–equally as important it is destructive in each moment of the present world. Faith, Spirit, works, and the like belong to earth, gifts in light of God's salvific decree.[23] Faith communicates the divine decision so the temporal present may be constituted as meaningful. If one is convinced of the justifying power of works in general, including works of the law, the ethical act becomes a practical impossibility. The conviction that good works have something to do with one's own eternal fate acts as a mirror upon the light of works, reflecting their benefit back upon the person who acts. Even the world's best love themselves more than their neighbor[24] and any works performed with the end of personal salvation in mind are in fact works of self-love, a charity that begins and ends at home. Their value for the neighbor is incidental to their true purpose. That is to say they are not good works any longer because their aim is self-enhancement and not love of neighbor. A good work cannot be performed for the purpose of self-profit.[25] To add any personal salvific efficacy to the theology of good works ravages the very work it seeks to supplement:

> If works are sought after as a means to righteousness, are burdened with this perverse leviathan, and are done under the false impression that through them one is justified, they are made necessary and freedom and faith are destroyed; and this addition to them makes them no longer good but truly damnable works. They are not free, and they blaspheme the grace of God since to justify and to save by faith belongs to the grace of God alone.[26]

Luther is emphatic–a good work even requires one to forget heaven altogether, desiring the good even if there were no hell or salvation:

> a kingdom awaits the godly, even though they themselves neither seek it nor think of it...What is more, if they did good works for the sake of obtaining the Kingdom, they would never obtain it, but would rather belong among the ungodly who with an evil and mercenary eye "seek their own" even in God. But the children of God do good with a will that is disinterested, not seeking any reward, but only the glory and will of God, and being ready to do good even if–an impossible supposition–there were neither a kingdom nor a hell.[27]

Only if God's grace eradicates all personal benefits to one's works can these works be truly good, for only then can they be done solely for one's neighbor and for praise of God. *Only because we have no freedom at all with respect to our heavenly destiny is it possible to have true freedom on earth.* In the quotation from *Freedom of a Christian* earlier, we should not bypass the fact that Luther charges legalism, which apparently appreciated the free will, with destroying freedom. Moreover, earthly righteousness involves the communication of "wisdom, power, righteousness, goodness–and freedom too,"[28] but these gifts presuppose lack of freedom to change one's ultimate destiny of salvation. Grace does not rule out earthly freedom but creates it.

While legalism lacked certainty, antinomianism was deceived into thinking it was certain. Because faith is that gift of God which knows one's salvation and because the "knowledge of faith consists in assurance"[29] of God's fidelity to that promise, Luther's polemic against antinomianism seems self-contradictory. After all, as Luther understood them, the antinomians were so certain of their own salvation as to feel free of any demands. But "a kingdom awaits the godly, although *they themselves neither seek it nor think of it*." Witness also Calvin: "For he who ponders within himself what God the Father is like toward us has cause enough, even if there be no hell, to dread offending him more gravely than any death."[30] This the antinomians could not admit. If the legalists stood accused of acting well because they wanted heaven, the antinomians acted badly because they believed they would certainly possess heaven. In both cases, however, heaven and one's own place within it are the aim, the object of thought. World, neighbor, God, all are viewed as means for the self's attainment of a future good. An antinomian interpretation of Luther's doctrine of grace is evidence of only one thing–that the self remains the primary concern–and this is precisely the problem the certainty of God's predestination is intended to overcome. Predestination removes the mirror between self and other so that the other can be truly recognized as an other and not merely as an instrument for the self's own benefit.

The antinomians, however, obliterate the other even more fully than the legalists did and this is proof that they too are among the condemned. Certainty of salvation is given not so that one may rest comfortably but so that one may approach the other and serve. Self-involvement is overcome, not accentuated;[31] one is freed from the world for the purpose of work in the world or more biblically put, "whoever would save his life will lose it; and whoever loses his life for my sake, he will save it." This is why, after all critique of legalism, the maxims of the law return in the Reformers' thought as a guide to conduct under the Spirit.

Predestination and the Creation of Freedom

Consideration of the legal and antinomian alternatives clarifies the temporal operation of the Reformation doctrine of predestination. The eternal, unchangeable declaration of salvation, in which faith has confidence, frees one from the past. To be sure, the bare events of the past cannot be changed. Certainty of salvation does, however, alter the past's meaning–instead of its being a prison of irremovable guilt from which the tender conscience cannot escape, the elect are assured that the past lacks condemning power. This claim is common to all doctrines and experiences of forgiveness.[33] Predestinarianism in its Reformation form, though, also has the effect of freeing one from anxiety over one's destiny. Salvation is assured and consequently one is freed to attend to the temporal future not for the purpose of achieving one's final glory but in order to combat the sin which remains inwardly and externally. The Reformers emphasize our present knowledge of God's forgiving decree in order to free the present for the future and from the past. For Luther at least, this is the only way in which love is truly possible for it alone can truly recognize both that the other is a neighbor and the neighbor an other.

Moreover, knowledge of predestination provides the only possibility for responsible combat against paralysis. If the unforeseeable outcome of one's act and thought are viewed as matters of ultimate destiny, effecting eternal salvation and damnation in any way, how can one avoid being frozen and inactive except in simple matters in which the effects of action can be foreseen with relative certainty? One is respon sible for the consequences of action as well as the act itself—faced with disastrous effects, it is not enough to say "I didn't mean to."[34] Freedom's fear that it will fail to reach its intended object is conquered because the eternal is not an object of striving at all. Rather, the eternal decree is the condition of all strivings, assuring the elect that irrespective of actions' success or failure, eternal destiny remains unchanged.

The alteration of the human relation to time in the Reformers' under-standing of predestination results in a new understanding of, or perhaps obliteration of, the religious object of desire.[35] Since predestinarianism removes the motive to keep the self's benefit in view, it also alters one's relation to God. It is no longer the case, as it was for Augustine, that one seeks the enjoyment of things insofar as through them one can enjoy God. Nor does one seek the final enjoyment of the contemplation of God. In a real sense "you are now sitting in paradise" because "You have all in superabundance, whatever your heart desires."[36] The quota-tion is from Luther although it was Calvin who made this presence to heaven the cornerstone of sacramental theology. If the presence of God is already enjoyed and if one is assured a place in paradise, God is no longer the object of attainment in moral decision-making but its back-ground. Moral action cannot obtain anything from God it has not already received. In consequence, the world is opened; it has a value in its own right that is distinct from its value to the self. One acts proxi-mately for neighbor and earth. This is why Luther's predestinarian doc-trine of grace, which first appears to make the world irrelevant, instead demands his extensive reflections on worldly questions.

To be sure the world is not desacralized by the Reformers (although Weber perceptively noted how that result grew from Protestantism[37]), for faith acts perpetually to give thanks to God.[38] It is no accident of thought, however, that "thanksgiving" is the meaning given to "remem-brance" by Luther in the sacramental debates with his Protestant oppo-nents. Remembrance is not merely inward recollection but a duty of external proclamation of God born of thanksgiving:

Although I receive no other benefit from it, I still want to be present to the praise and glory of my God...I still desire to receive the sacrament for this reason, that by such reception I might confess and bear witness that I also am one who would praise and thank God, and therefore desire to receive the sacrament to the glory of God. Such reception shall be my remembrance with which I think of and thank him for his grace shown me in Christ.[39]

The attainment of God, in whatever form, has been shifted from future realization to a past gift known in the present. As such, God is removed from the aims of moral striving; instead, God is the retrospective ground through whom neighbor and world, and consequently one's care for neighbor and world, are given significance.

This is a crucial difference between the Reformers, on one hand, and the determinism/freedom dispute, on the other. The issue in the latter is whether or not there is freedom to make choices between this or that object which stands in front of us and whether the ability or inability to make and effect such decisions bears on moral responsibility for what is chosen. In any event the argument revolves around a freedom or lack of freedom with respect to particular objects in front of us. The issue becomes: "Is the will free in some sense to choose to pursue God?" The problem is the possibility of pursuing and attaining objects not yet utterly present to the free actor. From within the confines of this debate we may ask about one's destiny toward God but we continue to assume that God is an object of striving to which God's self leads us.[40]

In contrast, the Reformation conception of predestination declares the utter presence of the revealed God to believers. The reflective focus of attention does not rest on a choice of objects in front of us, the highest of which is God, but rather on what underlies any choice. If faith's knowledge of God's salvation grounds the decision then it is a good choice; otherwise it is not. An important point is that the problem is not necessarily contained in the decision between external objects. The charitable and the mean-spirited can each give equal money to the same cause but with a quite different purpose—and it is this motivation which is the subject of the doctrine of predestination. The inward rather than the external dimension of life is highlighted. Moreover, Luther and Calvin were certain that without confidence in one's own salvation truly moral choice would be impossible precisely because the self's salvific relation to God would continually be placed between self and other as an object of desire. Only by relocating that salvific relation behind, below, or above (but not in front of) the believer could the truly good work be possible—and freedom too.

The emphasis upon the inward dimension of action implies two important distinctions between the Reformation understanding of pre-

Human and Divine Agency

destination and doctrines of "compatibilism." In the first place, it is not
the case that the Spirit under the reign of grace forces the actor to make
some particular choice, though there may well be new possibilities
opened or old possibilities closed under the influence of the Spirit.
Often the same act is possible whether the will is "ridden" by God or
the devil. In any event the most that can be said generally is that there
is a certain range of actions which may emerge from the elect in obedience to the Spirit; the Spirit does not force this act with this purpose at
this time and no other. Second, it is important to remember that one is
engaged in a battle of flesh against Spirit–sin remains in the elect. This
means that even the elect frequently disobey the demands of the Spirit
and submit to the designs of fleshly pride, self-interest, and so on. The
Spirit's conquest of the heart is a slow and faltering process.

The Contemporary Meaning of Predestination

Already we have betrayed considerable sympathy with the
Reformers. To argue, however, that predestination has been misunder-
stood is not to show why a different approach matters. It is now incum-
bent upon us to indicate the contemporary intelligibility and significance of a modified notion of predestination. Interpreted in line with the
existential cast we have given to the Reformers' notion, one might say
that all who are fundamentally confident of the meaningfulness of existence, the final good intentions of Being underlying our existence, are
predestinarians. It is not necessary as it was for the Reformers that
explicit adherence be given to such a doctrine (in fact the logical outcome of the Reformers' own emphasis leads to the doctrine's recession
from explicit consciousness).

Such a confidence in one's finally meaningful destiny serves precisely the same functions it served for the Reformers. If present, this
confidence removes what we called the mirror of the self from the distance which separates self and other so that the other can truly be recognized and treated as an other rather than merely as a means to one's
own advantage. In addition, confidence of eternal meaning is the condition for the free acts which are risky and potentially historically significant. Whatever the outcome of action–and even if all penultimate
meanings are destroyed entirely–one is confident that the intrusion of
eternity upon the present is available in the next present. We are exhort-
ed to "Sin courageously, but believe more courageously"[41] because era-
sure of these penultimate meanings cannot remove with it one's final
destiny in the divine life. Predestination remains the pre- or sub-moral
ground of morality and freedom.

Why use the term "predestination?" It is not necessary and if a more
evocative word can be found, so much the better. But "predestination"

has two advantages. First, it surrounds the present with the past (pre-) and the future (destination). Second, it has the advantage of pointing out the inaccessibility of this confidence to conscious decision. One is not "free" to wake in the morning and decide "Life has meaning." One may try, of course, but such an effort cannot succeed. The explosion of self-help literature is a negative illustration of the basic non-decision for meaning or meaninglessness in each life. A good deal of that literature prescribes techniques by which life might be made meaningful. It has, however, become a circular market of endless voracious demand. For as one therapy fails to deliver the promise of salvation, its former adherents shift to another, and another, etc. This is not to say these methods are not helpful to some. But self-help cannot be effective unless it is underlain by a basic security underneath all the insecurities of existence. And this is an attitude, a mood, a confidence which simply cannot be prescribed or produced by worldly hands. It must appear independent of all conscious striving. It is grace. One may choose external goods but it is not possible to choose inner trust, confidence, or security, that good which underlies the choices between relative goods. Luther's response to Erasmus is to the point: "'Your faith has made you well' [Luke 17:19]–do you hear 'your'? Explain it to mean 'you produce faith'; then you have proved free choice."[42] Or, as Austin Farrer says, and here he is in the center of Reformation thought, "We cannot take seriously men who talk as though they were free to entertain metaphysical beliefs, or not to entertain them; to say (in the extreme case) 'No, I don't think we will have God, thank you,' or to say 'Yes, let's have him.' For either we believe or we do not."[43]

This underivability of basic confidence from external, empirical factors also shows the clear difference between it and the debate between determinists and libertarians. Also, the terms of that debate are relocated. In the first place, both sides are convinced of the importance of their position. Does not the very virulence of the argument show that both are willing to argue for the rights of truth and morality–and is this not some indication of a core confidence in the meaning of truth and morality themselves? Second, the resolution of the argument makes no necessary difference to whether or not the adherents of either position are possessed by the fundamental confidence or despair which grounds and carries all action. The determinist can be despairing, certainly, for he or she can feel the world as nothing but a mass of mechanized cogs in a gigantic machine of causality. Libertarians are inclined to think the determinist must be despair-filled. It is not so. Determinists might as easily assert that determinism is the only way to keep the world from destruction, asserting thereby a comfort in determinism.[44] On the other hand, those who struggle most mightily for the cause of freedom seem to believe that freedom provides the *a priori* of all meaning. But if freedom can be exhilarating it can also be terrifying and we should probably have noticed by now that many who are utterly convinced of their freedom and moral responsibility are consumed by despair—as, indeed, was Luther prior to his formulation of justification by grace alone. As a society we seem to wish for less and less freedom just because it has become so meaningless for so many. We shall soon find that the more authoritarian answer of the last decade cannot produce confidence in the meaningfulness of existence either. The essential point is this: the core non-decision of meaning or futility is not subject to the freedom/determinism debate but subjects the results of that discussion to itself. Faith cannot be reasoned into or argued toward—it can only be lived and felt.

The question of predestination must be considered apart from its usual inclusion in the issue of determinism and freedom. Considered as a claim about the whole of a person and not an assertion about finite causality, the central tenet of the Reformation understanding of predestination remains existentially descriptive, morally creative, and a condition for meaningful freedom in the world. Far from being the utter negation of freedom, predestinarianism is instead an indispensable condition for the existence of a freedom which has meaning, a freedom which must itself be freed from the arbitrariness of mere choices, each one as meaningless as the next. Only a core conviction that our choices contribute to or detract from a life that is not pointless but stands under the redeeming meaning-producing grace of God can save us from either simple arbitrariness in which choice is maintained but means nothing or a sense of despair that feels excluded from, and therefore tries unsuccessfully to produce for itself, the fulfillments of life. In the end, one either believes in the importance of existence and in one's inclusion in the promises of life or one does not—and that belief is not and cannot be itself subject to finite partial choices, though it grounds all truly free choices.

Notes

1. The substantial differences between each of these thinkers' interpretation of what predestination means are not immediately relevant. In general, the difference between the "softer" predestinarians of the Roman Catholic tradition and the strict double predestinarianism of Luther and Calvin is determined by their different theologies of grace and especially their answers to whether grace is an inward possession of the elect.

2. On this question of predestination, as on many others, the differ-

ences between Luther and Calvin have been substantially and artificially inflated. Indeed, it is a favorite tack of Lutherans to cast most of the blame for double predestinarianism in Calvin's direction. This is unfortunate since it tends both to be gratuitously insulting to Calvin and obscures the basic direction of Luther's thought. On all of the issues that nourish the theological conclusion of "predestination," such as the doctrines of sin, grace, and faith, one must cut with an exceedingly fine scalpel to distinguish Luther and Calvin. Thus, the two are approached as virtually identical here, although one or the other may have a clearer formulation of the same point. I am deeply grateful to Thomas J. Davis for the long hours spent to heighten my own appreciation for Calvin.

3. Parts of the treatment of Luther are drawn from Kyle A. Pasewark, *A Theology of Power: Being Beyond Domination* (Minneapolis: Fortress Press, 1992).

4. In addition to the quotations which follow, see Martin Luther, *The Bondage of the Will* in *Luther's Works*, vol. 33, *Career of the Reformer III*, trans. and ed. Philip S. Watson (Philadelphia: Fortress Press, 1972), 73-74, 87, 103-108, 118-19, 285; Martin Luther, *Luthers Werke*, 18 Band (Weimar: Hermann Böhlaus Nachfolger, 1908), 641-42, 651, 661-64, 671-73, 781. See also the excellent discussion in Gerhard Ebeling, *Luther: An Introduction to his Thought*, trans. R. A. Wilson (Philadelphia: Fortress Press, 1970), 218-25. For a summary of interpretations which do take Luther's predestinarian claims as assertions about causality, see Harry J. McSorley, *Luther: Right or Wrong?* (New York: Newman Press, 1969; Minneapolis: Augsburg, 1969), 297-366.

5. *Luther, Bondage of the Will*, 239; *Luthers Werke*, 18:751.

6. *Luther, Bondage of the Will*, 197; *Luthers Werke*, 18:723.

7. *Luther, Bondage of the Will*, 70; *Luthers Werke*, 18:638.

8. *Luther, Bondage of the Will*, 87; *Luthers Werke*, 18:651.

9. This was noticed by Ernst Troeltsch, *The Social Teaching of the Christian Churches*, vol. 2, trans. Olive Wyon (London: George Allen and Unwin; New York: Macmillan, 1931; reprint, Chicago: University of Chicago Press, 1981), 470, and more recently, albeit unsympathetically, by Juan Luis Segundo, *The Liberation of Theology*, trans. John Drury (Maryknoll, NY: Orbis Books, 1976), 143.

10. Martin Luther, *Against Latomus*, in *Luther's Works*, vol. 32, *Career of the Reformer II*, trans. George Lindbeck, ed. George W. Forell (Philadelphia: Fortress Press, 1958), 208; Martin Luther, *Luthers Werke*, 8 Band (Weimar: Hermann Böhlaus Nachfolger, 1889), 92-93.

11. Luther, *Against Latomus*, 227; *Luthers Werke*, 8:106.

12. Martin Luther, *Disputation Concerning Justification*, in *Luther's Works*, vol. 34, *Career of the Reformer IV*, trans. and ed. Lewis W. Spitz (Philadelphia: Muhlenberg Press, 1960), 164; Martin Luther, *Luthers*

Werke, 39 Band (I) (Weimar: Hermann Böhlaus Nachfolger, 1926), 95.
13. Luther, *Against Latomus*, 228-29; *Luthers Werke*, 8:106-107.
14. On Luther's early Catholic opponents, see David V.N. Bagchi, *Luther's Earliest Opponents: Catholic Controversialists, 1518-1525* (Minneapolis: Fortress Press, 1991), 147-80.
15. Luther, *Against Latomus*, 177; *Luthers Werke* 8:70.
16. Luther, *Against Latomus*, 151-95; *Luthers Werke*, 8:53-83. Also see Martin Luther, *The Freedom of a Christian*, in *Luther's Works*, vol. 31, *Career of the Reformer I*, trans. W. A. Lambert, rev. and ed. Harold J. Grimm (Philadelphia: Fortress Press, 1957), 349; Martin Luther, *Luthers Werke*, 7 Band (Weimar: Hermann Böhlaus Nachfolger, 1897), 53.
17. Luther, *Bondage of the Will*, 68; *Luthers Werke*, 18:636.
18. See especially Luther, *Bondage of the Will*, 64-87, 171-74; *Luthers Werke*, 18:634-51, 706-708.
19. Luther, *Bondage of the Will*, 158; *Luthers Werke*, 18:698. That "no power but to spurn grace" and "no power at all" are equivalent expressions, is shown in *Bondage of the Will*, 286; *Luthers Werke*, 18:781.
20. Luther, *Bondage of the Will*, 65-66; *Luthers Werke*, 18:635.
21. Martin Luther, *The Epistle of St. Paul to the Colossians on the Fifth Sunday after Epiphany*, in *The Sermons of Martin Luther*, vol. 7, *Sermons on Epistle Texts for Epiphany, Easter, and Pentecost*, trans. John Nicholas Lenker et al., ed. John Nicholas Lenker (Minneapolis: The Luther Press, 1909; reprint, Grand Rapids, MI: Baker Book House, 1988), 79-84 (page references are to reprint edition); Martin Luther, *Luthers Werke*, 17 Band (II) (Weimar: Hermann Böhlaus Nachfolger, 1927), 112-16. See also, Luther, *Against Latomus*, 207-51; *Luthers Werke* 8:92-122.
22. Luther, *Bondage of the Will*, 109, 113, 125; *Luthers Werke*, 18:665, 667, 676.
23. The important distinction between grace and gift is drawn most carefully in *Against Latomus*.
24. Martin Luther, *Lectures on Hebrews*, in *Luther's Works*, vol. 29, *Lectures on Titus, Philemon, and Hebrews*, trans. Walter A. Hansen, ed. Jaroslav Pelikan (St. Louis: Concordia Publishing House, 1968), 118-19; Martin Luther, *Luthers Werke*, 57 Band (III) (Weimar: Hermann Böhlaus Nachfolger, 1939), 108-109.
25. Luther, *Freedom of a Christian*, 370; *Luthers Werke*, 7:68.
26. Luther, *Freedom of a Christian*, 363; *Luthers Werke*, 7:63. See also, Martin Luther, *Lectures on Galatians, 1535*, in *Luther's Works*, vol. 26, *Lectures on Galatians, 1535, Chapters 1-4*, trans. and ed. Jaroslav Pelikan (St. Louis: Concordia Publishing House, 1963), 116-

17; Martin Luther, *Luthers Werke*, 40 Band [I] (Weimar: Hermann Böhlaus Nachfolger, 1911), 208-209.

27. Luther, *Bondage of the Will*, 152-53; *Luthers Werke*, 18:694.

28. Martin Luther, *The Two Kinds of Righteousness*, in *Luther's Works*, vol. 31, *Career of the Reformer I*, trans. Lowell J. Satre, ed. Harold J. Grimm (Philadelphia: Fortress Press, 1957), 301; Martin Luther, *Luthers Werke*, 2 Band (Weimar: Hermann Böhlaus Nachfolger, 1884), 148.

29. John Calvin, *Institutes of the Christian Religion*, vol. 1, trans. Ford Lewis Battles, ed. John T. McNeill, The Library of Christian Classics, vol. 20 (Philadelphia: Westminster Press, 1960), 3.2.14, p. 560.

30. Ibid., 3.2.26, p. 572.

31. "Overcome" in the measure that one is faithful. The battle between sin and the Spirit continues in the believer and the world. Luther is not so naive as to believe that the perfectly faithful person exists. The continuing conflict between sin and God's gifts is absolutely central to Luther's thought; unfortunately, it is a theme we cannot explore here.

32. The most poetic expression of this is found in Luther, *Lectures on Galatians, 1535*, 8; *Luthers Werke*, 40[I]:46-47.

33. See, for example, the fascinating argument of Hannah Arendt, *The Human Condition* (Chicago: University of Chicago Press, 1958), 236-47.

34. The callousness of such exclusive attention to subjective intention is shown brilliantly by John Updike's Pulitzer Prize-winning portrayals of "Rabbit" Angstrom. Rabbit leaves in his wake a swath of destruction from which he escapes responsibility by assertion of harmless intent.

35. It is perhaps not accidental that the great atheists of the nineteenth century, notably Feuerbach, appeared on Protestant soil.

36. Martin Luther, *A Beautiful Sermon on the Reception of the Holy Sacrament*, in *Sermons of Martin Luther*, vol. 2, *Sermons on Gospel Texts for Epiphany, Lent, and Easter*, trans. John Nicholas Lenker et al., ed. John Nicholas Lenker (Minneapolis: Lutherans in all Lands, 1906; reprint, Grand Rapids, MI: Baker Book House, 1988), 232 (page references are to reprint edition); Martin Luther, *Luthers Werke*, 12 Band (Weimar: Hermann Böhlaus Nachfolger, 1891), 487.

37. Max Weber, *The Protestant Ethic and the Spirit of Capitalism*, trans. Talcott Parsons (New York: Charles Scribner's Sons, 1958).

38. Martin Luther, *Treatise on Good Works*, in *Luther's Works*, vol. 44, *The Christian in Society I*, trans. W. A. Lambert, rev. and ed. James Atkinson (Philadelphia: Fortress Press, 1966), 44; Martin Luther,

Luthers Werke, 6 Band (Weimar: Hermann Böhlaus Nachfolger, 1888), 221. See also Luther, *Freedom of a Christian*, 350-59; *Luthers Werke*, 7:54-60.

39. Martin Luther, *Admonition Concerning the Sacrament of the Body and Blood of Our Lord*, in *Luther's Works*, vol. 38, *Word and Sacrament IV*, trans. and ed. Martin E. Lehmann (Philadelphia: Fortress Press, 1971), 109; Martin Luther, *Luthers Werke*, 30 Band (II) (Weimar: Hermann Böhlaus Nachfolger, 1909), 604.

40. A good example of this is Austin Farrer, *The Brink of Mystery* (London: SPCK Press, 1976), 98-99.

41. Luther, quoted in McSorley, *Luther: Right or Wrong?*, 302.

42. Luther, *Bondage of the Will*, 232; *Luthers Werke*, 18:747.

43. Austin Farrer, *The Freedom of the Will*, (New York: Charles Scribner's Sons, 1960), 307-308.

44. How it would be possible for the determinist to know this in an undetermined way is unclear. In fact, this is a central problem with determinist epistemology–it cannot include itself in its own determinist understanding, but must act as if it sees the world from beyond and above its own framework.

Chapter 4

Kant, Luther, and Erasmus on the Freedom of the Will

Elizabeth Galbraith

Introduction

This essay is a reflection on the theological significance of the free will/determinism debate. Its main aim is to show that Kant represents a sharp break with the Reformation on free will in relation to evil, grace, and salvation, continuing instead a line of thought articulated by Erasmus of Rotterdam and later developed by Austin Farrer. However, neither Kant's nor Farrer's theological rendering of free will escapes the free will/ determinism issue. I will articulate that issue as found in Kant and Farrer and suggest a resolution by drawing on the work of Donald Davidson.

In the first section of the paper Kant's conception of free will is contrasted with that of his Reformation predecessor, Luther, and in the second section, compared with that of Luther's critic at the time of the Reformation, Erasmus of Rotterdam. The similarity of Kant's (and Erasmus') approach to free will to that of Farrer is then highlighted. In the third section it is suggested that, although Kant's position leaves the free will/determinism debate unresolved, Donald Davidson's work offers an explanation as to how Kant's understanding of free will can be reconciled with determinism in nature.

The Comparison Between Kant and Luther

Much German literature, especially at the beginning of this century, draws a comparison between Kant and Luther.[1] Kant has been referred to, not only as the Philosopher of Protestantism, but also, as the fulfiller of what Luther had initiated with the Reformation. Such over-optimistic comparisons can be dispensed with by showing that there is a dichotomy between Luther and Kant on what amounts for both to be the most significant concern of religion. The shared central concern is the value of free will, with regard to which the thought of Kant simply cannot be reconciled with that of Luther.

Luther's evaluation of freedom is best illustrated in a well known debate over the freedom of the will which took place between himself and Erasmus of Rotterdam.[2] Luther provides a brief summary of his opinion in saying that "free choice is nothing but a slave of sin, death, and Satan, it does nothing and is not capable of doing or attempting to do anything but Evil."[3] In order to understand this claim it is necessary to consider the distinction Luther makes between human freedom and God-given spiritual righteousness. Human free choice alone is lacking in spiritual righteousness. Thus: "And of the things without the spirit is that very power of free choice...Free choice by itself is so blind that it is not even aware of sin, but has need of the law to teach it."[4]

Such freedom belongs to the world of flesh and sin. According to Luther, when Isaiah in Chapter 40, verse 6, says "that all flesh is grass," he means all that belongs to the person: reason, judgment, and what is most excellent in human nature.[5] Therefore, in Luther's opinion, "if we take free choice, or take whatever may be regarded as the highest or the lowest in a people, Isaiah calls it all flesh and grass."[6] Freedom of this kind is freedom of the flesh in distinction to freedom of the spirit. In Luther's view his opinion is supported by St. John's claim that "what is born of the flesh is flesh, and what is born of the spirit is spirit."[7]

Human freedom alone has very little worth; it is scarcely distinct from sin itself. One could even say that human freedom and God-given spiritual righteousness, the latter being that which is bestowed upon human nature as a gift of God, are in conflict. Hence, "free choice is nothing else but the supreme enemy of righteousness."[8] This is because it is a slave to sin.

In fact, Luther believes that free choice without God-given spiritual righteousness is determined by Satan, and spiritual freedom is determined by God. Therefore, both kinds of freedom are in fact predetermined either by Satan or by God. Luther even goes so far as to say:

> I was wrong in saying that free choice before grace is a reality only in name. I should have said simply: "free choice is in reality a fiction, or a name without reality."...everything (as Wycliff's article condemned at Constance rightly teaches) happens by absolute necessity.[9]

Luther's allusion to absolute necessity in the above makes it clear that he believes in predestination. Human freedom apart from God amounts to no more than a predisposition to sin, and is in fact determined by Satan. Human freedom has no value whatsoever in relation to spiritual righteousness or human salvation. As far as salvation is concerned, Luther claims that "we must therefore go all out and completely deny free choice, referring everything to God."[10] Luther's view is that everything in relation to salvation is determined through the will of God. This view cannot be reconciled with that of Kant.

First, and most significantly, Kant values human freedom as indispensable to human dignity. Freedom is "the one sole and original right that belongs to every human being by virtue of their humanity."[11] Freedom is a presupposition of human action: "Man acts according to the idea of freedom, he acts as if he were free, and *eo ipso* he is free."[12]

Kant also attributes a much higher status to the freedom of the human will than the Lutheran account. Far from being determined by either Satan or God, freedom amounts to self determination. According to Kant, we must attribute to every being endowed with reason and a will this property of determining themselves to action under the idea of their own freedom.[13] And accordingly, when I ask myself what my duty is, "I ask only what I now have to do, and in that, freedom is a necessary practical presupposition and an idea, under which alone I can regard the command of reason as valid."[14]

According to Kant, freedom of the will is independence from a foreign will. He speaks of "independence from the constraint of another's will,"[15] and stresses that "reason must look upon itself as the author of its own principles independently of alien influences. Therefore as practical reason, or as the will of a rational being, it must be regarded by itself as free."[16] There is no better example of the distinction which lies between the views of Luther and Kant than in Kant's appraisal of what he refers to as *fatalism:*

> Fatalism in general...transforms all human actions into a mere puppet show, and totally annuls the conception of obligation. It is that which is against the ought or the imperative. It is impossible and inconsistent, and much more leaves us with nothing to do, than to wait and to observe what kind of decisions God, by interceding in and through the natural way of things, will effect in us, not however, what we from ourselves as authors can and should do.[17]

The kind of attitude which Kant describes here as *fatalist* is precisely that which Luther maintains with regard to freedom through faith, when he claims that "God works through us, and free choice is nothing."[18] According to Kant, without freedom of the will we are marionettes. The Lutheran view regarding spiritual righteousness makes us little more than marionettes. Although we seem to be free, our spiritual righteousness and the moral acts which go with it are determined by God. In Luther's opinion, we do not have the liberty necessary to lead the moral life without God. For Kant, the kind of predestination Luther proposes presupposes "an immoral order of nature."[19] In other words, we must have liberty if the moral life is to make sense. Thus there is no way in which Kant can submit to Luther's concept of predestination.

Secondly, whereas for Luther human free choice is tied to sin, for Kant it is a freedom to do good as well as evil. Free will at its best is the capacity to overcome sin:

> As a free will, and thus not only without co-operating with sensuous impulses but even rejecting all of them and checking all inclinations so far as they could be antagonistic to the law, it is determined merely by the law.[20]

The law referred to is the moral law. Whereas for Luther free will is bound to sin, with Kant free will is bound to the moral law. Being bound to the moral law does not, however, imply determination by the will of another, but rather self determination in accordance with the moral law. Human freedom is bound to the moral law in the sense that "if the freedom of the will is presupposed, morality, together with its principle, follows by mere analysis of the concept of freedom."[21] Moreover, "morality must be derived solely from the property of freedom."[22] In other words, without freedom morality would be illusory. Freedom is also tied to autonomy, for "what else then can the freedom of the will be but autonomy, that is, the property which the will has of being a law to itself."[23] That is, being your own master, not simply being subject to the law of another. Even the moral law for Kant is the law of one's own nature rather than a law imposed by another. Thus, in contrast to Luther, self determination, morality, and autonomy are all closely tied to Kant's notion of human freedom.

This divergence in the understanding of the notion of freedom has even more far reaching implications, some of which are highlighted in Luther's debate with Erasmus over the freedom of the will. Upon closer reading it becomes clear that the debate between Luther and Erasmus is not just about freedom, but about grace and salvation as well. Thus, according to Luther, "grace is preached therefore free choice is abolished; the help of grace is commended therefore free choice is destroyed."[24] Furthermore, "the righteousness of faith comes from grace apart from the law. The expression apart from excludes works, moral righteousness, and preparation for grace."[25] This suggests that for

Luther, divine grace and human freedom are contradictory concepts, in the sense that, when grace is given, human freedom is ruled out.

However, one might ask why it is that grace rules out freedom and works in preparation for salvation? The answer for Luther is quite clear, since "what need is there of the Spirit or of Christ or of God if free choice can overcome the motions of the mind towards evil."[26] What Luther means is that to suggest that human effort is necessary to overcome evil and gain righteousness cheapens grace by implicitly neglecting the significance of the life and death of Jesus. The reconciliation of persons with God is made possible only by the atonement of Jesus. It is God's gift to humans, given at the immeasurable cost to God of the death of the Son. Hence the idea that people can merit salvation by exercising freedom of choice is nothing short of blasphemous. The exercise of freedom is irrelevant to salvation since for those saved through Jesus Christ, salvation is a certainty apart from works.

B.A. Gerrish has suggested that Luther's theology operates with an opposition between grace and reason. In this context, the opposition is actually between grace and freedom. Luther's theology of grace separates him radically from Kant, whose understanding of free will in relation to grace will be dealt with more fully in the next section. For the moment it is necessary only to point out that in contrast to Luther, Kant could never accept the idea that grace might rule out free will. If he is to allow the notion of grace, it must work in co-operation with the human will.

One might conclude from the above that the difference between Kant's perspective and that of Luther is so great because Luther is dealing with the question of freedom from within a religious perspective (that of the Christian tradition which emphasizes the role of Christ in relation to human salvation), whereas Kant is not. However, nothing could be further from the truth. As will be shown in the second part of this paper, Kant's discussion of freedom cannot be properly understood independent of his perspective on religion.

The Comparison Between Kant and Erasmus

The main source used to contrast Luther's perspective with that of Kant has been Luther's famous debate with Erasmus of Rotterdam. It is therefore interesting to note that the stance taken by Erasmus in that debate has striking affinities with Kant's later position. In fact, from a rereading of this text it seems reasonable to suppose that, as far as freedom in relation to salvation is concerned, the main religious forerunner of Kant is in fact Erasmus. On the main point where Kant cannot agree with Luther, namely concerning free will and salvation, his thought is similar to that of Erasmus. In order to show this, Erasmus' view as presented in the debate on the freedom of the will with Luther will be analyzed, and then compared with the Kantian equivalent.

According to Erasmus, freedom is "a power of the human will by which a person can apply himself to the things which lead to eternal salvation, or turn away from them."[27] Kant is entirely in agreement with Erasmus on this point of the relationship between freedom and salvation. Free choice is for Kant the ability to choose between evil and good, the good being that which leads to salvation, the evil that which detracts from it.[28] Erasmus also suggests that "if the will had not been free, sin could not have been imputed, for sin would cease to be sin if it were not voluntary."[29] The thought here is that if there were no freedom of the will, then there would be no sin either, because evil actions would never be chosen, they would simply be the result of our natural impulses. Moreover, if there were no freedom of choice, then there would be no moral responsibility; there would be no attribution of either good or evil. Sin is, and must be, the result of a free choice. Thus, Erasmus not only defends free will, but also uses the idea of freedom to stress the fact of moral responsibility as a necessary condition of salvation.

Such a conception of freedom also appears to be the essential component of moral responsibility according to Kant. As Kadowaki puts it, the leading question for Kant was, "if persons didn't have free will, how could they be evil?"[30] It also follows from this, that as Erasmus argues, "if a person is not the author of good works then they are not the author of bad works either."[31] Thus, if there is no freedom of the will and all good is attributable to God, as Luther had maintained, then on Erasmus' view we would have to attribute all evil to God also. Most significantly, Erasmus advocates the biblical command "work out your own salvation in fear and trembling,"[32] which is a major imperative in Kant's *Religion Within the Limits of Reason Alone*.[33]

Erasmus also recognizes the conflict of good and evil in the individual, for he holds to the idea in Romans 7:18 that "I can will what is right, but I cannot do it."[34] Erasmus claims that in this passage St. Paul was affirming our power to will what is good even in circumstances where we eventually succumb to evil. This idea is reflected in Kant's claim that an evil disposition can exist together with a good will.[35] The substantive issue between Luther and Erasmus is really the one relating to whether salvation is the result of human effort and God-given grace in cooperation, which is Erasmus' position, or God-given grace alone, which is Luther's position. Luther accused Erasmus of speaking about freedom in relation to salvation, without mention of grace. He was charging Erasmus with the claim that freedom unaided by God's grace can achieve salvation. This accusation is false. Erasmus is not trying to rule out Godly grace, for he admits that although the human will is not powerless, it cannot attain its end without grace.[36] From this it is clear that Erasmus does not intend to disparage grace, only to establish freedom and human responsibility. What he cannot allow is grace to the exclusion of human effort. Exactly the same is the case for Kant, who in the *Religion Within the Limits of Reason Alone* makes it clear that we have every right to hope for God's assistance in order that we may achieve salvation, but "only by qualifying for it through our own efforts to fulfill every human duty."[37]

One might argue that Erasmus is finally separated from Kant in his admission that "those who support free choice nonetheless admit that a soul which is obstinate in evil cannot be softened into true repentance without the help of heavenly grace."[38] By this he means that grace is needed before an obstinate and evil will can turn towards the good. However, as Allen Wood has argued convincingly in *Kant's Moral Religion*, divine forgiveness and human repentance are both notions at work in Kant's interpretation of religion.[39] When Kant refers to the overcoming of evil, he speaks of the necessity of a "change of heart." This "change of heart" is achieved through what Kant refers to as the "supersensible principle in human nature." Although Kant does not give an extensive explanation of the "supersensible principle," it appears to be something which is both human and yet at the same time beyond sensible human nature.[40]

In many ways Kant's notion of the supersensible principle bears direct relation to much Roman Catholic theology which conceives of grace as working through human nature. Bearing this in mind, it is also interesting to note the distinction used in Roman Catholic theology between prevenient and peculiar grace, a distinction which Erasmus makes use of in the debate on free will. He claims that peculiar grace is present in those who strive for moral improvement,[41] whereas prevenient grace is the extra help that God gives to the person.[42] The former is that which enables the human to move from the evil to the good, the latter that which complements a person's moral efforts in order that they may achieve salvation.

In this we can also see a direct parallel with Kant. We can compare Kant's notion of the supersensible in human nature with peculiar grace, and the help which God gives after we have striven for moral perfection with prevenient grace. Kant does not rule out peculiar grace, or the possibility of prevenient grace; he simply stresses the need for human effort in co-operation with grace.

According to Luther, after the fall of humankind human freedom is nothing but the freedom to sin. In contrast, Erasmus holds that even after the fall persons can choose the good. Erasmus is therefore an optimist about the possibility of moral improvement. However, he never, as

Luther wrongly suggests, thinks that this is possible without at least peculiar grace. Rather, if people do as much as lies within them, God's assisting grace will be made available, for divine grace "always accompanies human effort."[43] This claim is reflected in Kant's *Religion Within the Limits of Reason Alone* where he says that if we do as much as we can to become better people, we can hope for the help of God in those aspects of our lives where we are lacking.[44]

So far as freedom, grace, and salvation are concerned, Kant and Erasmus are in agreement: salvation without freedom and moral responsibility is not possible. In Erasmus' opinion, the question of free will exposed Luther's fatalism.[45] As was shown earlier, Kant argued strongly against fatalism. Heavenly grace can be assumed, but only in connection with moral effort. Salvation and moral attainment go together.

As shown above, Kant's perspective on freedom is concerned with grace and salvation, but in a way which is at odds with the thought of Luther. It is now possible to compare Kant's position with that of Farrer. For both Kant and Farrer the recognition of grace cannot undermine an appreciation of free will. Neither Kant nor Farrer can entertain the idea of human beings as simply pawns in some supernatural game. It is rather that through our free will we are able to cooperate with God's gracious action. In Farrer's opinion free acts are also the organs for the reception of God's grace. Precisely the same is the case with Kant. Both Farrer and Kant believe that we have a human responsibility to fulfill God's will rather than live in a kind of passive dependence that waits for God to do everything. Without this human free will and the moral responsibility it entails, we would be enslaved. But this is ever and always a matter of human agency in cooperation with God-given grace. God's will is verified and known only in the doing of his will in furthering his kingdom here on earth.

Thus, the Kantian insistence upon freedom of the will in relation and mutual cooperation with divine grace is not in these respects too far removed from Farrer's God of grace. Farrer might also be thought to improve upon the Kantian understanding of free will in co-operation with grace. According to Farrer, it is when we act to the highest degree of our freedom that we become most aware of the fact that divine activity comes through into the creature. In a sense then, our most free acts are offprints or expressive of the divine will itself. Similarly, it is just where we cease to conceive our dependence upon God that we begin to live it. Such cooperation between the human and divine has been described in relation to Farrer's perspective as a "coinciding with God's action in one's own life." It might similarly be thought of in terms of "double agency," human and divine, and reflects the supreme mystery of freedom–human and divine.[46]

Kant and Recent Philosophical Work on Free Will

From the above it should be clear that both Farrer and Kant are strong advocates of free will, especially in relation to salvation. All the more surprising, therefore, that Kant also accepted determinism in nature. In fact, it is Farrer himself who, in an article in the *Dictionary of the History of Ideas*, characterizes Kant's position with regard to free will and determinism as follows: Kant was forced to think deterministically about physical and mental processes, when making them an object of study. But Kant also maintained that we are called to exercise free and responsible choices in favor of the moral law. Therefore, Kant seems to favor both free will and determinism. However, rather than give an explanation as to how our power to exercise free choice fits in with the actual order of nature Kant simply maintained that such things are beyond our comprehension. Thus, Kant's position with regard to the problem of free will and determinism appears to be a rational and systematic agnosticism.

Such agnosticism is no solution to the free will/determinism issue. Fortunately, however, recent philosophical work in the area of free will and determinism offers some explanation as to how Kant's understanding of free will can be reconciled with determinism in nature. Furthermore, the philosophical work referred to reflects convictions to some extent already present in Farrer's defense of free will.

Integral to Kant's whole approach to determinism and freedom is a distinction between what he refers to as the phenomenal and intelligible worlds, and corresponding to this distinction, those between desire and reason, compulsion and autonomy. Whether or not there are in fact two worlds, or whether the distinction is just a figure of speech, is not our present concern, which is simply to explain and assess Kant's position. In Kant's opinion, determinism is a fact of the phenomenal world, which is the world of desires, compulsion, and determining causes. Free will, by contrast, belongs to the intelligible, or noumenal world, which is a world of reason as distinct from desires, and of free causality. The noumenal world is also the realm in which moral actions, based in free will and autonomy, find their being. This may sound like a rather inappropriate attempt to, as it were, have the best of both worlds; that is, to favor both freedom and determinism without giving any explanation as to how the two are to be reconciled. However, recent work in the area of freedom and determinism suggests that, regardless of how implausible the notions of phenomenal and noumenal worlds may be, Kant's claims are not as unfounded as they may at first seem.

Thomas Nagel has argued convincingly that desires and wants do not provide the only reasons for acting.[47] Something other than desires may, in some instances, lie at the source of action. This fact becomes impor-

tant when one considers the claim made by Donald Davidson, that reasons are causes of action, and can provide the rational explanation for
actions.[48] If one applies this interpretation of reasons as causes to Kant's
distinction, it would suggest two different kinds of causes of action,
those determined by desires, and those determined by reasons.
Following on from this, one might say that desire causation relates to
the phenomenal realm, and reason causation relates to the intelligible
realm. The former has to do with compulsion, the latter with that of free
causation. One might also conclude from this that the kind of free
choice referred to by Luther would, on Kant's understanding, be a case
of determined causation, and the free will referred to by Kant would be
a matter of free causation. In other words, on a Kantian account,
Lutheran free will would amount to determinism.

By applying the theory of reason as a cause of action to the nature of
duty, which was so important for Kant's account of free will, we can
assume that the practical judgment "I ought to do something" includes
the acceptance of a reason for doing it. We require no alternative explanation in terms of desires or wants, which belong to the determined
realm. Thus, doing our duty is not necessarily the result of some prior
motivating factor in our nature, such as a desire or a want. Rather, it can
be the result of a free causality determined by, for instance, a value
judgment. And if reasons are causes, then moral actions are not just
mere determined happenings, and people are not mere victims of their
determined natures. Moral values can be reasons for acting, and can
motivate us quite independently of, or at least notwithstanding, our
desires. This helps explain why we sometimes are motivated to do
things morally worthy, irrespective of our selfish desire to do otherwise.

More interesting, however, is Davidson's further claim that freedom
cannot be analyzed without appeal to intentions, and that intentions are
not fully explicable in determinist terms. This is because intentions are
connected to the notion of purpose, which is not analyzable within a
deterministic framework. For example, value judgments, or purposeful
intentions are never satisfactorily explained in determinist terms. The
result of this is not that some events are uncaused, but that some human
actions resist incorporation into a closed deterministic system. Nagel
puts the point well when he suggests that the self which acts and is the
object of moral judgment is threatened with dissolution by the absorp-
tion of its acts into the class of events.[49]

The kind of compatibilism[50] between determinism in nature and
intentional, albeit *caused* human activity advocated by Davidson does
seem a plausible explanation of Kant's position with regard to free will
and determinism. Unfortunately, there is little evidence to suggest that
Kant would be any happier to accept a compatibilist stance on the free

will/determinism issue than would Farrer. What is clear is that both Kant and Farrer felt so strongly about human freedom that they would be reluctant to accept any position which might appear to undermine free will. As a result, one is left with a difficult choice between an agnosticism which offers no solution to the free will/determinism debate or an attempted solution which possibly Kant and certainly Farrer would not be entirely happy with. In this respect I am inclined to follow Allen Wood, who has convincingly argued that irrespective of Kant's reluctance to compromise human freedom, compatibilism does appear to be the most coherent stance given his interpretation of free will and determinism.[51]And the same might be said of Farrer.

Conclusion

Kant was willing to accept determinism in nature, but he also pinpointed the areas in which deterministic interpretations are least satisfactory, namely, those of morality and religion. My attempt to defend Kant's acceptance of determinism with regard to the physical world, and at the same time allow him a notion of free will, is bound to the very idea that human behavior, especially moral and religious behavior, is not always reducible to physical explanation. As conscious, reflective and reasonable beings, we cannot be fully appreciated in terms of a physical system, especially when we are acting according to the moral law, in obedience to God's will, or choosing between good and evil.

When we are acting with some purpose or end in view, we appeal to a purposive scheme which alone makes human behavior comprehensible. It is within this purposive scheme that the intentional activity intrinsic to the nature of free will belongs. On both Kant's and Farrer's reading of such a purposive scheme, it is a scheme reflecting God's purpose for us. It is a scheme which contains the notions of moral responsibility, grace, and salvation. And given that the kind of free will which is necessary to intentional behavior is that which makes us not only free to choose what we do, but also answerable for our behavior, it follows for both Farrer and Kant that it is God to whom we are answerable, just as it is God who has given us the freedom which makes us so.

Notes

1. See: B. Bauch, *Luther und Kant* (Berlin, 1904).
Ernst Katzer, *Luther und Kant* (Gießen, 1910).
Friedrich Paulsen, "Kant der Philosoph des Protestantismus," *Kantstudien* 4 (1900): 1-31.
Horst Schülke, *Kants und Luthers Ethik* (Greifswald,

1937).
Theodor Siegfried, "Luther und Kant," *Lutherjahrbuch* 9 (1927); *Luther und Kant: Ein geistesgeschichtlicher Vergleich im Anschluß an den Gewissensbegriff* (Gießen, 1930).
2. See Luther, "De Servo Arbitrio" (The Bondage of the Will), trans. and ed. P.S. Watson and B. Drewery, and Erasmus, "De Libero Arbitrio" (The Freedom of the Will), trans. and ed. E.G. Rupp, and A.N. Marlow, S.C.M., in *Luther and Erasmus:Free Will and Salvation*, 1969.
3. *Luther and Erasmus:Free Will and Salvation*, 317.
4. Ibid., 305.
5. Ibid., 271.
6. Ibid.
7. Ibid., 270. Cf. John 3: 6.
8. Ibid., 296.
9. Ibid., 13, and Luther's reference to this, 219.
10. Ibid., 291.
11. References to the German text of Kant's works are to the *Gesammelte Schriften*, ed. Der Königlich Preußischen Akademie der Wissenschaften, Berlin, Reimer, 1905 onwards. These are indicated in the footnotes as KW, with volume and page number, after which the English translation, where available, follows. See KW 6, 237; *The Metaphysical Elements of Justice*, part one of *The Metaphysic of Morals, Division of the Theory of Justice*, trans. with an introduction by John Ladd (Bobbs-Merrill Co,1965), 43-44.
12. KW 28, 1068; *Lectures on Philosophical Theology*, trans. A. W. Wood (Ithaca: Cornell University Press, 1978), 105.
13. KW 6, 449; *Groundwork*, 116.
14. KW 8, 13; My translation: Ich frage nur, was ich nun zu tun habe, und da ist die Freiheit eine notwendige praktische Voraussetzung und eine Idee, unter der ich allein Gebote der Vernunft als gültig ansehen kann.
15. KW 4, 237; *The Metaphysical Elements of Justice*, 43-44.
16. Ibid., 448; *Groundwork,*116.
17. KW 8, 13; My translation: Der allgemeine Fatalism...alles menschliche Tun und lassen in bloßes Marionettenspiel verwandelt, den Begriff von Verbindlichkeit gänzlich aufhebe, das dagegen das Sollen oder der Imperativ, der das praktische Gesetz vom Naturgesetz unterscheidet, uns auch in der Idee gänzlich außerhalb der Naturkette setze, indem er, ohne unseren Willen als frei zu denken, unmöglich und ungereimt ist, vielmehr uns alsdann nichts übrigbleibt, als abzuwarten und zu beobachten, was Gott vermittelst der Natursachen in uns für Entschließungen wirken werde, nicht aber was wir von selbst als

Urheber tun können und sollen.

18. *Luther and Erasmus: Free Will and Salvation*, 289.

19. KW 28, 1116; *Lectures on Philosophical Theology*, 159.

20. KW 5, 72; *Critique of Practical Reason*, trans. L.W. Beck, (Macmillan Publishing Co., 1986), 75.

21. KW 4, 447; *Groundwork*, 115.

22. Ibid.

23. Ibid.; *Groundwork*, 114.

24. *Luther and Erasmus: Free Will and Salvation*, 290.

25. Ibid., 307.

26. Ibid., 188.

27. Ibid., 47.

28. KW 6, 51-52. Cf. 83; *Religion Within the Limits of Reason Alone*, trans. T. M. Greene and H. Hoyt (Hudson: Harper and Row, 1960); Book I, General Observation, p.47. Cf. Book II, Section Two, p.78.

29. *Luther and Erasmus: Free Will and Salvation*, 50

30. Takuji Kadowaki "Das Radikal Böse bei Kant" (Diss., Bonn, 1960), 26. My translation: Wenn der Mensch in der Willkür nicht frei wäre, wie könnte er böse sein?

31. *Luther and Erasmus: Free Will and Salvation*, 92.

32. Ibid., 73, 81. Cf. Phil. 2:12

33. KW VI, 68; *Religion*, Book II, Section 1, C, 62. Cf. Phil. 2:12.

34. *Luther and Erasmus: Free Will and Salvation*, 63. Cf. Rom. 7:18. See KW VI, 29; *Religion*, Book I, ii., 25.

35. KW VI, 37; *Religion*, Book 1, iii., 32.

36. *Luther and Erasmus: Free Will and Salvation*, 79.

37. KW VI, 118; *Religion*, Book III ,Division One, vii, 108.

38. *Luther and Erasmus: Free Will and Salvation*, 73.

39. Ithaca and London: Cornell University Press, 1970, 240-248.

40. KW VII, 46-47; *The Conflict of the Faculties,* trans. and introduction by M.J. Gregor (Abaris, 1979), 81-83.

41. *Luther and Erasmus: Free Will and Salvation*, 49, 52.

42. Ibid., 52, 66, 84.

43. Ibid., 15.

44. KW VI, 51-52; *Religion*, Book I, General Observation, 47.

45. *Luther and Erasmus: Free Will and Salvation*, Introduction, 9.

46. See *Faith and Speculation* (London: Adam and Charles Black, 1967), especially Chapter IV, where Farrer worked out his final views on free will and grace.

47. See *The Possibility of Altruism*, (Oxford: Oxford University Press, 1970).

48. See *Essays on Actions and Events*, (Oxford: Oxford University Press, 1980).

49. It is interesting to note that in his defense of free will, Farrer himself stressed that a full explanation of human conduct in purely physical terms was not possible. He made the point that determinants of physical nature and constitution do not rule out the possibility of creative volition.

50. Otherwise referred to as soft determinism.

51. See *Self and Nature in Kant's Philosophy* (Ithaca: Cornell University Press, 1984), Chapter III.

Section II:
Freedom and Agency–Finite and Infinite

Chapter 5

Finite and Infinite Freedom in Farrer and von Balthasar

Brian Hebblethwaite

Introduction

In this essay I extend my reflections on the free will defense in theodicy–or the kind of freedom inherent in human personal existence which allows us to explain why God cannot *ensure* that all goes well in his creation.[1] Whatever else it entails, freedom in humans, at least in the conditions of our earthly pilgrimage, means the freedom to choose evil as well as good. One cannot here on earth have the latter–human moral goodness–without the risk of the former–wickedness or the abuse of freedom. The plausibility of the free will defense depends upon our ability to sustain this sense of significant freedom, whereby finite agents like ourselves can be held responsible, praised or blamed for our actions, and indeed for the sort of people we become.

In our present case, the "could have done otherwise," essential to freedom in normal conditions, importantly includes the real possibility of taking the wrong course, succumbing to temptation, even allowing one to become ensnared in structures of radical evil from which one cannot escape without help, whether human or divine. In this sense, significant freedom has to be defended against all forms of determinism, but especially against the kind of compatibilism so powerfully argued by J.L. Mackie, and so eloquently elaborated in a series of books by Daniel C. Dennett, especially in *Elbow Room*.[2] I explore and defend this significant freedom in this essay with the aid of Austin Farrer's Gifford Lectures, *The Freedom of the Will*.[3]

But reflection on the exigencies of finite human freedom leads me to ponder, by way of contrast, the nature of infinite divine freedom. God's freedom cannot, of course, entail the freedom to do good or evil; for God is, in essence, absolutely and perfectly good. God's action is bound to flow from his nature as perfect Love. But, if so, does not the threat of a higher determinism raise its head? Are not God's actions, necessarily, always the best possible, and thus not really free? It seems that for God, like Mrs. Thatcher, there is no alternative.

So my second concern is to explore the nature of infinite divine freedom and to try to spell out the sense in which it is indeed the very paradigm of true freedom. Such a topic requires both philosophical and theological awareness. That is why I turn again and again to that philosophical theologian par excellence, Austin Farrer, digging out occasional remarks on God's freedom not only from the Gifford lectures but from his other books and articles. But I have found it necessary to secure the theological side of my explorations even more extensively than by reference to Farrer alone. That is why I shall be turning to the writings of Hans Urs von Balthasar, and in particular to the long section on "Infinite and Finite Freedom" in Volume II of his *Theodramatik*, published in English under the title *Theo-drama*.[4]

But, clearly, I cannot rest with contrasting explorations of the nature of finite human freedom, liable to wrong choice, on the one hand, and of infinite divine freedom, necessarily acting for the best, on the other. For human beings are made in the image of God. Their destiny is to be conformed to the divine likeness, and while they will remain finite centers of freedom, believe they will be so "divinized" through incorporation into the risen body of Christ that eventually, in heaven, they too will come to act, freely and spontaneously, always for the best in the blessed company of the communion of saints. There they will have lost that liability to go astray which seems characteristic of the moral life on earth, and which is required for the free will defense in theodicy to work. So my third concern in this paper is with the question how it can be that finite freedom, when conformed to infinite freedom, can still be thought of as freedom. A further question follows any successful answer to this one, namely, why that happy state of finite creatures freely responding perfectly to one another and to God, cannot be achieved directly, without the arduous process of formation in which we find ourselves at present, where freedom, as I say, entails the liability to err.

A fourth area of concern is that of the active relation between infinite and finite freedom from the divine side. Again, with the help of both Farrer and von Balthasar, I shall attempt to say something about the way God's freedom can be seen to be at work in the creation of a world containing free finite agents, and also about the way God freely acts, by grace, in and through the free thoughts and acts of those who love him, and place themselves at his disposal.

Finite Human Freedom in the Making

First, then, let us consider the nature of finite human freedom as we find it in this present, formative, phase of the creative process, where, it seems, we are indeed confronted with the choice between good and evil. Farrer has urged correctly that we should not restrict the scope of freedom in humans to the relatively narrow area of important moral struggle and choice. Our freedom is much more pervasive and all-embracing. It is involved in all thought and action. Of course my control of what I think and do, and my ability to do X or to refrain from doing X, are not absolute; I am a finite creature, hedged about with factors, environmental and hereditary, that are given, not chosen. I am a conditioned being, both externally and internally.

But, for the libertarian, these factors separately or in combination, are only in certain spheres of my life uniquely determining, for example, my physical stature. By contrast, in thought and deliberation, I stand back from these factors, known and unknown, and consider what to believe and what to do. In action, I choose a particular path between branching alternatives. In artistic creativity too–perhaps supremely so–I use given materials and powers to invent something new and theoretically unpredictable. On human voluntary action, I quote Farrer's lapidary summary: "What can be more voluntary than a project with nothing against it, immediately seized by the whole energy of our will; when for example, on a day of leisure, we embrace an invitation to visit the person whom we love?"[5]

Let us look more closely at this example. For this is just the sort of case that the compatibilist, such as Dennett, tries to assimilate to a sophisticated stimulus/response situation in an advanced computer or robot, and to describe, in causal terms, as the inevitable effect of a set of necessary and sufficient conditions. Conscious acquiescence to a welcome invitation is thus regarded as the necessary outcome, in a highly sophisticated organism–a human being–of the total input (internal and external) at a given time. Eventually the development of artificial intelligence will enable us to construct exactly similar "conscious" stimulus/response situations in a silicon-based artifact. Of course, it is advances in computer technology and the hope of progress towards artificial intelligence that have given a new lease of life to theoretical determinism. If consciousness and rationality can indeed be simulated in this way and analyzed in causal terms as our highly developed means of registering relevant input and of triggering appropriate response, then freedom in the libertarian sense of the conscious power to act or refrain whatever the input, or to react in one of many different ways given the same input, is indeed illusory.

But Dennett's treatment of consciousness and rationality–most recently in his magnum opus, *Consciousness Explained*[6]–does not convince. The assimilation of reasons to causes and of consciousness to the receiving end of feedback mechanisms does not begin to do justice to what it is trying to explain. A set of reasons, however, powerful and "compelling" as we somewhat rashly say, does not in fact necessitate. Where conscious evaluation of reasons for action plays its role, there is always that element of responsible control that leaves it up to us whether to respond appropriately or not and in which way.

The very meaning of "sufficiency" in talk of sufficient conditions changes where rational action is concerned. In genuinely causal situations a set of sufficient conditions are those from which the outcome necessarily follows. But in a case of voluntary action, the grounds may be sufficient to elicit an appropriate response, but only in the sense of being enough to explain that response. Other responses remain quite possible, some more, some less intelligible. If I insult you, and you slap my face, the insult is "sufficient" to explain your reaction. But it does not necessitate it. You might have exercised forbearance.

These possibilities of alternative action are latent in an unambiguous case like Farrer's of my embracing an invitation to visit a loved friend, but they are there notwithstanding. Even if no contrary reason, motive, or desire intervenes, it is still up to me whether I initiate the natural and obvious response. The sufficiency of the circumstances still does not compel. To take an even more extreme example–an example to which we shall return–a violinist in a great orchestra playing a Beethoven symphony freely plays the notes before him in the score. He could just stop or break out into a different piece altogether. The fact that he doesn't and won't does not make his playing necessary or inevitable. He is not like a series of digital imprints on a compact disc which comes out with the Beethoven willy-nilly.

The voluntariness of our actions remains even when the alternative possibilities are latent; but of course the pervasive fact of our freedom is the more evident in the more ambiguous circumstances of conflicting reasons for action or of tension between reason and desire. And it is because we frequently find ourselves in such circumstances that choice for us is so often choice between good and evil. In other words, the freedom to choose between good and evil, essential to the free will defense in theodicy, does not belong to the essence of finite freedom as such. It is entailed by significant finite freedom in certain circumstances, namely those of ambiguity and conflict.

Therefore, the key question in theodicy becomes, not why freedom is so important. It obviously is. Freedom belongs to the essence of agency and personal existence in any and all circumstances. The key question in theodicy is why God sets out finite freedom in such ambiguous and conflicting circumstances that it necessarily involves the choice between good and evil?

When we turn to von Balthasar's more explicitly theological analysis of finite freedom, we find two pillars or poles to finite freedom–one, freedom as autonomous motion, the other, freedom as consent. We are at present concerned with the first of these–the genuine autonomy of the finite agent, to whom is given by God the power of self-determination. This is a basic presupposition for the whole biblical drama, says von Balthasar. "Christianity had continually to vindicate its authentic form by defending this point against the determinism and fatalism of the ancient world...["7] I have claimed that we are in no different case today. Our identity as finite personal agents, our ethical responsibility, our derived powers of creativity, all depend upon our being autonomous selves–even though this entails the risk of egocentric self-possession and the embracing of inappropriate aims and objects as our good. The other pole of finite freedom consists in the self-realization which comes from self-surrender to our true and highest good and finding our true selves in relation to each other and to God. More will be said about this second pole later. At present our interest focuses on the necessity to finite freedom of the first pole, genuine autonomy, the basic capacity to choose between alternative possibilities.

On the theodicy question–why God sets our finite freedom in ambiguous conditions which make it inevitable that choice, for us, includes choice between good and evil–Farrer has rather more to say than von Balthasar. He develops a basically "Irenaean" theodicy, designed to show that only some such matrix as a law-governed, evolving, yet open and flexible physical world can provide the necessary conditions for the formation and growth of finite persons. It is the very conditions of our formation that at the same time render us liable to temptation and to the lure of egocentricity. It is finite freedom in these necessary conditions that is, inevitably, at risk to abuse and wrong choice.

Von Balthasar, a greater traditionalist that Farrer where the doctrine of creation is concerned, also shows some awareness of the unavoidable risks entailed in giving finite persons that necessary first pole of finite freedom–our autonomous power of self-determination. God's finite creatures, writes von Balthasar,[8] "only gain room for freedom...if God, in allowing them freedom, withdraws to a certain extent and becomes latent." This "making room" for his free creatures "yields the possibility of profound error in the realm of the finite." "Foreground goods are available, obscuring our view of goods that are greater but more distant and harder to acquire." So again it is not the nature of finite freedom as

such that accounts for our liability to err. It is rather the necessary setting of autonomous creatures in an environment where their highest
good is hidden that explains why choice, for us, involves choice
between good and evil.

Much of the larger part of von Balthasar's treatment concerns the
second pole of finite freedom–the freedom in relation to God for which
we were made. But before tuning to this definitive aspect of finite freedom, I want to consider the nature of God's infinite freedom itself.

God's Infinite Freedom

Philosophers have often used the concept of God as a heuristic
device in order to bring out, by contrast, the limited, finite nature of our
human faculties. Thus Immanuel Kant, despite his theoretical agnosticism, contrasts our human "ectypal understanding" with God's "arche-
typal understanding" which knows the world intuitively in making it.[9]
This recalls the medieval adage, often cited against those who would
offer us a spectatorial model of God's omniscience: *scientia Dei causa
rerum.* I shall return to this theme at a later stage, but certainly the
divine will, unlike the human, is not to be thought of as exercised in
relation to any already given realities or laws. God does not exist in an
environment that limits his creative powers and acts.

Both Farrer and von Balthasar stress the unconditionedness and
absoluteness of the divine will. However, this is not only a question of
God's acts in creation. Unconditioned will is what God is in himself.
Both theologians quote the Plotinian definition of infinite freedom:
God's "will is identical with him; he will be what he is, and he is what
he will be."[10] Farrer explicity links this voluntarist concept of God's
essence with the question of God's understanding. Perfect understanding and perfect will would be identical. Only an absolute will could be
both spontaneous and intelligent, apprehending what he enacts and
enacting what he apprehends.[11]

It has to be said that the Plotinian definition by itself yields little
informational content. When we read in Farrer's *Faith and Speculation*
that God "is all he wills to be, and will to be all he is; for his act is himself, and his act is free," we may well feel that we are not much the
wiser concerning who or what we are talking about. In fact, of course,
both Farrer and von Balthasar say much more than this about the one
they speak of as unconditioned will. For Farrer, God is of course creator
of the world; but Farrer goes on to insist on God's prior actuality as transcendent incorporeal spirit, and that, for Christians at least, God is not
to be conceived as "action in vacuo, that is, action with out interplay."
Christians believe in a "Trinity of Persons in Unity of Substance."[12]

Von Balthasar begins his treatment of infinite freedom with the

revealed truth that absolute freedom consists not only in God's self-possession, but in God's limitless self-surrender in the mutual interrelations
of the Trinity. Absolute freedom consists in love given and love
received within the triune God. Love is God's nature–essentially and
necessarily so. It is this that gives content to the bare assertion that God
is all he wills to be and wills to be all he is. Only on the basis of this
prior interchange of love in God does God's free act of creation and
God's free acts within creation take the form of self-giving love.

But if we are constrained to speak here of God's necessary goodness
and love, how can his acts–either within God's Triune being or ad
extra–be thought of as genuinely free, let along paradigmatically so?
Are we not driven into that higher theological determinism where all
God's acts necessarily express his nature? Necessarily God exists and
loves in his inner Trinitarian reciprocity. Necessarily God creates; for
that creativity of new centers of freedom and love expresses his essential nature. And necessarily God acts for the best in relation to what he
had made. Thus it seems there are no real alternatives.

However this is totally to misunderstand the nature of absolute perfection. Even Keith Ward, who in his fine book, *Divine Action*, shows
clearly that God's creativity is expressed freely and contingently in what
he creates and in the manner in which he acts in relation to the creatures
he had made, still feels driven to speak of creation itself–some creation
or other–as necessary to God.[13] Farrer and von Balthasar are much near-
er the mark in insisting on the free spontaneity of God's very act of creation. Both, as we shall see, use the model of artistic creativity–the creation of a novel, a drama, or an opera–for God's free act of creation. Von
Balthasar also insists on God's inner Trinitarian love as perfectly free:
"The divine hypostases know and interpenetrate each other to the very
same degree that each of them opens up to the other, in absolute freedom."[14] Indeed, this Trinitarian infinite freedom is the basis of God's free
acts of creation and of binding his creatures to himself.

Far from acting out of necessity, we might say that God, out of his
great love, necessarily acts freely in quite unpredictable, creative, and
contingent ways. This is as true of God's inventive, creative acts as it is
of God's responses to what his creatures freely do. In neither case is
there only one best act which God must necessarily perform. There are
innumerable, good, creative, possibilities–though, as we shall see, they
cannot, in the nature of the case, be specified in advance, even by omniscience. And there are innumerable, loving, ways of responding to what
creatures do, inspiring and assisting them by grace, and bringing good
out of evil when they go astray.

Finite Freedom in the End

Before pursuing the topic of the model of artistic creativity which both Farrer and von Balthasar employ for God's act of creation, I want to turn back to the question of finite freedom and its second pillar or pole–what von Balthaser dubs freedom as consent–our true freedom, that is, as we come to realize our God-given nature in freely surrendering ourselves to each other and our Maker. It is in and through the spontaneity of self-giving love that we are drawn closer to the image and likeness of God.

The contrast between finite and infinite is, of course, never wholly overcome. Our freedom is conditioned by a given natural and social environment and supremely by the givenness of our Creator's being and intention. Even in eternity we remain derivatively free and *pro*-creative. God's freedom is unconditioned and the very source and goal of our finite self-realization. It is by participation in infinite freedom that finite freedom comes to fruition; and, given the *nature* of infinite freedom, that means participation in love–love of other human beings and love of God. As von Balthasar puts the matter:

> ...finite freedom can fulfill itself in infinite freedom and in no other way. If letting be belongs to the nature of infinite freedom...there is no danger of finite freedom, which cannot fulfil itself on its own account (because it cannot...attain its absolute goal by its own power), becoming alienated from itself in the realm of the Infinite. It can only be what it is, that is, an image of infinite freedom, imbued with a freedom of its own, by getting in tune with the (Trinitarian) "law" of absolute freedom (of self-surrender): and this law is not foreign to it...but most authentically to its own.[15]

Having stressed God's latency and hiddenness in connection with the first pole of finite freedom–autonomy–von Balthasar goes on to stress God's providence in connection with the second pole of finite freedom–our self-realization in God. Having let us be, God draws us, uncoercively and freely, to himself. This process constitutes the *drama* of creation and redemption. Unlike Karl Barth, who tends to place all the action on God's side, von Balthasar stresses *both* God's action in the creation and perfection of a world of finite life, and the myriad forms of creaturely creative acts and achievements, under God's providential care. The vast riches of human culture and literary and artistic creativity are all grist for von Balthasar's mill at this point. They are all aspects of theo-drama–divine as well as human creativity.

Therefore, finite freedom fulfills itself only by participation in infinite freedom. This sets no *arbitrary* limit on human autonomy. On the contrary, left to itself, a Promethean self-assertion of human autonomy

self-destructs. It is the very nature of finite freedom to find self-realization in giving itself to the other, or in mystical experience, *in the power
of the Spirit*, that is, of infinite freedom.

Earlier, I used the analogy of a player in a great orchestra, freely con-
tributing to the performance of a symphony. The analogy indicates, up
to a point, how shared participation in a given project in no way takes
away freedom. It also suggests how, in a perfected and unambiguous
environment, a free response can and will be given, with no further risk
of rebellion or falling away. But this analogy will need to be comple-
mented by other stories illustrative of the effects of grace, in equally
free acts of mutual love, intellectual discovery, or original creativity.

The Relation Between Infinite and Finite Freedom

This leads us on to the fourth of my main concerns, the active relation between God's infinite freedom and the finite freedom of his creatures. As I have pointed out already, both Farrer and von Balthasar
employ the model of artistic creativity to try to capture something of the
nature of this relation. Farrer, in *A Science of God?*, employs the
"author" analogy:

> The Creator of the world is not to be compared with those bad novelists
> who make up the plot of their story first, and force the characters to carry
> it out, all against the grain of their natures. He is like the good novelist
> who has the wit to get a satisfying story out of the natural behavior of the
> characters he conceives. And how does he do it? By identifying himself
> with them and living them from within.[16]

The purpose of this analogy is to give substance to Farrer's key idea
of "double agency," of God's making the creature make itself; for the
characters in God's "novel"–the creation–are real live characters
endowed with finite freedom, learning for themselves, under God's
providence, the secret of their true freedom under God.

Von Balthasar employs a comparable analogy, though for a somewhat different purpose. In an extended footnote he writes:

> A consummate work of art, Mozart's Magic Flute, for example, stands
> before us as the product of an imaginable creative freedom. Does it make
> any sense to ask this work whether it might not have been even more per-
> fect? Obviously, the question can be put...but it is impossible to come up
> with any meaningful concrete suggestion as to the direction in which this
> improvement might be made. On the other hand, the work of art radiates
> so much freedom that it would be just as mistaken to label it "best" once
> and for all, in such a way that, had Mozart lived longer, he would have
> been unable to write a more perfect opera. It is well known, furthermore,

with what playful ease Mozart could insert new arias or delete existing ones...without thereby endangering the harmony of his work–which forbids us to separate the "necessity" of a work from the freedom which lends wings to it. Moreover, it is clear that part of the "perfection" of the Magic Flute is the incredible variety of the characters, scenes and musical forms, the lofty and the lowly, the tragic, heroic, burlesque and idyllic, pathos and the stolidly down-to-earth, profundity and absurdity...If a composer like God creates the opera of our world and puts the crucified and risen Son at its center, there must be no fault-finding and wondering if he could not have made it better. This is the standpoint from which to assess the value of what Leibniz, Malebranche and Rosmini have said about the world, as the "best possible," as well as Thomas' objections to the concept...[17]

Clearly von Balthasar, with this powerful analogy is trying to distance himself from two opposite errors–one, the view that God finds himself confronted with an existing range of possible worlds; the other, the view that God necessarily (by that higher determinism) creates the best possible world. The spontaneity, freedom, and contingency of artistic creation suggests that neither of these views can possible be right. Out of his sovereign freedom and self-giving love, God composes a thoroughly contingent work of surpassing beauty, notwithstanding its inevitable temporary tragedies on the way to perfection, and notwithstanding innumerable unknown and unknowable alternative possibilities that might have been created.

The author or composer analogy is well worth pondering and exploring in depth and at length. God's creativity along, I have said, invents a world endowed with genuine creaturely autonomy. God's infinite freedom is nowhere more evident than in letting such finite free creatures be and relating to them appropriately by providence and grace. Certainly, *scientia Dei causa rerum*. God knows his creatures in thus making them. But if he is in fact making them make themselves, then what God is doing is fashioning and relating to an open-futured and theoretically unpredictable world.

The attempt to rescue God's fore-knowledge of future free acts of autonomous creatures by a doctrine of "middle knowledge," whereby God only actualizes those futures, which, through his awareness of all counterfactuals of freedom, he knows will invite his predetermined responses, is futile in two respects. First, it requires a deterministic or compatibilist account of finite freedom after all. Only so could one make sense of the idea of the actualization of specific determinate futures. Secondly, it presupposes the coherence of the notion of knowing all possible individual persons in advance of their formation. This cannot be right. Granted, each individual is endowed from conception with a unique set of basic characteristics. But these are only the given material on the basis of which a new personality is formed.

The whole beauty of the gradual formation of new unique personalities lies in the fact that their newness and individuality are formed out of an actual life history of actual personal relations and responses to circumstance. A particular individual is theoretically unpredictable and unknowable in advance. The notion that all possible people are knowable in advance is comparable to the notion that all possible operas are knowable in advance and that composition is a matter of selection from that range.

Once again the theological determinist is failing to appreciate the astonishing creativity of God in fashioning a genuinely open-futured world, productive of unique personal, autonomous, lives. If the case of Jeremiah is cited against me–"Before I formed you in the womb I knew you, and before you were born I consecrated you; I appointed you a prophet to the nations"[18]–I can only reply that we cannot take this literally. It is poetic hyperbole, expressive of a powerful sense of vocation and an unshakable belief in providential guidance: but it could not literally have been so. The actual nature of God's creative act–infinite freedom's letting be of finite freedom–is belied by the suggestion that the character and personality of Jeremiah and his path through life in all its detail are predetermined and known by the Creator Spirit. That is simply not the nature of the theo-drama in the midst of which we find ourselves.

Both Farrer and von Balthasar have much to say about the way in which God, by his grace, without forcing or faking the story, without overriding the finite freedom of his creatures, wins their consent, and acts in and through them to build up the body of Christ on earth and eventually the communion of saints in heaven. This co-operation of grace and free will is the paradigm case of double agency for Austin Farrer. Keith Ward, in *Divine Action*, is quite wrong to interpret double agency as a matter of God's holding the whole system of finite causal powers in being while we exercise our God-given powers.[19] On the contrary, double agency, for Farrer, is a matter of God's bringing about his *particular* purposes in and through the autonomous energies and acts of creatures, without forcing or faking the story.

The paradox of grace and free will is the clearest example of this. Yet it remains a paradox, because the mystery of such divine creativity–the composition of a multifarious story or drama out of genuinely free created personal lives, themselves the source of derived creativity, is strictly impenetrable by human reason. We can experience it from within–we ourselves are part of that mystery–and we can come to realize that it is so. But we cannot "comprehend" it. We can only gesture at its nature through analogies like the author analogy or the composer analogy. As Farrer says, the modality of divine action remains hidden to us.

Reflection on Ward's misinterpretation of Farrer leads one to propose a theory of *triple* agency rather than *double* agency. For God does act creatively, holding the world and its powers in being while also acting by providence and grace in relation to his creatures' own agency. But it is the sense in which our free acts are at the same time God's free acts in us which leads Farrer to speak of double agency, not the more basic Creator/creature relation, which, as Ward says, is no paradox at all.

In his article "On the Divine Nature and the Nature of Divine Freedom,"[20] Thomas B. Talbott discusses many of the issues adumbrated here in a penetrating and illuminating way. In the interest of showing that God's freedom and the kind of human freedom required by the free will defense in theodicy are the same kind of freedom, he argues that we must, after all, ascribe to God the power to do evil even though we know that God's essential nature is such that he never will. On this assumption, freedom can be defined as the power to act or to refrain and is indeed common to both God and human beings.

Talbott's treatment of God's freedom is something of a tour de force. I suppose there is a somewhat abstract sense of God's power according to which God *could*, say, commit genocide. We become aware that the restrictions on divine omnipotence stemming from God's essential goodness are, logically speaking, different in kind from the restrictions stemming from logic itself. All the same, I think we can see that this brave attempt to hold divine and human freedom together in the sense of the autonomous power to act will not really work for purposes of theodicy. I too, following Farrer and von Balthasar, have tried to hold divine and human freedom together–but the real power to act or refrain is not a logical abstraction to be divorced from either divine or human nature. In God, the real power to act or refrain is seen in God's creativity, God's love, and God's grace. It is God's nature thus to act freely, both internally in the reciprocities and interpenetrations of the triune life of God, and externally, in creation and in relation to his creatures. Similarly, true human freedom is to be found in the real power to go out of ourselves in love of neighbor and of God, and in the countless infinite images of the divine creativity that make up human culture.

For theodicy, we need to be able to refer not to some *abstract* power to do good or evil common to both the human and the divine, but rather to a real liability in humans (but not in God) to go astray. I have suggested that the source of that liability lies in the conditions of human formation–the necessity of setting us at an "epistemic distance" (to quote John Hick)[21] from our Creator in an environment which, as well as forming us, inevitably tempts us away from our true and highest good.

Eventually, in the perfect consummation of heaven, that liability is finally to be overcome; and we hope to realize that likeness to the divine freedom which, whatever its abstract powers, has never had, and can never have, any such liability. Of course our liability to err in this formative stage of God's creative process presupposes the autonomy which does indeed mirror the divine autonomy. So autonomy plays a role in theodicy. But it is not autonomy as such that provides us with the free will defense. Rather, the chief explanatory force of the free will defense resides in the necessary conditions of the formation of finite autonomous persons. We do not need, therefore, to assimilate divine freedom to human freedom in respect of the power to do evil, as Talbott does.

The lesson of this essay is that finite freedom is to be assimilated to infinite freedom. Human beings, made in the image of God, reflect in their derived powers of self-determination something of the underived autonomy of their Maker. But God's infinite freedom is that of love given and received and expressed not only in mutual self-bestowal, but in the creation of innumerable finite centers of life and love. Finite freedom realizes the divine likeness, therefore, the more it participates in infinite freedom. As the conditions of their formation are transcended and finite persons are raised to the unambiguous state of the perfected, new creation, they will spontaneously and without further risk be drawn into the communion of saints. That final state of the blessed in heaven, which we can only gesture towards with the language of ecstasy, vision, mutuality, and love, must be deemed the more free and creative the more it both mirrors and participates in the freedom, creativity, and love of God.

Notes

1. See B. L. Hebblethwaite, "Freedom, Evil, and Farrer," *New Blackfriars* (April 1985).

2. Oxford: Clarendon Press, 1984.

3. A. M. Farrer, *The Freedom of the Will* (London: A. & C. Black, 1958).

4. San Francisco: Ignatius Press, 1990.

5. Farrer, *Freedom*, 111.

6. Boston: Little, Brown & Co., 1991.

7. Von Balthasar, *Theodramatik*, 215.

8. pp. 273f.

9. I. Kant, *Critique of Judgement*, Part II, trans. J.C. Meredith (Oxford: Clarendon Press, 1952), 62.

10. Von Balthasar, *Theodramatik* , 243, 314; A.M. Farrer, *Faith and*

Speculation (London: A. & C. Black, 1967), 118.

   11. See A.M. Farrer, *Finite and Infinite*, 2nd ed. (Westminster: Dacre Press, 1959), 294ff,

   12. Farrer, *Faith and Speculation*, 167.

   13. K. Ward, *Divine Action* (London: Collins, 1990), ch. 2.

   14. Von Balthasar, *Theodramatik*, 259.

   15. *loc.cit.*,

   16. A.M. Farrer, *A Science of God?* (London: Geoffrey Bles, 1966), 76. (In its American edition, this book was entitled *God is not Dead*.)

   17. Von Balthasar, *Theodramatik*, 269.

   18. Jer. 1:5.

   19. Ward, *Divine Action*, 51.

   20. *Faith and Philosophy* (January 1988).

   21. J.H. Hick, *God and the Universe of Faiths* (London: Collins, 1973), 54.

Chapter 6

The Supremely Free Agent

Edward Hugh Henderson

There is no recent philosophical theologian for whom the freedom of the will was more thematically important than Austin Farrer. His first book, *Finite and Infinite*,[1] built his defenses of metaphysics and traditional theology on the basis of an analysis of deliberate agency. His Gifford Lectures, *The Freedom of the Will*,[2] constitute another analysis of the will, updated to take into account developments in the philosophy of mind. His last books, *Faith and Speculation*[3] and *A Science of God?*[4], continue to make human free agency the starting point both for religious epistemology and for theistic metaphysics. The effect of Farrer's emphasis on the freedom of the will is a voluntaristic personalism in theology, whereby he affirms both a high view of divine transcendence and the reality of divine relativity to the world. This amounts to a dialectical incorporation of strands from both Thomistic and process theology.

Farrer wove these strands together to articulate and provide a philo-sophical background for the heart of traditional Christian theism. That heart I take to be a cluster of teachings that stress the responsiveness of God to the world: that there is one God; that the one God is a personal agent who has made himself known through particular actions in the world; that God's crowning revelation is in the action whereby he makes himself incarnate in the man, Jesus of Nazareth; and that the life, cruci-fixion, and resurrection of this Jesus are the principal things God has done to express divine love and effect divine redemption. Any philo-sophical theology that aims to support lived traditional faith, must render these beliefs intelligible. Farrer does it by means of a voluntaristic and personalistic idea of God as a supremely free and personal agent, Trinitarian in nature, transcendent, self-sufficient, creator of the world *ex nihilo*. For, he thought, a God who can be philosophically understood as the perfect, personal, and supremely free agent is a God who can be understood to wait upon and respond to creatures and who can be known by those responsive actions. My purpose here is to show how Farrer used this voluntaristic personalism so as to unite the high transcendence of traditional thought with the real relatedness of process thought.

Introduction

There are two main directions in the interpretation of Farrer's thought. One takes him as an English Neo-Thomist who translates the substance of Thomism into a twentieth century idiom so as to defend that substance against anti-metaphysical trends.[5] There are good reasons for this line of interpretation. When Farrer published his first book, *Finite and Infinite* (1943), he insisted that he was not out to say anything new about God, but to clarify and defend the traditional idea against difficulties thrown up by those twentieth century philosophical descendants of Hume and Kant, the logical positivists, who then reigned supreme at Oxford. Later he said in the "Revised Preface to the Second Edition" (1959), that when he wrote it he was "possessed by the Thomist vision and could not think it false." (p. ix)

Nearing the end of his philosophical career, Farrer was still arguing for traditional theism—and by this time doing it explicitly in opposition to the neo-classical theism recommended by Charles Hartshorne and other theological Whiteheadians. In fact, the question of process theology took a good bit of his attention in the last few years of his life. He concluded *Faith and Speculation*[6] by arguing against recent forms of world-soul theology, mentioning Hartshorne by name. He wrote in a letter just before *Faith and Speculation* came out, that he would "make no concession to those who wish to relativize God or to qualify his Prior Actuality."[7]

When he lectured at Perkins School of Theology where the process theologian, Schubert Ogden, was teaching, he presented the case of God's high transcendence to Ogden's students in order "to give them," he said, "something else to think about."[8] Spread between these extremes of his career are numerous sermons and several smaller works in practical theology in which Farrer clearly spoke for orthodoxy of belief and practice.[9] Surely all this adds up to reading Farrer as an apologist for traditional Christian theism.

In its most extreme form, this approach dismisses all process elements and plumps for a purely Thomistic reading. John Underwood Lewis has recently encouraged such a perspective in a review. Noting that some interpreters want to see him as a process thinker and recalling

Oxford tutorials on Aquinas, Lewis retorts that "Farrer is about as much a process theologian as was St. Athanasius."[10]

However, many readers have found that while Farrer's thought does defend traditional elements in the idea of God, it also resonates in partial harmony with process thought. This other direction in reading Farrer sees the earlier and more clearly Thomistic and Aristotelian shape of his thought as part of that "Aristotelian leaven" Farrer said he wanted to "purge" from his thought.[11] According to this reading, Farrer progressively thought his way out of the traditional understanding and more and more into an up-to-date theism. The task of the interpreter then becomes one of reading Farrer's earlier works through the filter of the anti-Aristotelian voluntarism of the later works, a reading that construes Farrer more and more as a friend of the process theology of Whitehead and Hartshorne.

Just as textual evidence can be given for reading Farrer as a Neo-Thomist simpliciter, so can it be also for reading him as a naturalistic process thinker. Even in the most Thomistic of his books, *Finite and Infinite*, he developed the theory that "to be is to operate" (*esse est operari*), a theory admittedly influenced by Henri Bergson and A.N. Whitehead.[12] In *Love Almighty and Ills Unlimited*,[13] he argued that in choosing to create a world of real finite creatures, God would have to take on certain limitations. Otherwise, God would be all, and creatures would be but contents of a divine dream. In *Faith and Speculation* he said that he was purging "the old Aristotelian leaven from the voluntarist metaphysics I sketched so many years ago in *Finite and Infinite*" (p. v), and he spoke of a "rethinking of scholastic positions" (p. vi). Chapter VII of the same book rejected the "formalist account" (p. 117) of the idea of God, the idea of "Being just being itself" (p. 116), and Chapter VIII criticized Aristotle's account of causation and the theology derived from it. There, in one of the rare instances in which he explicitly named a contemporary philosopher in print, Farrer discussed Hartshorne and acknowledged their agreement on the inadequacy of scholastic formalism in conceiving God.

In *A Science of God?*, Farrer described God's action in nature as a matter of "persuasion" rather than of "coercion,"[14] and went so far as to say that "God acts as the soul of the world."[15] Finally, in "The Prior Actuality of God," while arguing against process theology's dilution of God's prior actuality, he agreed to go *with* the retreat from absolutism.[16]

At its most extreme,[17] this second line of interpretation takes Farrer all the way into the camp of process naturalism. God becomes the soul or mind of the world, the world the *necessary* place and instrumentality of God's action. Inasmuch as "bodily extension and social coherence are fundamental in our sense of self-awareness,"[18] so, too, can God be conceived *only* in relation to the world as his body and to a society of other selves with whom he socially interacts. On this view, high-transcendence (including the existence of God above and before all worlds, the life of God-in-God understood by Christians as the life of the Blessed Trinity, and creation *ex nihilo*) is the residue of the Aristotelian leaven that Farrer sought to remove from his thought.

What are we to make of this conflict of interpretations? Most readers locate Farrer somewhere between these extremes, recognizing both traditional and process elements and resonances. Typical are John Glasse and Julian Hartt. Glasse speaks of "the process direction" of elements in Farrer's thought, noting that they remained in tension with the more traditional Thomist aspects.[19] Hartt says that though Farrer seemed "to share some of process's notions," he perplexed us by "dismissing it" and "non-dialectically reaffirming traditional or classical theism."[20]

I want to pitch my tent with those who avoid the two extreme interpretations of the upshot of Farrer's thought. But I disagree with Hartt's suggestion that Farrer's response to process theism was a "non-dialectical" reaffirmation of traditional theology. On the contrary, I think his response was dialectical. By that I mean that Farrer took into his philosophical theology certain ideas learned from Whitehead and Hartshorne as well as ideas learned from St. Thomas and the scholastic tradition. He did not *identify* St. Thomas's metaphysical theology with traditional Christian belief. He saw it, rather, as an effort to render philosophically intelligible the "faith of the fathers."

In one sense, Farrer regarded scholastic formalism as on a par with process thought. Both are abstract philosophical conceptions, a step removed from lived belief. The purpose of each should be to clarify, explain, and defend lived faith. The faith to be understood, therefore, is the faith people pray and live. Its heart is given in scripture, creed, and liturgy. And it is faith in a God who is the supremely free personal agent who reveals himself most clearly and completely in Jesus as the lover and redeemer of the world.

That being so, Farrer's point was not to defend Thomism as opposed to process thought, thereby "non-dialectically" affirming the one and rejecting the other. His point was to defend lived traditional faith. The way to do that, he saw, was to put the believer's idea of God as the supreme personal agent onto solid metaphysical ground. The scholastic Aristotelian metaphysics had not been able to do that. Neither, thought Farrer, had process panentheism. The former had conceived God's being apart from the world in such a way that God's loving responsiveness to the world could not be understood. The latter had conceived God's loving responsiveness in such a way that God could not be thought to enjoy a life apart from involvement in the world.

The point was to get an adequate understanding of divine transcendence together with an adequate understanding of divine relativity. Such a union would be a synthesis of Thomistic with process elements. I want to show that Farrer did in fact effect this synthesis by means of the idea of God as the supremely free agent. His position is closest to "open God" or "free will theism," although it is presented in Farrer's inimitable prose and uses the idea of double agency to understand God's action in the world, a view less friendly to the idea that God acts unilaterally and coercively to affect events in the world than "free will theism."[21]

That Farrer Affirmed Divine Relativity

Contrary to the straight Neo-Thomistic reading of Farrer, it is plain he thought process theism was right to stress that the God people worship must be a God who is affected by and in some ways dependent upon the world and creatures. In "The Prior Actuality of God," he addressed the question of divine relativity directly and clearly. He declares that he "retreats from the absolutist position," from that philosophical theology he calls, "scholastic formalism." He also asserts that he does not understand God as *ipsum esse* or *actus purus.*[22] Rejecting these formulations, Farrer can say–as, in fact, God's people at prayer, sacrament, and devoted service have always said -that God, in his very life and being as God, waits upon his creatures and is affected by them, that

> there is joy in the divine heart over a sinner's repentance; (that) God obtains his desire when he recreates a wayward creation to truth and happiness...; that a satisfaction forming part of that joy which is the life of God is relative to his creature's actions–for it is concerned with it; and dependent upon the creature's actions–for the creature might withhold it. ("PAG," 178)

Farrer generalizes the point to cover all of God's dealings with free persons.

> Not only God's acts of forgiveness, but his whole purpose for mankind is concerned with what man can be brought freely to do, and dependent upon such cooperation or consent as they are willing to offer. ("PAG," 178)

And then he goes still further, taking into his thought even more of the process theologian's insistence upon divine relativity as essential to God's being God to the world.

> If the march of God's purpose through history must wait for the footdragging and malingering of human multitudes, is it not equally evident that God's purpose in natural evolution is a slow persuasion of brute ele-

ments which waits for and works through their inborn capacities? If there is any divine purpose anywhere in the world, it is a purpose relative to the action of the world's constituents, and dependent upon the forthcomingness of that action. ("PAG," 178-179; emphasis added)

These words, written *after* both *Faith and Speculation* and *A Science of God?*, show quite clearly that Farrer accepts the position, fundamental to process theism, that a God worthy to be worshiped and called supremely perfect is a God who must act *in relation to* and *be affected by* and in certain respects *dependent upon* his creatures. Nor is Farrer's agreement with process thought limited to holding that God must be patient only to his *human* creatures; Farrer generalizes the idea to mean that God must be relative to and dependent upon *all* the world's constituents. For Farrer, too, relativity to the world is fundamentally characteristic of God's action in the world.

But how did Farrer incorporate this favorite theme of the process theologians? Not, as the extreme process interpretation would have it, in a way that makes God's whole existence and life dependent upon having some world he did not create, some world that would serve as the body and instrumentality of his agency; and not in a way that makes it impossible for God to enjoy life and fulfillment apart from his interactions with the world. Rather, in a way that also affirms God's high transcendence: God as the being who is the absolutely perfect personal agent, utterly transcending the world, condescending out of love to let it be *ex nihilo*, loving it and redeeming it but also enjoying in himself a full, perfect, and concretely fulfilled life, whose perfection is independent of this or any world.

However, it is not enough just to assert that one believes both divine relativity and high transcendence. A philosophical way of thinking their union is required. We must look to the late works to see how Farrer accomplishes the synthesis.

That Farrer Affirmed High Transcendence

In *A Science of God?*, where Farrer says that "God's mind lives in all the world as my feeling 'soul' lives in my whole body," he notes emphatically that "It is better...to say "*acts as* the Soul of the World than to say *is* the Soul of the World." (ASG?, 85, emphasis added) Why is it better to say "acts as" rather than "is"? Because, Farrer immediately says, we must be careful *not* to say or imply that God is *essentially* related to the world, that God's being or consciousness is dependent upon there being a world already there, or that God's action is confined to the world. "To suggest that (God) is tied to the world system in any such fashion," Farrer claims, "is to make nonsense of our whole discovery of the divine." (ASG?, 85-86) I will spell out the implications.

A. God is not Essentially Embodied

It makes nonsense of our whole discovery of the divine to say that God is *essentially* the soul of a body, the world. But if not *essentially* the soul of the world, then it is not necessary to God's being God that God be in relation to a world. And, because for God to be is to act, if it is not necessary to God's being, then it is not necessary to God's acting that there be a world to serve as the instrument of God's action.

It is true that in *The Freedom of the Will* Farrer defends a view of human agency according to which we must take ourselves not as mental reality plus material reality, but as psychophysical unities. The idea was not new. He had defended it also in *Finite and Infinite*. He was never a Cartesian metaphysical dualist. For Farrer, *esse est operari*. That means that what we classify as material is also to be understood as operation on the model of our experience of human agency. This makes it possible for us to conceive of divine agency apart from bodily instrumentality, though we cannot think that way about ourselves. Farrer makes it very plain in *Faith and Speculation*.

> To say that, *with us*, mind is embodied, is to say that our personal action is geared to the working of many minute actions themselves organizing actions yet more minute. And naturally, for *our* personal action is one arising out of the world; it is not, *like God's*, that out of which the world arises. His action, being prior and creative is free and simple. Surely to believe in God is to believe exactly this. (FS, 166-167; emphasis added)

B. God is Fully Apart from the World

If God's being or action is not dependent on a world and is not to be confined to the world, then surely methodological agnosticism does not hold us back from saying that God is essentially and fully God apart from being in relation with a world. We must be agnostic about the concrete shape and content of God's life in God. We cannot describe it or specify it except insofar as it may in part and through the limits of our existence be expressed in God's actions in the world. But we cannot deny *that* there is God-in-God.

C. God Creates the World Ex Nihilo

The extreme process reading denies that Farrer affirms creation *ex nihilo*, but Farrer's words show that that reading is wrong. In *A Science of God?*, Farrer speaks of God as "creator and cause of whatever system there is in the world." (ASG?, 86) Process theism also says that God is the creator and cause of all *system* in the world, but it limits God's causal creative action to the system or order of things. It denies that God is also the cause of there being any world at all, that God is the cause of whatever there is to be ordered. Farrer, on the other hand, argues that in order for God to be the creator and cause of order in the world, God must transcend and be prior to the being of the world: "To be this (creator and cause of system in the world) he must stand above it, *and come before it*. If *God's thought thinks the world into being*, his mind cannot essentially *be* the soul of the world." (ASG?, 86; emphasis added)

Creation *ex nihilo* is so surely intended here that the Latin tag need not be tied on to mark it. God does not shape the world from preexistent materials; he comes before it. Of course that does not have to mean coming temporally before it; it is logical and, especially, ontological priority that matter. God is responsible for the being, the existence, of the world; but God's being, on the other hand, is not dependent on that of the world. And if these words do not secure the interpretation, there are others. Farrer notes earlier in the book that Jewish and Christian Bible readers, in thinking of God's creative action in shaping the world, "were brought face to face with a creative power so absolute that nothing could be left outside its scope; not even the first matter and primary stuff of the world." (ASG?, 40) And again, "God is the cause of the world's *existence*, and...he has woven nature from the bottom up." (ASG?, 73; emphasis added)

That means from the very bottom, the absolute bottom. Nothing is there as constituents from which other things are formed that does not depend already upon God for its existence. Farrer does hold that we cannot get back to the absolute beginning of creation to know that at some time something suddenly appeared and was where previously there was only God. Nor can we separate God's action in causing existence from God's action in shaping and forming what exists. But that does not mean that we cannot affirm creation *ex nihilo*. The evidence of creation is near at hand. Wherever we look we find going operations that are other than God, operating as themselves. But if we have eyes to see we also see God's action in their action, making them at once both to be and to be what they are. Creation *ex nihilo* means not that we can locate a time before which there was nothing but God. It means that the world depends upon God's action for its existence, while God does not depend upon the world for his.

Farrer could be agnostic about creation *ex nihilo* only if he held that it is possible for something to exist in utter and complete independence of God's creative action. Process theologians say not only that that is a possibility; they say it is the truth. Farrer, on the other hand, says that there cannot possibly be anything that does not depend upon God for its existence. That is an affirmation of creation *ex nihilo*.

D. The Playwright Analogy

If more evidence of Farrer's affirmation of high transcendence is needed, we can find it in the Perkins/LSU lecture, the very lecture in which the retreat from absolutism was announced. There Farrer distinguishes his own from the standard process position by means of minimizing and maximizing versions of an allegory. The process position is represented by the minimizing story, Farrer's own position by the maximizing one. On the minimizing version, a playwright-producer is prevented by a witch's curse from having any life apart from a play which he or she gets out of the players by leading them along and letting them be themselves. The playwright's prior actuality consists in having his or her own ideas, initiative, and goals, and acting to persuade, lead, and encourage the players to get a play out of becoming themselves. This allegorically expresses the notion of double agency: God acting in the actions of creatures in a way that gets a world out of them without coercing them against the grain of nature.

The maximizing story, Farrer says, "is not to be so maximal as to constitute a return to the scholastic absolutism; we have agreed to go with the trend in discarding that." ("PAG," 179-180) Farrer is saying that he will not make the playwright a coercive determiner such that the players have no independence from the playwright. Nor will the playwright be so removed from the actors that he or she is unable to get a play out of them by responding to and working with them in their freedom. To get the maximizing story, which would allegorically express the God with the greatest prior actuality, Farrer removes the witch's curse that binds the playwright in the minimizing story. In the maximizing story

> The playwright is not condemned to confine his active existence within the production of plays. *Quite apart from* and *prior to*, his activity as producer-playwright, he has a personal life of his own. Indeed, if the playwright had not lived outside his plays, he would have nothing to put into them. It is the content of the life he has lived offstage that moves him to make the dramatic representation. There is no need for him to make it, *he could live his life and be himself without making it.* In fact he *chooses* to make it, and it is very intelligible that he should so choose. In so far as he puts himself into the play-business, he relativizes his actions to the being and the performance of his actors, just as in the other story, no more and no less. But his *prior actuality* in respect of the play is not simply his *initiative* in creating it but *his life exterior to it; a life out of which flows his creation of it.* ("PAG," 180; emphasis added)

That allegory, Farrer says, shows that the substance of traditional theology is not dependent upon the scholastic formalism of St. Thomas and his successors. Clearly the intention is to preserve a high doctrine of transcendence. It is also to show that the high doctrine is not inconsistent with God's relativizing himself to his creatures. It is problematical to assert both *actus purus* and divine responsiveness, but that is not the same thing as asserting both the life of God exterior to creation and a life of divine responsiveness. Why? Because God is understood not as *actus purus* or *ipsum esse*, but as the supremely free and perfect personal agent.

We can further clarify how Farrer effected the synthesis by looking at some ways Farrer's theology, while rejecting *actus purus*, nevertheless retained other elements characteristic of Thomistic thought.

Thomistic Strands in the Late Farrer

A. *Doing Theology from the Bottom Up*

Farrer is faithful to St. Thomas's cosmological or empirical approach to philosophy. Knowledge of God begins from our experience of things, events, persons, and our living with them in the world. Their and our operation is such that we may come to see them or certain features of them as effects of God's action and thereby as signs of his reality. This is doing theology from the bottom up, not from the top down; *a posteriori*, not *a priori*.

There is a difference between the empirical approaches of St. Thomas and Farrer, however. Farrer describes the difference in *Faith and Speculation*. It is the difference between the "formalist" and the "voluntarist" approaches (FS, 116-117). In choosing the voluntarist, Farrer takes the *more* empirical of the two ways. Each approach finds finite things in need of explanation. Why are they at all and why are they as they are? Each thinks that no answer is satisfactory until we arrive at God as one who needs no explanation. But St. Thomas does it through the distinction between *esse et essentia*, which gives us God as "the Supreme Existence in himself, outside and above the series of finites rising toward him." (FS, 116) Farrer, on the other hand, does it through the idea that *esse est operari* and that the clearest kind of *operari* we can know is that of ourselves acting freely. Taken as the path from the bottom of the world to God, it gives us God as an agent, as one who acts, not God as being just being itself.

Despite the difference, note that the same form of thought is involved. In each case the resolution of a question about finite things is seen to depend on the reality of something utterly different from them, something that is not *aliquid mundi*.

In doing their theology from the bottom up, both St. Thomas and

Farrer make implicit use of St. Anselm's formula, "God is the being than which no greater can be thought." Not that they think the existence of God can be proved from the formula or that the formula implicitly contains the whole divine nature, but that it is a regulative principle or, to use more contemporary terms, part of the grammar of thought about God. We can ultimately explain the modalities of finite being only if we do it in terms of a being that cannot itself need explanation. That can only be a being than which no greater can be thought. The rule tells us not to attribute to God characteristics that would make God need explanation by a yet greater being. St. Thomas follows the rule when he says that God must be pure being. Farrer follows it when he uses, from his first book to his last, human free agency as the only analogy for thinking the nature of God. We know our own being best and most fundamentally in knowing it as operation that rises to clarity and explicitness in our conscious and deliberate choices and voluntary actions. The being of God, therefore, also can be most reasonably understood as voluntary agency. God's agency, on the other hand, must be different from ours, not merely in the degree of knowledge on which it is based, of love out of which it arises, or of freedom in which it is enacted. God is the perfect or unconditioned will, the supremely free agent:

> God must be such that he can will for every sort of creature once it is created, and also will what created forms there shall be. Such a will can only be defined by its unrestricted freedom. *It is not the will of a determinate being, operating within a certain charter of function or scope of effect. It is all that it does, and it chooses to be all that it is.* (FS 111; emphasis added)

How close Farrer is to St. Thomas here! For St. Thomas, we must not attribute to God a determinate essence that would in any way restrict God's *esse*. For Farrer, we must not attribute to God any determination that would restrict God's will. We shall see that the slight difference makes "all the difference." Yet it seems right to say that Farrer still follows very much the spirit of St. Thomas.

B. God is not in a Genus

Farrer's theological thought is fundamentally shaped by St. Thomas's position that God is not a kind—or a member of a class of which there could possibly be other members. God is unique, *sui generis*. Explicitly stressed in *Finite and Infinite*, the terms appear less in the later works. Nevertheless, the principle pervades Farrer's thought. Perhaps we should see it as another expression of the rule we were just discussing, that in thinking up to God we must not say of him anything that would make him less than the supremely perfect being. When Thomas says of God that his existence must be the same as his essence, he is ruling out the possibility that God could be a member of a larger class. And when Farrer says that God must be Undetermined Will, he is doing likewise.

That Farrer continues in his late works to assume God's uniqueness is especially clear in discussions of "double agency." The idea that God acts in the actions of his creatures without coercing them or destroying their reality as things that are other than God is *not* a theory or an explanation of *how* God's action works and takes effect. Nor is the idea an assertion of absurdity, of a contradiction: two agents in one action. It is neither explanation nor contradiction because the relation of God to creatures is itself understood to be a unique relation. It is not an instance of any relations that hold among finite things. Among *finite* things there are no pure cases of double agency, though relations involving personal communications like those of teacher and student, are able to suggest it and serve as images for it. Thus, the uniqueness of God and of God's relations with creatures, which Farrer set forth in *Finite and Infinite* as the uniqueness of "the cosmological relation," remains in his later thought.

C. The Analogy of Being

The analogy of being puts St. Thomas's metaphysics of *esse et essentia* into a cautious empirical theology. We cannot know God as God is in himself; we can know him in terms of finite things, but only also as utterly other than they. The analogy of being preserves that otherness. According to it we can say, for example: God's goodness is to God's being as human goodness is to human being. Farrer defended the doctrine in *Finite and Infinite*, but because in *Faith and Speculation* he no longer thought in terms of *esse et essentia*, we cannot suppose that he continued to hold the doctrine in that same form. Charles Conti, who presses the extreme process reading, thinks that Farrer either dropped the appeal to analogy altogether or at least minimized its role. I think, however, that this element of his earlier Thomism was still very much alive and very important. It is dialectically subsumed within Farrer's metaphysic of will. In the very portion of in which Farrer was focussed on purging the Aristotelianism from his theology, he declared that

> ...there is no question of our bypassing analogy; for to think about God is to think of living act, to which our own action is the only possible clue. (FS, 129)

Therefore, rather than the analogy of being, Farrer gives us the analogy of will or agency. As our characteristics are to our operating, so, too, for God. God is the Perfect Personal Agent. Yet, thinking about God as analogous to human agents does not in itself give us the knowledge of God's individual personhood or of his particular acts. It lets us say things such as that God is "the undetermined Determinator, the Sovereign Will and ultimate Power" (FS, 129) or "the God who is all he wills to be, and wills to be all he is." (FS, 118) These are abstract formulae, ways of representing God in terms of what we know best and as qualified by the principle that God is not a kind but is greater and better than anything that could conceivably share properties with other things.

Nevertheless, Farrer argues that making will or operation our fundamental metaphysical principle and the basis of our analogical thought about God is a gain over the more abstract analogy of being. For where God is known through the personal analogy, the analogy is not only a form of speculation, it is given substance by being the form of faithful life. God as the supremely free and perfect agent

> is a reality not to be objectively observed (how could it be?) but performed or lived; and so the believer escapes from dependence on mere analogical inference in the same way as the believer in other personal existence escapes from it; for he lives the belief, a belief which, admittedly, has an analogical shape. (FS, 129-130)

So it is that Farrer's appeal to the analogy of personal agency gives us a God about whom we have something to do.

Divine Relativity

I have argued so far that despite an acknowledged retreat from absolutism, Farrer continued to maintain that God is the being who is full and perfect in himself, creating the world *ex nihilo* as an action of supremely free and creative will; and I have argued that Farrer remained quite under the tutelage of St. Thomas, doing theology empirically, affirming God's uniqueness, and claiming knowledge by analogy. The other side of the argument is that his theology also took into itself a point basic to process theology, namely, that an understanding of God worthily suited to theistic religion must express God's loving and responsive relation with his creatures.

Farrer's original achievement is that he found a clear way to include God's loving relativity without seeming to make God's transcendence impossible and that he found at the same time a way to include God's transcendence without seeming to make nonsense of his relativity. He did this through a philosophical theology that bases its metaphysic directly on the conviction and analysis of human free will and person-hood. Free intelligent agency enacted in a society of free intelligent agents is allowed to do direct metaphysical duty.

The Farrer of *Finite and Infinite* thought it was necessary to interpret the lived experience of agency in terms of St. Thomas's metaphysic of substance, *ens, essentia,* and *esse* before it could be made to yield theo-logical fruit. But after *The Freedom of the Will* he thought that interpre-tation unnecessary, even counterproductive. We can put the knowledge we have of persons as free agents immediately to work. In general meta-physics it yields the understanding that *esse est operari* and in theology the understanding that God is the Supreme and Perfect Personal Agent, the Undetermined Will, the one who is all he sees it best to be.

What "Personal Agency" gives us, however, is an analogy or an image, not a description or explanation that either excludes other images or reduces all things to membership in a single class. Nevertheless, it is a master image; and it claims a privileged place. Its privilege is due to its being the experience-based image with an attend-ing grammar through which we inescapably live and are. Part of the ten-sion between Farrer and process theology is that Farrer refuses to define the essential form of operation and then to say that all entities must sim-ply and ultimately be isomorphic with each other as possessing that one basic form, whereas process thinkers usually do hold to such an iso-morphism. Consequently, for process thought *all* things, from the most minute of physical entities and energies to God, are held to be occasions of experience or societies of occasions of experience. All are species of the same class, sharing the same universal essential form. The result is both pansychism and naturalism: pansychism because it takes all things as feeling and experiencing things, and naturalism because it takes God as a member of an all-inclusive natural kind. Farrer intentionally and advisedly avoids both pansychism and naturalistic reductionism. And he does it by taking human personal agency as the privileged image for understanding that which alone can be the reason why things are and have the modalities they have.

The personal agent who can be that reason can only be one that nei-ther needs nor admits explanation for itself other than its own agency. It will be the Unconditioned Will or the Agent who is all it wills to be and wills to be all it is. We ought not to think that these expressions of God are descriptions of God's own life as it is in itself. They are abstract philosophical applications of the personal image. God remains an abyss of mystery, but the personal image is the best philosophy can do. We can be confident that God is *at least* Supremely Personal and Free.

Now it is just this understanding of God that allows Farrer to include that basic process point that a God worthy of worship must be a God who lets its creatures be free and responds to them with loving care. For if God is the Perfect Personal Agent, he is a God who can freely relativize himself to creatures, first by choosing to let them be, and then by waiting upon them, letting them be themselves and responding to what they are and do. This is a God who can enjoy a life in God, independent of engagement with a world, yet who can also be the creator of all else that is and live a life of loving relation to it.

This is exactly the point made by the playwright allegory. The playwright-producer gets the players on the stage, Farrer says, and leads them by "hints and suggestions" to become their characters and thereby to make the play. The playwright does not coerce the characters or force them against their natures, but rather makes use of what they are. He or she is dependent upon their free responses and must wait upon them for the fulfillment of his or her design and intention. Yet the playwright-producer is so close to the players as to be *in* them and in their acting and thereby to act as the "soul" of the play.

There, as I read Farrer, is his proposal about God's transcendence and relativity. They are brought together dialectically through the image of God as the Perfect Personal Agent.

This same personalism has further consequences for standing themes in Christian faith and philosophy. Two of these have special importance in understanding Farrer's view of God's transcendence and perfection as against the Neo-Thomistic and the process interpretations. One consequence is that personalistic theism places knowledge by reason and knowledge by revelation on a continuum. The other is that the doctrine of the Trinity gives content to the general claim of God's perfection apart from creation–and does so in a way that is consistent with Farrer's empirical and practical emphasis. I will take them in order.

The God of Revelation is the God of Reason

One of the clear advantages of philosophical personalism in theology is that it bridges the gap between the God of the philosophers and the God of Abraham, Isaac, and Jacob.[23] It establishes a foundation for and logical orientation toward traditional doctrines of lived faith. It makes the appeal to revelation intelligible. As philosophers we may know God in general terms as the "Supremely Perfect Agent who is all that he wills to be and wills to be all that he is." But if that general characterization is true, we can hope to know God more richly and concretely by knowing who God has willed to be in relation to the world. For agents are known by their actions, by what they do and by how and to what end they do it. This, of course, is exactly what believers in the God of Abraham, Isaac, and Jacob have claimed for generations–that God is encountered in the world, acting to make himself known, commanding, loving, redeeming, and sanctifying. While it may be difficult to explain how a God conceived as Pure Actuality can be so engaged in the world, it is exactly what one *must* say of a God conceived as the Perfect Agent. If God is an agent, we must know him by what he does.

One might think that this very feature of God's existence as a personal agent imposes so severe a limit on our ability to know God apart from his actions that we cannot speak of a life of God apart from God's actions in the world. That is exactly what Conti, in the extreme process reading of Farrer's personalism, thinks. Such a reading blocks the claim that this personalistic theism well incorporates the traditional belief in God's high transcendence. While I agree that we must always maintain a healthy agnosticism about God-in-God apart from this and all worlds, I believe also that on Farrer's approach we may claim that God does enjoy such a life and that we can make some meaningful claims about it.

The idea of God above and before all worlds is not simply the consequence of a speculative philosophy that was ill-suited to express the truths of Christianity; it is an idea that is very much called for by the God who is known by what he does. The high view of divine transcendence is the rightful outworking of the idea of the God of Abraham, Isaac, and Jacob.

From the personalist standpoint we can say that rational and revealed theology are opposite ends on a continuous spectrum. We know human agents by what they do, and this in two ways. One: because we experience the effects of their actions, we know that they exist, that they are real. Two: because the things human agents do are particular, we know from them the particular characters of the persons who do them. The same is true of God. Because of God's actions we know that God exists; and because the things God does are particular, we know from them the particular character of God. Philosophy or natural theology, pursuing the knowledge of God "from the bottom up," is concerned with those general characteristics of the world that are available to all whose experience is open to recognizing them. Arguments from the contingency of the world and its features and modalities, such as design and moral meaning, are, in fact, arguments from certain general or pervasive effects of God's actions. To recognize the existential insufficiency of things in the world is to experience them as effects of God. To recognize the contingency of the natural order discovered by the sciences or the moral nature of human social life is to experience them as effects of God. Because these effects are general features of things or of large classes of things, they can be known to observant and curious inquirers. What is known of God through such general features is known of God by philosophy or reason. And God's character as known through them is articulated in such terms as "God is creator," "God is designer," "God is the source and foundation of morality," and so on. In a meaningful sense, these characteristics of God are *revealed*, for anything that is the effect of action can be said to re-veal or dis-close the will and character of the agent. But they are revealed to minds attending to general features of things.

God's action is not limited, however, to what God does to establish and sustain the general order of things. It extends also to such particular actions as the calling of Abraham, the appearance to Moses, the various events of the Exodus, the establishment of covenants, the inspiration of the prophets, and, of special importance for Christians, the life, ministry, crucifixion, and resurrection of Jesus. These all reflect events and human actions that allow of interpretation as effects of God's action. Such particular events are limited to particular times and places and can be experienced only by those who are, so to speak, in the right place at the right time, though they can be recognized, reported, and interpreted by others.

Some such events even come to be ritualized so that others can become participants in them. The effectiveness of God's action is thereby extended. God is revealed in such cases in more particular and concrete ways than in the general features of the world, yet the particular action of God becomes generally available to humankind through them. In such sacramental cooperations with the grace of God's action, we gain a richer and more intimate knowledge of the person who is God than is possible from the discovery of the general effects that reveal God to reason.

Yet in both kinds of experience, God's person and character are revealed to us through what God does. So we come to know not only that God is creator and orderer of the world, but that God is one who desires communion with us, who has expectations of us, who commands us, who loves, redeems, and sanctifies us. Such discoveries about who God is and what he is doing are formalized as doctrines in creeds, canons, and confessions. We come thereby to know God as the Father Almighty, Creator of heaven and earth; as the eternally begotten Son who was made incarnate in Jesus of Nazareth; and as the Holy Spirit who enlivens us with the life of God; and so on. Nor is this knowledge of God merely or mainly a sheerly intellectual matter. It is urgently and helpfully practical. It gives us a God who is the Supremely Perfect Person into relation with whom we are called to enter actively and intentionally. For

> his life is personal to him, it is not ours;...he has a will after which we enquire, a judgment to which we submit, a forgiveness we implore, a succor we seek;...(and) the personal character of our relation with him is the

very form of it, not a metaphorical trapping which can be thought away while any substance remains. (FS, p. 47)

The Perfect Personal Agent revealed to us through reason is thus further revealed in particular actions as we relate ourselves to him. The gap between reason and revelation is closed.

The Trinity

In affirming the general (or philosophical) revelation of a life of God-in-God, independent of this and all created worlds, Farrer argued also that one of the particular revelations of God enables Christians to attribute intelligible content to that high transcendent life of God. I refer to the revelation of God, through the life of Christ and in the experience of the Church, as Trinity. If God is Trinity of Persons, then the life of God-in-God is not that of a being just being itself, closed in on itself with no life to live. It is a life of perfect love: perfectly given, perfectly received, perfectly returned, perfectly fulfilled.

Conti, in developing his process-oriented interpretation, has rightly argued that Farrer came to reject the idea that there could be a personal subject without other personal subjects. And this conclusion at first seems to count against the belief in God's self-sufficiency and independence. Being a person is an essentially social matter. We are what we are only through being in relation with others. This would seem to mean, if we conceive God as a personal agent, that the idea of God existing in himself, enjoying life in himself and having no relation to anything outside himself, is vacuous. Conti has argued, therefore, that the idea of a life of God-in-God and apart from the world is the same as the idea that God is being just being itself in plenitude, pure actuality.

Farrer did not think so. Had he thought the idea of the life of God-in-God a corollary of the Aristotelian-Plotinian theology as adapted into Christianity, he might have rejected the idea as empty and unintelligible. But he did not. He saw it as intelligible for Christian understanding because of the doctrine of the Trinity. For the doctrine of the Trinity is the recognition that the God who is the creator, redeemer, sanctifier is a God who includes within the divine nature a fulfillment of personal being *as* social. If God is revealed to us as a Personal Agent, and if the very grammar by which we distinguish God from finite agents in the world justifies us in saying that God is the Perfect Personal Agent, then we must not deny of God the perfection of characteristics essential to the human agency we know. But human agents are essentially social. Hence, we cannot deny the sociality of God. We must instead think of God as perfecting within himself the social nature of agency. The social being of human persons is perfectly fulfilled in God.

Farrer is quite explicit about this, both in the Perkins/LSU lecture
and in *Faith and Speculation*. In the former he notes that the maximizing version of the playwright analogy shows that the traditional idea of
God's transcendence of all worlds is independent of "the special forms
of scholastic Aristotelianism." ("PAG," 180) It is not only that we can
tell allegories that do not depend on scholastic Aristotelianism. It is that
Christians in the doctrine of the Trinity have a way of thinking God's
high transcendence–and a way that does not require us to deny the
social nature of persons:

> The doctrine of a life of God in God, above and before all worlds, *can* be
> thought, and by Christians commonly *is* thought, in purely personal
> terms; it is the fellowship of Blessed Trinity. The Trinity is the substance
> of personal being and the pattern of personal relation; and it is this sub-
> stance, this pattern, which God is pleased to reproduce, to represent, and
> to extend in his creation. ("PAG," 180)

Farrer makes the same point in *Faith and Speculation*. There he
acknowledges that we cannot intelligibly conceive of "action *in vacuo*,
that is, action without interplay." (FS, 167) It is a concession to process
thought and to twentieth century philosophy of mind. But he does *not*
say that therefore we cannot intelligibly conceive of God as having a
life above and beyond his life in relation to this and all worlds. He does
the very opposite. He argues that Christians, because of the particular
actions of God they have interpreted as revealing the Trinity, are able to
affirm the life of God-in-God without asserting action *in vacuo*:

> ...to Christians at least it has not appeared that the Godhead self-disclosed
> to them exhibits so desolating and inconceivable a solitude. They believe
> Trinity of Persons in Unity of Substance. (FS, 167)

We may ask, however, whether that claim is permissable to Farrer in
view of the epistemology of interaction. How can we claim to know that
God exists above and before all worlds if all our knowledge is through
what God does in this world? Farrer sees no problem with this, nor do
I. It is intelligible in terms of Farrer's personalism to say that one knows
through a person's actions in relation to oneself what that person's character is apart from the relation.

The maximizing allegory makes that very point. The players in that
story will directly know the playwright-producer only as he works with
them, but they are not precluded from thinking that he could have a life
outside the play-producing business or even from thinking that the character he displays in producing the play tells something of what his life

apart from the play would be like. Their knowledge of his independent life would be schematic, of course! But it makes sense to think they could know from their experience that he is not limited to the play and that his life apart must exhibit the character they experience in him in the play.

Similarly, the knowledge of the world's ontological insufficiency justifies us in thinking it the effect of creation *ex nihilo* by a supremely free Personal Agent. And, if creation is the free choice of God, God must have being as God apart from the activity of creating. The knowledge is minimal, schematic in the extreme. But if our experience of what God does extends to incarnation, and to the ministry, crucifixion, and resurrection of Jesus for the redemption and sanctification of the world, then we can intelligibly say that this God must enjoy, all apart from the world, the fulfillment and perfection of personal life, including its social nature. Saying that God enjoys, independently of God's relations with the world, the fellowship of Blessed Trinity preserves the necessary agnosticism that humility requires. For we are not claiming to be able to describe the life of God-in-God *as it is for God*. We can only speak of God's being and life *apart* from the world on the basis of what we know from the revelations this God makes of himself *in* the world.

But the knowledge of God as Trinity above and before all worlds meets Farrer's practical empirical criterion for meaningful talk. It gives us a God in relation to whom we can act, and who gives us directions, so to speak, about what to do. It is an often voiced idea in Farrer's works, and it finds eloquent expression in "The Prior Actuality of God." Referring to the life of God apart from the world as the life of the Trinity, he says

> Ask the orthodox Christian why he supposes these things to be so, and
> he will tell you they are to him the immediate objects of his faith and the
> direct form of his salvation. If he can be said to know anything *qua*
> Christian it is his adoption into divine sonship...The Son-by-Nature
> makes us sons-by-adoption through taking our condition and associating
> us with himself. So he lifts us into fellowship with God, shares with us
> the Society which is the divine beatitude, and causes us to hang on the
> skirts of the divine eternity, to drink immortal joy forever. ("PAG," 180)

I have tried to show, using ample passages from Farrer's later works, that Farrer dialectically subsumed elements of traditional Thomistic natural theology and elements of process theology to construct an original philosophical theory from the standpoint of which reason and revelation are placed on a continuum and the heart of traditional belief made defensible. I hope the discussion has shown that the idea of God as the Supremely Free Agent is worthy of further attention, particularly as providing a philosophical understanding both consistent with and supportive of lived traditional faith.

Notes

1. Austin M. Farrer, *Finite and Infinite, A Philosophical Essay* (Westminster: Dacre Press, 1943). Hereafter referred to as FI. Published in a second edition with a "Revised Preface" by the same publisher in 1959, by Macmillan and Humanities presses in 1966, and by Seabury Press in 1979.

2. Austin M. Farrer, *The Freedom of the Will*, Gifford Lectures Delivered in the University of Edinburgh, 1957 (London: Adam and Charles Black, 1958).

3. Austin M. Farrer, *Faith and Speculation, an Essay in Philosophical Theology,* containing the Deems Lectures for 1964 (London and New York: Adam and Charles Black and New York University Press, 1967). Hereafter referred to as FS.

4. Austin M. Farrer, *A Science of God?* (London: Bles, 1966). Published in the United States as *God is Not Dead* (Morehouse-Barlow; 1966). Hereafter referred to as ASG?

5. See, for example, E. L. Mascall, *Existence and Analogy* (London: Dartman, Longman and Todd, 1949). Mascall discusses the responses of early reviewers of Farrer's *Finite and Infinite*, noting that they are divided on the extent to which the book is Thomist.

6. See Chapters X and XI of FS.

7. Letter to the author, 24 March, 1966.

8. Letter to the author, 4 February, 1967.

9. Farrer's sermons can be found in five volumes, four published after his death:

> *Said or Sung* (London: Faith Press, 1960), published in the U.S. as *A Faith of Our Own*, with Preface by C.S. Lewis (World Publishing Co., 1960).
> *A Celebration of Faith*, ed. Leslie Houlden (London: Hodder and Stoughton, 1972).
> *The Brink of Mystery*, ed. Charles Conti (London: SPCK, 1976).
> *The End of Man*, ed. Charles Conti (London: SPCK, 1976).
> *Austin Farrer: The Essential Sermons*, ed. Leslie Houlden (London: SPCK, 1991).

The short works in apologetic and practical theology which make clear Farrer's allegiance to orthodox faith and practice are:

> *The Crown of the Year: Weekly Paragraphs for the Holy Sacrament*

(Westminster: Dacre Press, 1952).
Lord I Believe: Suggestions for Turning the Creed into Prayer
(London: Faith Press, 1958). Published in an enlarged edition by
SPCK, 1962, and reprinted for publication in the U.S. by Cowley
Publications, 1989.
Saving Belief (London: Hodder and Stoughton, 1964).

10. John Underwood Lewis, review of *Divine Action: Studies
Inspired by the Philosophical Theology of Austin Farrer*, edited and
with introduction by Brian Hebblethwaite and Edward Henderson
(Edinburgh: T & T Clark Ltd, 1990) in *Theology Today*, 48, no. 3
(October 1991): 348-352.
11. FS, p. v.
12. Letter to the author, 24 March, 1966.
13. Austin M. Farrer, *Love Almighty and Ills Unlimited*, containing
the Nathaniel Taylor Lectures for 1961 (London: Collins, 1962).
Published by Fontana Books in 1966.
14. ASG?, 88.
15. ASG?, 85.
16. Austin M. Farrer, "The Prior Actuality of God," a lecture given
in the Perkins School of Theology of Southern Methodist University
and in The Louisiana State University; October 1966. Published in
Reflective Faith, ed. Charles Conti (London: SPCK, 1972), 178-192.
The lecture is hereafter referred to as the Perkins/LSU lecture and as
"PAG." Page numbers refer to *Reflective Faith*. This lecture is most
important to the assessment of Farrer's position in relation to process
theology. It was delivered after both *Faith and Speculation* and *A
Science of God?* had been written, though the former was not in print
until 1967.
17. The most extreme process interpretation of Farrer is given by
Charles Conti in *Metaphysical Personalism: An Analysis of Austin
Farrer's Theistic Metaphysics* (Oxford: The Clarendon Press, 1995)
and in several unpublished papers. A more moderate discussion, which
nevertheless takes the process strand in Farrer's thought seriously, is
Robert King's *The Meaning of God* (London: SCM Press, 1974).
Russell Aldwinckle explored the process direction in a paper, "Process
Thinking and the Prior Actuality of God," given at the Keble College
conference on Farrer's thought, March 1983.
18. Conti, "God as the 'Perfection' of Agency."
19. John Glasse, "Doing Theology Metaphysically: Austin Farrer"
in *Harvard Theological Review* 59, no. 4 (October 1966): 319-350.
20. Julian Hartt, "Austin Farrer as Philosophical Theologian: A
Retrospective and Appreciation" in *For God and Clarity: New Essays*

in Honor of Austin Farrer, edited by Jeffrey C. Eaton and Ann Loades (Allison Park, PA: Pickwick Publications, 1983), 1-22. This and other essays in the book were first presented to the Second International Conference on the Thought of Austin Farrer, held in Princeton Theological Seminary, January, 1981.

21. See William Hasker, *God, Time and Knowledge* (Ithaca, N.Y.: Cornell University Press, 1989) and Keith Ward, *Holding Fast to God: A Reply to Don Cupitt* (London: SPCK, 1982), chap.3. And for a systematic treatment from the perspectives of different theologically oriented disciplines, see Clark Pinnock, Richard Rice, John Sanders, William Hasker, and David Basinger, *The Openness of God: A Biblical Challenge to the Traditional Understanding of God* (Downers Grove, IL: InterVarsity Press and Carlisle, UK: The Paternoster Press, 1994.

22. In addition to "PAG," his words in his letter to the author, March 24, 1966 are helpful:

> I no longer wish to define God as *Actus Purus* (though I wouldn't want to say he was *Actus Impurus*!). I would define him rather as the Being who wills to be all that he is, and is all that he wills to be; which comes nearer to *Causa Sui* than to *Actus Purus.*–I make no concessions to those who wish to relatavize God or to qualify his Prior Actuality.

23. It was an extended discussion, printed and oral, with Charles Conti that finally brought this part of Farrer's thought into focus for me. It is an idea for which I am most indebted to him.

Chapter 7

A Look at Austin Farrer's Theory of Agency

W. Mark Richardson

Introduction

Over thirty years after the death of the Oxford philosopher and theologian Austin Farrer, many are still attracted to his work. His writings as a whole are rich with suggestive leads, expressive of a consistent point of view (though surely one which undergoes revision as well), and focused on topics that remain in the forefront of philosophical theology. This is especially true of his work on human agency. The goal of this essay is to provide a broad outline of Farrer's views on human agency as presented in the 1957 Gifford Lectures, his last major work on the topic (referred to here by the published title, *The Freedom of the Will*).

We are presently in a period in intellectual history when issues in the philosophy of mind have surfaced with tremendous intensity. Largely due to the advances in cognitive sciences and neurosciences, philosophers and theologians alike are reconsidering the relationship between theory and data in the foreground of these sciences and the disciplines which provide a framework for interpreting the data.

One important watershed in modern philosophy of mind in the British-American context is the 1949 publication of Gilbert Ryle's, *The Concept of Mind*. This work delivered a resounding blow to dualistic conceptions of mind-brain, and offered a constructive alternative we now call philosophical behaviorism. Although many transitions have occurred in the philosophy of mind since Ryle's famous work, it can justly be cited as a critical turning point toward the present day dominance of monistic philosophies of the human person, which are especially relatable to empirical studies.

Austin Farrer is important in this context in two respects: He is perhaps the first British philosophical theologian to offer a position on the
theological implications of Ryle's views, and he himself registered on
the side of a monistic position. He ably demonstrated the importance of
philosophical bridge questions which must be resolved before interpreting empirical issues related to mind-brain research, and he offered ideas
which were empirically open in his day, and worth revisiting in our
own.

The challenge before him was to show how a theory which purports
that human beings emerge from natural processes could support a strong
view of human agency, and also satisfy the relational and moral prereq-
uisites of personal theism. His conclusions were more optimistic than
those drawn in most contemporary monistic philosophies of mind and
action.

However, it is not clear that Farrer met adequately the challenge of
his compatibilist contemporaries. *Compatibilism* is the view that a
wholly causally determined world, including the processes in which
human actions consist, is compatible with free will. This position is
often defended by defining freedom in a less than robust way, say, as the
absence of constraint. As such, one is free to *do what one wants,* but this
says nothing about whether one is free to *want what one wants.*
Ironically, one of Farrer's more interesting *theological* concepts–"double agency," which is the idea that there can be two distinct agents, one
divine the other human, of a single finite action–may signal a problem
left unanswered in the incompatibilist/compatibilist debate. Farrer's
concept and my criticism will be clearer as I proceed.

My remarks first will be expository, followed by a critical response.
Regarding the latter, I will state my conclusions in advance: I believe
that the greatest strength of his theory of human agency is found in the
use he makes of it in later work regarding the formation and sustaining
of theistic belief. A necessary condition for the personal theism he
espouses is the active, intentional orientation of the human agent in relation to God. Farrer grounds human identity in agency–not in consciousness–and this important distinction is reflected both in the substance of his theology and his religious epistemology.

Philosophy of Mind and Philosophy of Agency

Farrer's Philosophy of Mind: Its Background and Historical Context

Farrer's *The Freedom of the Will* (1958) came out of the English context not long after Gilbert Ryle's *The Concept of Mind* (1949), and dur-

ing a renewed interest in the philosophy of mind that continues to this day. It was the era when G.E.M. Anscombe, J.L. Austin, Stuart Hampshire, A.I. Melden, Gilbert Ryle, and Peter Strawson were among the prominent figures in philosophy of mind and action. To appreciate Farrer's contribution it will be important to summarize briefly this philosophical context.

The influence of 20th century science, and its philosophical cousin, logical positivism, had already cut away at widely held dualistic assumptions about the mind-body relation. Mind-body dualism–long a favorite in Western philosophy, and still commonly assumed on the popular level today–pictures the "mind" as a nonspatial entity or substance residing in the body. It is the source of consciousness, thought, will, emotion, feeling, and all the higher attributes we associate with personal existence. Descartes's version of metaphysical dualism is perhaps the best known. In keeping with the mechanistic worldview of his day, Descartes thought of the human body as a machine, vitalized by a thinking, willing substance–the mind. Indeed, the most self evident of truths, according to Descartes, was that the self is a thinking substance.

In Descartes's and other mind-body dualisms, mind and body interact constantly. For example, physical sensations cause seeing, hearing, and tactile experience; reciprocally, the mind's desires, beliefs, and intentions, formed in response to experience in the world, cause bodily movement. Dualistic theories account well for the human experience of introspection, the mystery of sense qualia (e.g., the experience of color), belief in immortality of the soul, and the experience of willful action. But they raise a number of problems as well.

Ryle's lasting mark (certainly more lasting than his behavioral theory of mind) was his persuasive criticism of mind-body dualism. He undermined the assumption that mind and body were entities that could be compared, contrasted, or in any sense viewed as distinct and interacting things. This, he believed, is a "category mistake," analogous to the way in which a comparison between Magdalene College and Oxford University would be a confusion of categories. "Mind," countered Ryle, refers to specialized capacities of human beings, and human beings are unified living organisms characterized by intelligent bodily action.

Dualism has taken knocks from other critics as well, whose arguments I will pose here in the form of questions: Where is the mind located? How can a non-physical entity (the mind) causally interact with a physical entity (the body)? Dualists identify persons essentially as minds, and minds as separate substances. But how is a disembodied person conceivable? That is, how are thought, memory, sensation, action in the world, possible without bodies? When does this separate substance enter the body: at conception, at later stages *in utero*, at birth, in early childhood? Finally, in the evolutionary context (where changes occur that only over the long term produce species differentiation), at what point did mind/spirit emerge? These questions signal difficulties with dualism that a number of contemporary philosophers have named.

As the influence of mind-body dualism faded among English and American philosophers, one of the mid-century alternatives to emerge was behaviorism. The philosophical behaviorists thought that the essential features of mind were observable, extrinsic features. Thus, for example, when we refer to "intentions," we are not talking about some inner conscious state; rather, we are making predictions about behavior. Likewise, desires and beliefs do not essentially refer to some interior mind-stuff that possesses desires and beliefs; rather, they refer to dispositions to act in particular ways.

This turn to ostensive language for talking about the human mind and human action (in keeping with positivistic forebears) had clear deterministic implications. The stimulus-response scheme underlying it left no room for free will as an effective aspect in human behavior. Furthermore, the focus on strictly observable characteristics of mind left much of the richness of human conscious experience unexplained: for example, thought processes that have no observable, behavioral correlates; and, mental background conditions of an action that are not fully exhausted by behavior descriptions.

Thus, while Ryle's attack on dualism may have shifted the ground in some very important ways for all future philosophy of mind, his behaviorist alternative was short lived because of this failure to account for internal states. Farrer was among those who accepted the conclusions about dualism, but rejected the behaviorism. I will take up his response in more detail later, but first it is important briefly to mention other place markers in philosophy of mind that followed.

One commonly held position on the paradox of freedom and determinism during this period was a return to a new form of dualism: the linguistic dualism represented by A.I. Melden. According to this view our various and contrasting descriptions of the same human action–one issuing in reasons for an action, the other in causes for the bodily movements corresponding to the action–are logically distinct and therefore incommensurable. For example, if John raises his arm and moves it forward I can explain the action on the basis of reasons and intentions (he is throwing a ball to Jack), or a scientific observer may explain it on the basis of physical causes (sensory input that triggered the firing of neurons in the central nervous system as executive response to the environment). There is nothing quantifiable or measurable about the beliefs and desires, or the voluntary aspects of John throwing a ball. However, if it were possible to hook John up to equipment that measured neural impulses, then in theory it would be possible to measure the sequence of events in the brain and nervous system from the point of John's choosing to throw to the conclusion of the act. The measurements may be said to line up exactly with the observed movement we have named an intentional action, but there is no way to show any one-to-one correlation between descriptions of various aspects of an intentional action and units of neurophysical activity. That is, there is no single neurophysical sequence that lines up exactly with "the intention to throw."

So how can we relate reasons and intentions (mental and personal language) to production within the brain and nervous system (scientific and causal language)? The linguistic dualists said that we can't. Philosophically speaking, the incommensurability is the last word on the topic, and we must simply live with the practical fact of dual (or multiple) descriptions that match the internal and external perspectives on a single event. This is simply to recognize one of the unique features of an ontology that includes minds in the world. This too was satisfying for some, but unsettling for many others. It begged the question of how to reconcile the conflicting metaphysical implications arising from the different levels of description: i.e., 1) the determinism implicit in causal descriptions, and the personal freedom implicit in descriptions centered in reasons, intentions, decisions, and so forth; 2) the ontological implications of having two "true" descriptions of the same phenomenon that are necessarily irreconcilable.

Finally, we must look at physicalistic philosophies of mind in Farrer's day that dominate the field today. "Physicalism" here will be a covering term for a range of theories, some sharply distinguishable, others only subtly so. One of the most common is "identity theory." Simply put, identity theorists claim that mental states just *are* physical states of the brain and central nervous system. This is so, they claim, even though it is difficult to disabuse ourselves of common sense assumptions to the contrary. For example, it is difficult to imagine how a particular belief is identical with excitations in a particular region of the neo-cortex.

Identity theorists claim that analogous identities occur between scientific and ordinary language descriptions all the time. Paul Churchland notes some common examples: high pitched sound is the same as high oscillatory frequency of compression waves; warmth and coolness of a body are the same as high and low average molecular kinetic energy in the body; lightning is identical with large-scale electron discharges in the atmosphere.[1]

These theorists are optimistic about finding physical roots to all phenomena we associate with intelligent, willful, purposive life as human beings, and for their support they point to a number of things: 1) the physical origins of all life; 2) the neural dependence of all known mental phenomena; and, 3) the accelerating success rate of the neurosciences in recent years in finding bio-physical roots of behavior, and in unravelling previous mysteries about many mental phenomena.[2]

The obvious problem (at least on the surface) for identity theories is that by reducing introspective states, the experienced quality of phenomena, the sense of purpose and meaning, and all intentional content of action, to physiological states, the *content* of mental states loses all explanatory significance in human life. Indeed, for most identity theorists, the physiological level of description is causally sufficient for explaining behavior. Mental state types will some day be mapped entirely with physical state types, and one wonders at this point whether the mental will be regarded as anything but epiphenomenal.

Another problem for the identity theorists is to explain how mental types, for example, the intention to lift one's arm, can be realized via more than one way physically. This problem of "multiple realizability" suggests the need for something more subtle than the identity theories offer.

These problems cannot be addressed in detail here. I shall simply conclude by saying that theories of mind have advanced in recent decades to several new stages, among them being functionalism, a descendant of behaviorism and perhaps the most popular theory today among philosophers, psychologists, and cognitive scientists. Functionalism holds that mental states are defined in terms of their causal relations to 1) input from the environment, 2) other internal processes, and 3) executive output directed toward the environment.

Another position, eliminative materialism, is a strong version of identity theory, which holds that common sense mental concepts about cognition and action are radically misleading, and suggests further that this conceptuality will eventually be replaced by new psychological taxonomy based in the neurosciences.

This partial and very brief framework is enough to provide a context for Farrer and his fit within it. He took an interesting middle ground, wishing to get beyond dualism and its failures, but also sympathetic with the desire to preserve a strong sense of free will that was not maintained under the identity theories.

Farrer explicitly rejected Cartesian mind-body dualism, and as for linguistic dualism, his position was that if our world is one then there ought to be coherent and intelligible linkage between our various descriptions of it. This represents the orthodoxy of the British natural theology tradition that had influenced him. He attempted to press toward a more unified picture of the mind-brain relation, and rejected the linguistic dualists' conclusion. He stated, "Do we make it a linguistic rule never to attempt the relating to one another of our different descriptions? Surely that way schizophrenia lies."³

Thus, he accepted the basic unity of personal existence espoused by Ryle. Persons are *not* essentially souls that reside in and interact with bodies, but rather unified beings characterized by intelligent and purposive bodily action.⁴

In order to get at the unity, Farrer examined the workings of *thought*, as a principal feature of mentality to show how it is a specialized form of *action*. Thought, he concluded, is like a tennis stroke, except that the latter is an observable bodily movement. Both the tennis stroke and thought have their respective neurophysiological correlates. He said, "All mental events are physical events, derived from physical causes, and carrying physical effects."⁵

But to accept the thesis of personal unity is not the same as accepting behaviorism. Farrer took an interest in aspects of mind that behaviorism had ignored—for example, how to account for bodily movements (e.g., reflex actions) that have no conscious mental correlates; or how to account for mental actions (e.g., calculating, or deliberating) that have no observable bodily expressions. As later functionalists would agree, behaviorism leaves gaps in the picture.

Farrer also rejected the reductionistic tendencies of behaviorism—the assumption that mentality is fully comprehended in observable bodily effects. Affirming the privileged epistemic status of self-knowledge, he held that the direct experience of action ought to control the form of our explanation of it. This means that to understand what one does under given circumstances, one must know the reasons that one might cite to answer "why" one so acted. He refused to let go of those higher aspects of experienced personal unity—rationality, self-consciousness, intentionality, purposiveness—in his understanding of action. So the tension for Farrer was in asserting the physical basis of mind without accepting a reductionistic interpretation of this claim.

Here it is important to emphasize that Farrer accepted the view that mind emerges from natural processes. Thus, as nature develops more complex patterns and systems of energy, so also the specialization and sophistication of creaturely capacities increases. In terms of human mentality, one thinks of the emergence of 1) the capacity for language, which in turn makes it possible 2) to hold multiple beliefs and desires informed by background conditions, 3) to anticipate future possibilities, 4) to make and change valuations about things and states of affairs, and thus to act purposively, and 5) to choose among alternative courses of action as one interacts with the environment, and thus to act innovatively in new and changing circumstances. Thus "mind," in a theory that emphasizes personal unity, expresses natural capacities. When Farrer referred to the "soul," he meant that "the whole bodily system is capable of responding to meaning... is alive with consciousness." This was a rather imprecise way of avoiding the Cartesian implications of "soul" without having yet worked out an alternative in detail.

Unlike the eliminative materialists, in Farrer's emergent view of the mind, the physical system is capable of responding to "meaning," not just "mechanism:"

> ...the actualizing of one pattern of action may be consequent on previous patterned actions not in virtue of physical efficacy but in virtue of what they mean.[6]

Human beings are not just complicated stimulus-response organisms whose behavior can be fully anticipated in antecedents. An adequate understanding of personal action must consider the sociolinguistic and personal-intentional factors. There may always be sufficient reasons for an action *ex post facto*, which include these factors, but there can be no predictive function in our explanations of action. We may anticipate the actions of others on the basis of their personal histories, and on the basis of what Farrer called "connaturality," but these are not predictions in the technical sense.

With these general features in mind, I will comment on two unusual moves in Farrer's treatment of the philosophy of mind. First, he proposes a *tertium quid* between intentions on the mental level and the correlating minute forces in the neuro-physiological system. He called the third term "action-patterns," which are those large scale bodily movements, comprised of a vast amount of neurological activity, that correspond with our intentional representations of action. They refer to completely observable and physical units (e.g., the raising of an arm), but they are definable only by reference to both intentional and physiological aspects. That is, the beginning and end of an action-pattern is only defined by the intention (intentions are logically related to action, not contingently or causally related). The scale of measuring neural firings is too small, and the sequence too continuous, for making sense of beginnings and endings. Yet the action-pattern is completely physical, composed of a large sweep of activity in the brain and central nervous system.

The action-pattern, thought Farrer, helps us make sense of mental reference since we intend large units of bodily motion; we never "intend" neural firings. The action-patterns are the physical aspect of personal action, and in this sense not explainable strictly in terms of their minute physical constituents, except as they are exhibited in larger systems. This, he believed, was an example on the physical level of nonreducible phenomena that we refer to as "action" on the mental level.

A second interesting move is that he made predictions regarding physiological theory (at least in a very simple way), and thus left his own philosophy open to falsification. That is, he hypothesized precisely enough about what must be the case about the brain for an emergent theory to be true, that in principle one could find evidence sufficient to show that his hypothesis is wrong.[7]

Farrer noted that in his day there was much knowledge of the input (stimulus) and output (response) processes of the physical system, but very little understanding of the processes and mechanisms in the brain that make possible the transition between them.[8] He conjectured that there must be a highly sensitive mechanism in the cortex that makes the transition from input to execution, that formalizes stimulus and response, and that accounts for the human ability to respond to alternative courses of action on the basis of *meaning*.[9]

Those who take positions like Farrer's usually give some philosophical attention to the concepts of "meaning" and "intention." Farrer did also, but his comments are informal and scattered throughout *The Freedom of the Will* and other smaller essays written in the 1960's.

We get an idea of how Farrer defined "meaning" in an essay entitled "Signification."[10] Here he placed meaning in a voluntaristic and socially constructed context: it consists in the intention to communicate, and in effecting change in objects and states of affairs as understood within social conventions and practices in the pursuit of purposes. One particular statement illustrates the direction he took. He said that the exclamation, "Mad bull!"

> ...is not primarily significant [meaningful] because we know how to verify it, but because we propose to act upon it. E.g., I do not know how to verify a *fugiendum* ("a thing to be fled from") or rather, I have the lively fear that it will verify itself, namely as malevolent and horned: my aim is, so to act, that no verification may take place.[11]

Thus, to say that the brain is capable of responding to meaning is to say that it is responsive to the highest form of personal activity, expressed foremost in human valuations as we interact in the world in pursuit of value. For example, we are able to place human sympathy above physical urges, to place long term goods above the fulfillment of present needs. Farrer was sensitive to the rich nuances and various functions of human language. It does represent but also expresses active-interactive orientation of human behavior in general. It is a social form conveying the purposive and intentional content behind our behavior.

Meaning is simply not reducible to its method of verification as if the sole function of language were to represent.

We find Farrer's view of the relation of intention to action within *The Freedom of the Will*. There are three particularly important features of this relation that Farrer highlights. First, and in line with what has already been mentioned, *intentions define the unit of behavior, or set the boundaries of an action.* They are "architecturally" defined, to use Farrer's words, in that one intends a project in the round; one never intends, say, to set off certain neural firings in the head. For example, if one intends to go shopping, there is a coherent, well-defined unit of action with a beginning and end, that the intention represents–driving to the store, picking items off the shelf, purchasing them, and so forth. The boundaries of the action are socially intelligible, signifying a behavior that fulfills needs, desires, beliefs, and calls for certain interactions with the world that are socially understood.

This leads to a second and related point: *Intentions are logically, not causally, related to the actions they represent.* The boundaries of an action represented by the intention are logical boundaries in the sense that there are certain *results* of an action which logically are internal to the intention, and certain *consequences* which are external to the intention, and caused by the action. (E.g., I intend to honk the horn to alert the farmer who is about to cross the country road onto my path. But I do not intend to frighten his cattle, who upon hearing the horn go on a stampede and trample my car.) The "alerting" is a *result* of the intentional action, and intrinsic to it. The "stampeding" is a *consequence* of the intentional action and causally (not logically) related to it. In short, intention is a mental representation of action, and so an aspect of the action itself (the aspect of preference, the bodily movement being the aspect of execution).

Third, Farrer adopted the view that *intentions indicate the directedness of action toward a particular object or state of affairs,* a standard assumption about intentionality following Brentano. The object of our intentions is never the brain or nervous system, but rather a macroscopic effect in the agent's world of interaction. Again, intentions refer to the representation of, and initiative in, the action. They are not merely predictions or reports about behavior.

This sketch of Farrer's philosophy of mind expresses what he believed to be the "bottom line" conditions of agency which the theist has an interest in defending. That is, for there to be the capacity to act innovatively, to form purposes, to make and change valuations about objects and states of affairs, to have responsible and real relations among persons, including human interaction with God, then at least the above must be true of person. We notice that it is not a theory that hangs onto an "immortal soul," which possesses only a fortuitous relation to our bodies, but it *is* a theory that is uncompromising on the riches of human free will, within a roughly monist outlook. The genius of this is that it provides the real, empirical limiting conditions on freedom, but indeed treats them as *conditions* and not *determinants*.

Farrer's philosophy of mind, only sketched out briefly here, is tightly linked to important metaphysical and epistemological assumptions that guided his work. For example, aside from the obvious opposition to dualism (not just among his English contemporaries but evident in Continental existentialists of his day as well) he resisted the metaphysical extremes of atomism (which yields a view of persons as an aggregate of events with no identity over time), and idealism (yielding an all-embracing oneness of which finite minds are a manifestation). Farrer construed the world as a plurality of interacting systems of energy, each with its own integrity.

Two epistemological principles stand out: First, there is an active orientation to thought, and to mentality in general. Thus, we do not come into possession of explanations, we *make* them. Knowing involves an active process: knowing *how* to do things, and *where* to look. He believed this thesis to be opposed to the legacy of David Hume. In Hume's theory the self receives discrete sense impressions which the mind associates variously. Persons are, thus, passive recipients of stimuli occasioned by the world.

Second, Farrer held the thesis that experience is not "in the head," so to speak, but out there in the world where the pattern of one's intentional activity meets up with other systems of activity that qualify one's actions. Experience does not originate internally (i.e., in some mysterious entity called the mind) but in the actual interference and cooperation of one's own activity with other systems of energy. This also differs from Hume, for whom experience is framed within the passive-receptive model as the internal appropriation (in the mind) of impressions. This model stands behind the skeptical philosophers' question about, for example, how we know whether other minds exist. If experience is not an interaction but purely mental appropriation of impression, then doubt is cast on objective existence. This second epistemological principle of Farrer's had a profound effect on his later philosophical theology, and led to his conviction that theology is fundamentally practical and not contemplative in orientation. The primacy of the practical, active character of the divine-human relation leads us to the next section of this essay.

Farrer On Free Will

Much of the foregoing on Farrer's philosophy of mind has spilled over into implications about free will already. However, a few more remarks directly bearing on his notion of freedom will make the last section on its theological implications clearer.

So far I have described Farrer's view this way: the mind refers to capacities of the human being, who is a psycho-somatic unity; mentality refers to specialized kinds of activity, and intentional action is the essential characteristic of personal being. Once Farrer had asserted this stance his focus turns to the implications this has for the problem of free will.[12] His first task is to define on the most basic level what he means by free will: Is it doing what one wants in the absence of constraint? Is it the capacity to choose among alternative courses of action? Each of the above, though related to the other, has a different force, and each a different fit with compatibilist and libertarian theories. It should also be noted that both are very minimal conditions and not robust enough to capture all that matters to the theologian about freedom.[13]

For the purpose of this philosophical study, Farrer defended the version of freedom captured in the phrase "could have done otherwise," meaning that, for an agent who has acted freely, there were alternative courses of action and the agent had it within his or her power to choose either or any option among the alternatives in the same circumstances in which the agent chose. This is a minimal condition for still other developments of freedom. For example, to consent to the good presumes the capacity not to consent–i.e., a choice between alternatives. To have the will one wants to will, a version of Harry Frankfurt, would presume that there are choices of wills to have and one is able to will one and not another.

This definition fit with Farrer's basic contention that the emergence of personal existence requires a level of explanation beyond those that account for simpler levels of life. Human agency adds something– voluntary action–to the world the scientist describes. The past does not causally necessitate human action as we think of it doing in non-agent events.

Farrer's view is similar to the agent-causation theory popular in the sixties and espoused by Roderick Chisolm, Richard Taylor, and later by John Thorp and Richard Swinburne. "Agent-causation" signifies that at the level of conscious, intentional agency (i.e., human agency) it is no longer sufficient to conceive of action on the basis of a deterministic stream of cause-effect events that happen to pass through the person. In place of the covering law model of explanation (Hempel's deductive-nomological formalism) from which the question would be, "What caused A to do X?," and which places the event within a broader framework of laws and initial conditions, the agent-causation theorists insist we must introduce the intentional-purposive structure of human agency into explanation. Thus, the more informative question becomes, "What is A up to?" The force of the question carries the teleological bearing of action, and precisely this captures the form of the agent's experience of acting.

Note also, the dependence of such a framework on sociolinguistic conditions. The power of symbolic reference just is this ability to refer to things without causal-temporal relations necessary between the thing and the referring agent. All things considered, the agent-causation theorists do not believe that purposes and intentions can be translated into antecedent motivational forces that "determine" the agent to act as he or she acts. Somehow, they insist, the teleological aspect of intentional action is effective in the agent's choice to do one thing and not another. This common sense form of explanation is metaphysically ultimate.

Of course this view is hotly contested by the eliminative materialists, indeed most contemporary philosophers of mind. Some of these refuse to believe there is such a thing as a personal center or identity–the self as a coherent unified whole–from which long term purposes and creative actions can take shape. Their strategy, in contrast to agent-causation theorists, is to reduce mentality to observable physical components in the brain, isolate the function of each part, then show how the aggregate of parts and systems can account for the complex phenomena popularly known as intentional action. They take a purely third-person, observational perspective on the agent which yields a view of action that can be explained on terms that apply to all phenomena in the world, without exception.[14]

Notwithstanding the element of alternativeness in personal action, which opens the door to the possibility of novelty and creativity, the agent-causation theorists, and Farrer, believe that an agent's actions must be subject to some forms of regularity. Otherwise the actions would result from sheer chance and randomness, and this does not fit well with the agent's experience of bringing about his or her actions. Two kinds of regularity are at issue here: regarding the environment of human action we rightly assume the stability of, and constancy of features in, the environment with which we interact; regarding the human agent, we also assume regularity but the regularity derives from the agent's purposes. The element of purpose–the pursuit of the good–gives personal action continuity over a stretch of time. This, and not the framework of law-like necessity, provides the intelligibility of action.[15]

So the key features of the agent-causation model, shared by Farrer, are that agents: 1) have the power to make things happen, rather than simply undergo them, and 2) this power is exercised and directed by the agent on the basis of reasons and purposes which cannot be exhaustively translated into antecedent causal terms. This self-determination, in a sense, is an "interruption" of the causal chain by the agent who is able to hold alternative possibilities in balance and choose on the basis of purposes. Of course, this ability is itself directly dependent on the agent being a linguistic being (the necessary condition for being able to represent and hold in consciousness a range of motivating forces on our action), and mind being a social reality (the necessary condition for the formation of value, and having a moral existence).

Perhaps most important, it is dependent on there being a person-as-a-whole who determines purposes, who utilizes memories and associates them with present experience, who imputes meaning to activity on the basis of social conventions, and employs still other features of consciousness, and is not merely the aggregate of these as if they were independently functioning characteristics. Said Farrer, "If I succeed in putting my desires among objective facts, I do so by putting myself–the self which desires–among objective facts."[16] Reasons, desires, appetites, purposes, all motivating principles, are not sub-agential forces that resolve in action–they belong to the agent who, as a whole, forms intentions, and chooses a course of action. Human agents experience all of this from "inside" as subjects, and the agent-causation theorists take this to be metaphysically irreducible.[17]

Naturally, Farrer particularized this position with his own creative contribution. For instance, he believed that if one is to reject the application of the uniform sequence model of causation to human agency it was important to formulate an alternative explanation. His alternative took the form of examining our interpretation of the creative and novel actions of others whom we wish to understand.

In his discussion of this question he revitalized the notion of "connaturality," the idea that we share a common intentional structure with other human beings which is at the hub of our understanding of them. Humans are language users who are self-conscious, able to hold alternative sets of beliefs and desires collaterally, able to make and change their valuations of things and persons with whom they interact, and thus to form purposes. All of these shared features of human existence, and more, are presupposed in interactions with other persons, and are the basis for the shaping of one's understanding of them.

Thus, according to Farrer, we don't look for patterns of the other's past behavior from which to make explanations of their present actions, or predictions of future ones; this would be a quasi-causalist approach. Rather, we "feel the force" of our neighbor's action more immediately: "...our own active nature serves us less as a standard to which we refer our neighbor's conduct, than as a sensitive organ in which we feel it."[18] Again, he states, "It is because my own reactions to circumstances is self-varying over an amazing range that I can keep up with the turns and twists of my neighbor's intentions under the guidance of the visible signs his behavior affords."[19]

Farrer believed that one of the reasons why one cannot put a causal form on action is that the motivating principles of action have what he called a "free sequence" relation to choices of the agent. Motivating principles at the onset of action are determined. I don't initially choose for an appetite to erupt in given circumstances. But once particular appetites are brought to consciousness they are possessed by the agent in a new way, one which does not determine. For now we must consider the agent's own awareness of having these motives, and the kind of self-reflexive judgments (in principle unlimited) the agent may make about them. In this respect, Farrer believed that "consideration and choice follow their antecedents by a free sequence" and not a necessary one.[20]

As Farrer considered those aspects of human agency which are basic if the theology of personal theism–divine and human agents in relation–is to be true, he placed stress on the human capacity for innovation, among other things. The strongly libertarian strain of Farrer's thinking surfaces when he focuses on this topic. By innovativeness Farrer meant not just that human behavior is unpredictable, but that in the dynamic conditions of life, agents find unforeseen ways to meet longstanding purposes; they are not stuck by patterns of past actions forever shaping subsequent ones when similar conditions arise. Rather, persons have an enormous power to create new motive principles in the face of new objects and states of affairs, and power to make new associations between elements in the memory background. So, instead of dwelling on the conditioning of the past on choices in the present, Farrer claims that in new circumstances with new opportunity the agent "dilates on a project" as what he or she wants to do.[21] "Reason introduces an object for its own sake; decision advances into an open future and chooses what it will create.[22] And again, "...we view ourselves as sovereign in our own republic, competent to revise our edicts as we see fit."[23]

Comments such as these, made in defense of libertarian freedom, leave the impression that Farrer underestimated the constraints on human behavior, and minimized the complexity of human action–the constraining role of contextual factors (both environmental and within the agent) which are true of human agency even in its most free and elevated form.

Farrer's notion of freedom, in this respect, stands out from what one might call the Aristotelian monist theories, championed today by Donald Davidson. Like Aristotle's rationalized appetites, Davidson's causal theory conceives desires and beliefs of the agent as causes of action, though we have no way to formally correlate mental event types with their underlying physical correlates. Without going into the details of his theory, Davidson holds that each event called an action has a token-token correlation between the mental and physical descriptive levels:

> If the causes of a class of events (actions) fall in a certain class (reasons) and there is a law to back each singular causal statement, it does not follow that there is any law connecting events classified as reasons with events classified as actions–the classification may even be neurological, chemical or physical.[24]

I believe Farrer's own argument would have been stronger had he taken this position, and other conventionally causal theories of action of his own day, more seriously at a detailed level. Instead, some of his remarks suggest that mental capacities are sheer luminous powers unbound by context or unconstrained by past experience. One wonders just how "sovereign" we are over our own volitional domain when deeply embedded patterns of action (sometimes vicious ones) incline us toward actions we later regret, or so cloud the sense of reason that we do not even have regret. I think in particular of Thomas Tracy's poignant examples of this in reference to Saddam Hussein (*see Tracy in this volume*). I don't think Farrer himself was unaware of the sometimes self-imposed and other times context-imposed constraints. For him at stake was a philosophical point and not the empirical fine-tuning of it, and the point was this: no matter what the constraints and conditions, the human agent is not determined in the Davidsonian sense or the eliminative-materialist sense. One may feel the weight of the past as compulsion; yet the past predisposes but does not determine one's agency.

Perhaps a helpful supplement to Farrer's account, which also appreciates his goal, comes from Alasdair MacIntyre. MacIntyre holds that explanation of action *does* have a "characteristically and for the most part" causal form, but it is adjusted to the circumstances both of intentionality, and the social factors which mark human identity. So contrary to Farrer, a loosely causal picture enters into our understanding of actions of other agents. Our interpretation of action does involve an analogy from patterns of past experience to present instances. MacIntyre insists that the ability to be knowledgeably conscious of our inner lives depends on the ability to interact with social institutions, and to understand what the social practices we engage in impute to us. Rational action has observable, social standards which pass through the private, mental world of intentions. We first learn a practice of doing X by having meaning imputed to our behavior; then we learn the goal of doing X; finally we judge the appropriate application of X so that it becomes a form for our own intentional action. Relative to this perspective Farrer does not properly contextualize the psychology of intentions. We don't just "feel" our neighbor's intentions by virtue of our mutual power to intend. This is too abstract, and too dismissive of the context and structure of intentional action.

Despite this difference in outlook, MacIntyre shares Farrer's resistance to the approach of Davidson and others, for he does insist on the efficacy of mental content in choiceful action. If reasons learned in a sociolinguistic context, which give rise to intentions, cannot be regarded as specifying the cause which constitutes an action and gives coherence to a particular form of life, we would have to see the psychological aspect of human conduct as epiphenomenal. MacIntyre holds that explanatory generalizations at the psychological level do specify the causal link which is partially constitutive of the inner life of the reason-guided person. Says MacIntyre:

> By insisting that only universal law-like generalizations, of the kind which embody the canonical form of the statements at the core of the theoretical structures of physics and chemistry, can specify the causal linkage between reasons and actions, Davidson obscures the distinctiveness of the causality of reasons and reasoning in the human world. And he also obscures the link between the inner life of the mind and the social life of practices.[25]

In conclusion, I would offer this assessment of Farrer's argument for libertarian freedom: In the first section of *The Freedom of the Will* Farrer's operating assumption was that if the world is one, then our various descriptions of it ought to cohere. On the basis of this he made considerable effort to connect a philosophy of mind with at least some of the key neurophysiological knowledge of his day. However, when the argument shifts directly to the problem of freedom, in my judgment this standard is not sustained. He appears, instead, to take less seriously the weight of real opposing views, and to be more interested in illustrating his own premises. His vivid and compelling account of his position is admirable as such, but it is not the same as engaging directly the problems presented by physicalistic interpretations of neurosciences, which was part of his point of departure.

Nevertheless, there are moments of real brilliance and illumination in Farrer's treatment of free will. He had made some important adjustments to account for new philosophical insights of his day, and some of his perspectives constitute an advance for philosphical theologians. Often his characterizations of opposing views are insightful. On the constructive side, we see that the constitution of human agency in

Farrer's philosophy is complex. It includes value formation which gives rise to stable and enduring purposes upon which agents act. And it includes day to day decisions that express novelty and change in the face of new circumstances as the agent goes about fulfilling certain purposes. Without either of these features, much that is important to the theologian about agency is lost.

I am not sure he said enough to move the doubter out of his or her inertia on the dispute between libertarian and compatibilist freedom. In fact it may be that his own development of the key theological idea of double agency signaled a lack of resolution on this topic. This will be discussed in more detail in the next section. However, the constructive thesis which follows is that Farrer's theory of agency offers important insights into how we acquire and sustain theistic belief.

Free Will and Theology: The Problem of Double Agency

In his last major work in philosophical theology, *Faith and Speculation*, Farrer gathered much of the fruit of his work on free will and showed the activist implications it has for knowledge of God and life in relation to God. He addressed the central topic of theism–God's action in the world–and the complex problem of making God's sovereign will and a libertarian theory of human freedom an intelligible fit.

I believe that the weakness in Farrer's defense of libertarian (or incompatibilist) freedom shows up once we examine his theological notion of double agency. He attempts to show philosophically why it is impossible to know the mode of divine action. However, in working around the edges of the "causal joint" of God's action, certain difficulties will not go away. I think it is likely, for example, that his notion of "double agency," (which stands for two intentions, one divine, the other human, behind one finite act) fits at least as well with a compatibilist outlook on freedom as it does with the libertarian view. If, as I believe Farrer claims, God acts both in the sense of primary cause (he calls it "making things make themselves") and in terms of special actions in the world (here the meaning is ambiguous but one must assume that by divine persuasion of natural energies, effects occur which would otherwise not have occurred without the special divine intention), then the question of human freedom must be raised. For when a special action of God occurs that involves human beings, how can God's intention in the action be utterly sovereign if the human agents involved in the event are themselves free?

One can imagine cases where there is perfect alignment between God's persuasion of a human agent and the human agent's desire and choice to consent to the persuasion. One can argue in such cases that a persuasion does not determine, but conditions, the human action. This is good so far as it goes. But these are the easier cases of double agency.

Farrer own example or illustration of the idea of double agency, however, raises a difficulty regarding the paradox of divine and human freedom. His example is clearly *not* a case where the human agent chooses to consent to God's persuasion.[26] Assuming, as Farrer does, that God's particular actions in relation to finite agents is like a persuasion, what are we to make of the idea of persuasion when God's intention is not the one from which the human agent acts, when the human action is an *instrument* of divine intention but does not itself conform to divine intentions? Farrer illustrates with the biblical example of God's use of the Assyrians' aggression against Israel in order to judge the latter. Here we may say that God's intention is to chastise Israel for its sins; however, the Assyrian intention is surely not this, but rather acquisitiveness and political gain. So God has not "persuaded" the Assyrians (in the sense of convincing them to align their intentions with God's own); God has merely used the accidental coincidence of two quite different intentions.

If we were to draw this out it would look more like a hidden force on the motivating principles at work in the Assyrians, not a persuasion to share the divine intention that actively enters into the Assyrians' deliberative processes. This is hardly an ideal picture that a libertarian would want to present. Note Farrer's own words in the illustration: "The Assyrian was a rod in the hand of God's indignation, but he had no notion of being anything of the kind...If we can make out a prophetic theory about the mechanism of divine action, it lies in openness of men's thought to *pressures of which they are unaware*."[27]

It appears in Farrer's own example that, if the Assyrians really were the instrument of God's judgment on Israel (i.e., God affects change in the Assyrians in order for them to be such an instrument), then the Assyrians were not free in the most robust sense of acting on motivations about which they were conscious, or of deliberating among open possibilities. It may have been that all the features of human agency appeared to function in the Assyrians so far as they were aware, but if divine influence unknowingly underlies their actions, then the motivating springs of action were not brought to consciousness so as to be in the human agent's charge. For all they knew they acted on their own choice, but in fact, as Farrer says, there were "pressures of which they were unaware" affecting their decision. It is, I believe, fair to say that Farrer's example unwittingly signals that he had allowed compatibilism in the door in its theological form.

Free Will and Theology: Farrer's Contribution

In spite of these criticisms, I believe that Farrer presented a rich perspective on human agency, and that it highly influenced his later theological commitment to the priority of practical and moral, rather than rational and contemplative, aspects of theistic belief. If interaction is the principal way of knowing in the world–the cooperation and interference of natural forces with the agent's intentions in the field of his or her experience–then, as Farrer states in *Faith and Speculation*, the theist's question is not 1) "How closely does God correspond to my idea of God?" but rather 2) "What can I do about, or in response to, God?" (or "What must I do to be saved?"). These questions roughly correlate with different emphases in identifying the human person, the first stressing consciousness and correlating generally with rationalistic approaches to theology, the second stressing agency and correlating with a more practical orientation. So the contribution I speak of had to do with an aspect of the problem of how we acquire and sustain theistic belief.

Philosophical theology for the later Farrer becomes the examination of theistic belief as lived. This, of course, was consistent with the approach of empirical language philosophers of his day, but more important, it was a product of his own philosophy of agency. In following this method the pragmatic and voluntaristic themes regarding how we acquire and sustain theistic belief come to the foreground. We see the tie between theory of agency and the psychology of belief in two works, *Saving Belief*, and *Faith and Speculation*. Here he discussed the relation between "initial faith" and "actual faith." These terms are strikingly parallel to language he uses to describe "motives" in *The Freedom of the Will*.

In order to safeguard against the tendency to see all motives as "dispositions to act," Farrer described stages of motivation. What begins as a motive that is dispositional in force (from the agent's background), enters the rational and purposive considerations of the agent concomitantly with other motive principles, now belonging to the conscious agent as chosen principles of action, not merely as dispositions. For example, as I pass by a bakery the fragrance of the fresh bread and my present hunger bring about a desire to enter the bakery and make a purchase of my favorite bread. This "initial" motivation is not by choice; it arises from the physical force of hunger and the compelling sensation effected by the environment. However, once this motivation of desire surfaces, I may hold it in awareness alongside other motive principles, for example, the desire not to gain weight, or saving my change to buy flowers for my wife, etc. Farrer called these stages of motivation *initial* and *actual* respectively. Free actions arise from actual motivations. (This bears on my criticsm of Farrer on double agency. On his own description, the Assyrians acted with the background motivational conditions unaware and not fully understood.)

Initial and *actual* motives mark a distinction similar to that between *initial* faith and *actual* faith of the theist in Farrer's later writings. Farrer noted that the initial faith of the theist is like a disposition: it is a given tendency to believe based on one's background. We are born into forms of life, traditions, and so forth, where we interpret experience in light of the meaning imputed to them by others, and we pursue the good in certain prescribed ways. This constitutes one form of initial faith for Farrer. Other forms of initial faith might arise from compelling apprehensions of the divine from experience in the world.[28]

But Farrer's position goes beyond this. Active faith, a later stage, is the entering into active relations with God as known in finite effects. Here the initial persuasion becomes a chosen principle of action.

I think one might find an interesting contrast between someone like Richard Swinburne and Farrer on this construction of the acquisition of theistic belief. According to Swinburne, beliefs that we find initially compelling are placed alongside alternatives, and by a process of inductive reasoning which render certain probabilities, we discover either that it is responsible to trust (have faith in) our theistic orientation, or not. That is, the next step would be one of reasoning, and reasoning follows its own principles; it is not a voluntary process. (He is admittedly a follower of Hume on this point.) So, according to Swinburne, we must reach some resolve on propositional "belief-that" questions before there can be a satisfactory "belief in" posture.

Farrer did not reject the importance of having adequate reasons for theistic belief. He was not a fideist (one who makes a sharp division between faith and reason when it comes to belief commitments, and emphasizes faith in such matters and the incapacity of reason). But his examination of theistic belief, as lived, led to a perspective on the process that leads to such belief different from what we find in Swinburne. We assume that the initial faith of the theist is based on a persuasive force whether the believer has undergone a full scale process of inductive reasoning or not. But the way forward from this initial faith is the active pursuit of the will of God as interpreted in finite effects in the world. As Farrer said, "faith does not substitute for the evidence but places us in a position to appreciate the evidence."[29]

This active bearing toward the world in pursuit of the good places one in productive relations with the facts. Or again, "by embracing the good one becomes convinced of the fact." Thus, it is a voluntaristic stance which places one in the condition to receive the evidence.[30]

On live, momentous and open issues such as theistic belief, Swinburne discounted how in "actual faith" (to use Farrer's term) the active pursuit of the good places one in productive relations with the facts. This was a direct carryover from Farrer's theory of agency, and the epistemology of interaction he derived from it. One places oneself in the context where evidence is forthcoming. This presupposes the active intellect where thought proceeds, "...not as a train is controlled by the rails, but as an explorer is controlled by the countryside."[31]

By this point in his career Farrer was suspicious of supposed neutral and universal standards by which to judge beliefs on the scale of theism vs. atheism. At one point he said that life-in-God is not self evident in the way that speech activity makes life-in-community self evident. The world is ambiguous enough regarding rational consideration of evidence to justify theism and atheism alike.[32] The theist places certain value on the world with which he or she interacts based on the theistic conviction, and the effects of such interaction become the basis of assessing the value judgment. As Farrer says, "...in embracing the good which the gospel offers, he or she becomes convinced of the fact."[33] Thus, Farrer said, "We know natural agents by their interaction with us and therefore cannot extract a purely objective account of them..." Both regarding our knowledge of the physical world and our belief in God, "the ground of ignorance lies in the limited nature of an *active relation*, whether it be in relation to God's will, or our relations with physical activities."[34]

So the ground of "knowing" proposed by Farrer recognized the indispensibility of *value* discrimination in making claims about existents. Valuations take the lead in our assessment of existents. What is there in the world either confirms or disconfirms the value judgment as we interact with the object on the basis of it. Empirical evidence as such does not lead to serious assertions of existence without an accompanying acknowledgement of value. These value and evidential claims alike are asserted on the basis of action. Thus, Farrer was not optimistic about finding a singular acceptable standard for making judgments on questions such as theism vs. atheism because the valuational question can not be separated from determination of the facts. But he was more optimistic about the place of activist and practical principles in the coming to know real existents.[35]

Farrer succinctly stated the above insight regarding the active orientation of the believer in the following empirical maxim for religious epistemology:

> To know things is to exercise our actual relations with them. There can be no physical science without physical interference; no personal knowledge without personal intercourse; no thought about any reality about which we can do nothing but think.[36]

For theology specifically, this meant, "We can know nothing of God unless we can do something about him."

Regarding what one can do about God, Farrer's answer followed the traditional form of western theism: we can will the will of God. If the analogy of sovereign will is to be useful we must be able to interpret certain effects in the world as divine effects. The discernment of God's will in the world is obviously a complex matter constituted both by God's general purpose of "making things make themselves," but also by the lesser known particular purposes of God. Farrer drew on a wide range of human experience, including aesthetics, to describe our judgments of divine effects. [37]

Farrer's discussion of the background conditions of human intentionality sheds light on how the theist gains appreciation of divine will in the world. He insisted that the background content reflects the active orientation at the core of human identity. In thinking about another person, "my contemplation is not concerned with what my eyes can see, not with my friend's looks, but with his behavior."[38] He contended that the same is true in contemplating God: it is guided by a background of divine action, calling us into existence, acts of grace, forgiveness, renewal. "Thought of God is a summary of a tale that narrates the actions of God."[39] It is clear to all who have read Farrer's corpus that he believes this tale is told in scripture and in the ongoing life of the Christian community.

This conception of the background shows both psychological and epistemic links between 1) the history of the experience of a community with shared beliefs, and 2) the one's present active relations with an environment conceived as effects of God's activity. The whole wave of history laps against the shore of the present.[40]

I think that Farrer might have given us more in the way of criteria for judging our efforts to align our wills with God's. He said little about how we test whether one's active intention to will God's will is a misfire or an actual alignment with God's activity except to list certain subjective effects–nourishing, steadying, enlivening results of freely submitting to God's will. It would seem that a philosophical theology that centers on tradition, and on the coherence and intelligibility of theistic belief as lived, owes us more regarding the criteria for judging religious experience.[41]

Nevertheless, Farrer shows that his preference for performative knowing, drawn from his theory of agency, directly encourages the practical orientation of theism. The form "knowing how to" is just as basic as "knowing that" in the life of the theist. To discern divine intentions in natural effects, and to experience the enriching effects of aligning oneself with them, is a skill or practice of a person that is learned after consenting to God's will. Ostensive definition in the religious context becomes dependent on the more basic performative or experiential

form of knowledge.[42] The life of Christ or the lives of the saints is compelling evidence of divine-human relations only because theistic belief
is compelling in practice, either as a principle of interpretation, says
Farrer, or as that which renders the good. Regarding religious belief:
"The question is not whence it came, but why we should accept it; and
the second question cannot be answered by merely answering the
first."[43] We accept it because it works.

In summary, I would say that there are strong pragmatic tendencies
in Farrer's later philosophical theology, which provide opportunity to
compare and contrast his thought with the earlier William James, and
Hilary Putnam today. The similarities must be qualified. With James he
shared a voluntaristic orientation, but clearly he rejected James's idea
that we collectively make the future, and the idea that religion is a function of subjectivity. He was, at bottom, a theological realist who
remained traditional regarding the content of belief and held to the prior
actuality and activity of God. But he insisted that religion must be
something which works, and it must reflect our purposive relation to the
world. This latter point is a movement toward pragmatic principles.

Regarding Putnam, the clues for common ground come from his
work, *Reason, Truth and History*, wherein he states, "...our search for a
better conception of rationality is an intentional activity, which like
every activity that rises above habit and the following of inclination or
obsession is guided by our idea of the good."[44] Farrer would agree with
Putnam that intellectual judgment is an intentional activity which
involves our valuations. He is not so interested in overhauling our conception of rationality, but he would insist that a rigid, single-standard
criterion of meaning fails to distinguish kinds of objects that there are.
How we conceive things, our intentional activity in relation to them,
and our valuations, hold together in human knowing. It may be that our
interaction with the referent will bring about effects that cause us to
change our judgments about it, but the assessment itself is value ridden.

The good that Farrer sought was to enjoy life-in-God, and he claimed
that the active orientation of the finite agent was the means God had
chosen for such enjoyment. We know God by willing God's will,
intending to align ourselves with divine purposes as we recognize them
in finite effects. I conclude with a sentence from Farrer that expresses
this poignantly:

> You want to realize the mysterious immensity of God. And how will you
> set about it? By sitting with your head in your hands in a perfect fog,
> while you ask yourself what, if anything, you have the right to affirm? It
> will not get you far.[45]

Notes

1. Paul M. Churchland, *Matter and Consciousness*, (Cambridge, MA: MIT Press, 1984), 26.

2. Ibid., p.

3. *Freedom of the Will*, 63.

4. I have read in essays on Farrer that he had an "interactionist" view of the mind-body relation. This is misleading. In modern parlance interactionism is a form of dualism: something interacting with something else. If the mind is not an entity, but refers to specialized personal capacities (Farrer's position) then there is no *thing* to interact with the body. Farrer's comment, "...the whole physical system is alive with consciousness..." was his way in the absence of better words to avoid the interactionist view.

5. *Freedom of the Will*, 88.

6. *Freedom of the Will*, 100.

7. *Freedom of the Will*, 63, 82-85,100.

8. It so happens that this remains the case today. See Patricia Churchland, *Neurophilosophy*, (Cambridge, MA: MIT Press, 1989), 295.

9. Again, this would involve the capacity for language, and such derivative capacities as the withholding of response to initial motives and dispositions, the making of valuations and the forming of purposes, the holding of collateral beliefs and desires, and the weighing of alternative possibilities. Of course, as a philosophical theologian he was in no position to be precise about this matter, but the above conjecture is specific enough as a hypothesis to be tested. If this transitional function in the cortex exists, it will sooner or later be discovered, and this would augment the position Farrer takes. If such a function cannot be accounted for, this would weigh against the hypothesis. This would not mean that Farrer's larger thesis is wrong. Nevertheless, cumulatively, the success or failure of such hypotheses makes a difference.

10. This essay was written around 1953 and published in *Reflective Faith*, ed. Charles Conti.

11. *Reflective Faith*, 151.

12. Assuming correctly that the issue of freedom could not be addressed intelligibly apart from a theory of mind, Farrer did not even approach the title topic in *The Freedom of the Will* until he had dedicated five chapters to the mind-brain problem.

13. Note in particular the Thomistic stress on freedom as consent to God's goodness. This is not fully comprehended in either of the above philosophical options.

14. The problem with this view is that it so far does not satisfactorily deal with the universally human experience of subjectivity. It seems inadequate to say, as Dennett does, that the sense of self we experience directly is a deception generated in the West by the culture's preoccupation with "responsibility." One gets the impression that subjectivity is an embarrassment to the eliminativists' framework. Dennett's multiple drafts hypothesis is an alternative which eliminates a unity through personhood and establishes the sense of unity of other bases. See Daniel Dennett, *Consciousness Explained.*

15. Here I think the explanatory model offered by Diogenes Allen is helpful. He notes that in theoretical reasoning involving physical terms, when X occurs, and from the standpoint of the observer's knowledge, there is an open possibility of Y or not-Y following X, we have no explanation. When there is a logically complete explanation we can say *why* Y, and not not-Y, follows X. Practical reasoning differs in this respect: When a person does Y, and the reasons are for the most part universally understood so that it would not make sense anymore to ask, "Granted yours reasons, why did you do Y and not something else?" we accept the reason offered as explanation. But by this criterion more than one action with accompanying reasons may satisfy the inquirer. Allen's conclusion is that *ex post facto* such reasons do determine the action. But before the action occurs no possible reason for one act or another can specify what will necessarily be done. Diogenes Allen, "Deliberation and the Regularity of Behavior," *American Philosophical Quarterly* 9 (July 1972): 257.

16. *Freedom of the Will,* 201.

17. Norman Malcolm makes this point in an essay on pain; pains are not autonomous, atomic facts, but belong to the person whose background, context, and so forth, define the experience of pain. See his essay "Scientific Materialism and the Identity Theory," *The Mind-Brain Identity Theory,* C.V. Borst, ed. (London: MacMillan, 1970), 171-81.

18. *Freedom of the Will,* 152.

19. Ibid., 156-7.

20. Ibid., 225.

21. Ibid., 212.

22. Farrer, *Faith and Speculation,* 213.

23. *Freedom of the Will,* 164.

24. *Essays in Actions and Events* (Oxford: Clarendon Press, 1981), 17.

25. Alasdair MacIntyre, "The Intelligibility of Human Action," *Rationality, Relativism, and the Human Sciences,* J. Margolis, M. Krauz, R.M. Burian, eds. (Boston: Martinus Njhoff Publishers, 1986), 71.

26. *Faith and Speculation*, 61-65.

27. Ibid., 61. Emphasis mine.

28. One is reminded here of Norman Malcolm's remarks in the essay, "The Groundlessness of Religious Belief," *Reason and Religion*, Stuart Brown, ed., 147): "We grow into a framework, we don't *decide* to accept frameworks."

29. Farer, *Saving Belief*, 27.

30. This bears resemblance to a longstanding tradition usually associated with Anselm.

31. R.L. Franklin, *Free Will and Determinism*, 76. Since it is the pragmatic strain in Farrer that I am highlighting here, it is interesting to note the parallel between the Swinburne-Farrer constrast, and the W.K. Clifford-William James debate over the relation between will and belief.

32. *Faith and Speculation*, 128-9.

33. Ibid., 10.

34. Ibid., 79.

35. In this respect, Farrer anticipated some of the features of non-foundationalism emerging in contemporary philosophy and theology. He certainly recognized the power of the critical stance in shaping existential claims. This comes through clearly in his comment on the supposed division between empiricists and rationalists; he said:

> It is not more than a matter of defining at a particular point the relativity of our knowledge to our activity...The depth of mental color, the degree of diagrammatic fiction thus inevitably introduced into our picture of nature may be variously estimated. The variety of our estimates no longer places [rationalists and empiricists] in mutually opposed camps. *Faith and Speclation*, 18-19.

36. Faith and Speculation, 22.

37. Here we see a connection to William James's appeal for standards of empiricism that are appropriate to the object of inquiry. See *The Varieties of Religious Experience*.

38. *Faith and Speculation*, 31.

39. Ibid., 32.

40. Ibid., 97.

41. I have suggested in another essay that since Farrer explicitly says that "mind is a social reality," there ought to be social criteria for judging a person's experience of divine action. This might include an examination of the rich network of the believing community's assertions, and their logical relations both to one another and to the practices which constitute community life. In other words, some kind of speech-act

analysis could be applicable here.

42. Faith *and Speculation*, 123ff.
43. Ibid., 4.
44. Hilary Putnam, *Reason, Truth and History*, 136-7.
45. Farrer, *A Science of God?*, 126.

Chapter 8

Experience and Agency

Steven M. Duncan

In his book *The View from Nowhere*,[1] Thomas Nagel contrasts the subjective and objective perspectives on reality. The subjective viewpoint, identifiable with my particular perspective on the world, constitutes life as it is lived and appreciated from inside; it is what makes introspection and selfhood possible. The objective viewpoint, however, abstracts from one's own perspective, and indeed from all individual perspectives; it attempts to constitute itself as the view from nowhere, encompassing all reality from the God's-eye point of view. In our time, the objective point of view is most closely identified with the scientific perspective on reality.

Nagel's thesis is twofold. On the one hand, most of the classic philosophical problems such as the mind/body problem, the nature of the self, personal identity, the nature of knowledge, etc. can be explained by showing how they arise from the clash of these two perspectives, which, as it turns out, cannot be made to fit comfortably together. On the other hand, neither perspective is dispensable. While Nagel is concerned not to sell the objective point of view short, he insists that there are some features of reality which can be appreciated only from the subjective point of view.

One such feature is consciousness itself. Reiterating a position which he first articulated in his essay "What is it Like to be a Bat?",[2] Nagel argues that consciousness is irreducibly subjective and hence must forever lie beyond the grasp of science because the external, scientific point of view is completely committed to the objective "view from nowhere." Thus, behaviorists, eliminative materialists, and artificial intelligence notwithstanding, there are limits to what we can understand about the mind from the objective point of view.

When it comes to our experience of agency, one might suppose that Nagel would be equally sympathetic to the defender of free will. However, this is not the case; Nagel is all too ready to dismiss our subjective awareness of our own freedom as an illusion inevitably to be supplanted by an objective account of human action which integrates it without remainder into the causal order of nature. While making passing references to the agency theory and even to Austin Farrer's work as representative of that theory, he ultimately rejects it as incapable of explaining human action:

> If autonomy requires that the central element of choice be explained in a way that does not take us outside the point of view of the agent...then intentional explanation must simply come to an end when all available reasons have been given, and nothing else can take over where they leave off. But this seems to mean that an autonomous intentional explanation cannot explain precisely what it is supposed to explain, namely why I did what I did rather than the alternative that was causally open to me. It says I did it for certain reasons, but does not explain why I didn't decide not to do it for other reasons. It may render the action subjectively intelligible, but it does not explain why this rather than another equally possible and comparably intelligible action was done. This seems to be something for which there is no explanation, either intentional or causal.[3]

Thus, since free will is ultimately inexplicable, Nagel concludes that it must be impossible, an illusion produced by confusing the objective view from nowhere as it functions in action with the perspective of a Kantian noumenal self existing behind and beyond human experience and in complete independence of the causal order.[4]

The most natural response to this objection is to say that the demand for an explanation of free action is itself an illegitimate one. For if my action is free, there can be no further account of its occurrence beyond the fact that I chose to do it; to demand anything further would be to demand what amounts to an efficient cause prior to and external to one's choosing which determines what one's choice will be, which is in effect to demand that the action be shown to not be a free one after all. Thus, one might be inclined to reject Nagel's demand as unreasonable; still, one does not have to accept Nagel's position to be strongly inclined to suppose that if free will is as I describe it, then no sense can be made of the notion. If human action can be explained, then it is caused and very likely determined, and if it is inexplicable, then it is unintelligible and at best random. It seems we go wrong no matter which alternative we take.

This impasse is familiar to all students of the metaphysical problem of free will. Is there any way beyond it? I want to suggest that there is. Just as defenders of evolution routinely distinguish between the fact of evolution (for which there seems to be as much evidence as anyone would like) and evolutionary theory (which remains incomplete and controversial), and just as Nagel appeals to experience to establish that there is an inner life even though this may upset the materialist's theoretical apple cart,[5] so too the defender of free will needs to argue in the strongest possible terms that agency, however opaque it may be and remain to theory, is a fact that cannot be got around. This is what I propose to do in the present essay.

First, we need to try to isolate what it is about the free will problem that makes it so troublesome; I shall attempt to do this by reference to Farrer's notion of *natural mystery*.[6] Second, it needs to be shown that the free will problem really is a problem, not just an illusion, and that intentional or personalistic explanation is not so much an explanation as a description of an ineliminable feature of action as understood from the subjective point of view. In attempting to establish this I shall briefly consider the role of agency in deliberation. Thirdly, having established the putative fact of agency, I go on to argue that a) even though the possibility of illusion cannot be altogether eliminated, there is no strong reason for supposing that our experience of agency is an illusion, and b) that, since this is anomalous on the deterministic point of view, the experience of agency must be regarded as positive evidence for free will and against deterministic accounts of human action. In all of this, my debt to Farrer's *Freedom of the Will* will be obvious, even if I do not stop to acknowledge his influence at every point.

Free Will and Mystery

As I understand it, Farrer's account of natural mystery is as follows. What we call metaphysical problems are really mysteries, which arise out of experience but which involve the apprehension of unique realities which demand to be understood in their own terms and not in terms of anything else. The locus of a mystery is a real, metaphysical relation, either within a single individual (e.g., the relation between mind and body) or between two or more individuals (e.g., the relation between subject and object in the knowing act), which is revealed directly in experience and is not reducible either to a logical or a causal relation. Our awareness of these mysteries is pre-theoretical; indeed they are the realities which provide the starting points for philosophical reflection. At the same time, the intellectual difficulty inherent in a mystery is not one of explanation but rather of description. Since each mystery is unique, it can at best be analogically described by reference to other relations which it more or less resembles. No harm results so long as those analogies are taken seriously but not literally; however, there is a persistent tendency on the part of philosophers to take their chosen analogies as literal descriptions and this generates interminable puzzles and difficulties within the discipline.

How can we construe free will as a natural mystery? Perhaps the following will suffice. The locus of the free will problem is the relation between the grounds of action on the one hand and the actions themselves on the other. If there is to be free will, two conditions must be met: first, our actions need to be intelligibly connected to our motives and characters, else they will not be our acts. This means that our actions must have grounds. Secondly, these grounds must not give rise to our actions with logical or causal necessity, else they will not be free. There can be no doubt, then, that the relation between action and grounds for action on the hypothesis of free will not be quite the same as any other sort of relation upon which we might wish to model it. But the only relations of ground to consequent available to us as philosophers are those of premiss to conclusion and cause to effect. From the very nature of the case, then, these can at best provide analogies to the unique relation of ground to consequent in instances of free action; nevertheless, we are constrained to use them even as we attempt to remain cognizant of their limitations.

On this interpretation of the free will problem, free will is what Farrer called a natural mystery, and the intellectual difficulty about free will arises from the unique character of the relation of the ground to consequent in free action. To what extent is this account credible?

There is much in our everyday talk and experience to support this account of the nature of the free will problem. For example, the very notion of grounding in this context is itself ambiguous, for it can refer either to the epistemic relation of justification between beliefs or to the causal relation of "bringing about" between events, both of which are indispensable aspects of the intelligibility of an act. If I ask, "Why did you do that?", I may be asking what your motive was, or for a reason justifying your action, or both; and there may be either a single answer to both questions or two quite independent answers, depending on the circumstances. When we speak of the grounds of action, then, we are speaking about simply whatever it is that contributes to the intelligibility of action, and this covers things belonging to different categories.[7] This suggests that when we use the word "grounds" in this context, we are using it by analogy and not to refer to a logical or causal relation between the grounds of action and actions themselves.

Nor does experience support the claim that our actions have causes, at least if the usual candidates, e.g., desires, passions, reasons, etc. are under consideration. We can see this even in the simple, straightforward case of desire. In the case of animals, we may suppose that desires are causes in the same way that the motion of one billiard ball is the cause of the motion of another billiard ball, i.e., by the exercise of direct, immediate influence of the one upon the other. An animal's felt tendency toward some behavior or other is immediately followed up by an endeavor to enact it, unless this is somehow prevented. It is the awareness that makes possible the objectification of our desires and other motives, which creates the psychic distance between myself and my desires necessary to hold them in check (at least for the moment) and to make them potential objects of choice. But in that case, desire as a ground for my action is at best analogous to the standard case of causation because it lacks the immediacy and necessity we associate with the relation between cause and effect.[8] One both feels the desire for, e.g., a Popsicle, and is aware that one has that desire. It is this that makes selfhood and deliberation possible, and that is the basis for what Nagel calls autonomy, the objectification of our desires and other motives, which creates psychic distance between my self and my desires, mediating them, at least for the moment (as when, e.g., one loans money to a friend or relative on a promise of repayment even though one knows full well on the basis of past experience that it will not be repaid). But in that case, desire as a ground for my action is at best analogous to the standard case of causation.

Desires and other motives differ from standard instances of causation in another way as well. In cases of causation involving multiple, simultaneously competing elements all of the same order, we expect that causal influence will be proportional to the degree of motive force ("causal power") exerted by each element; to put it more simply, we anticipate that a stronger force will typically beat a weaker force. Where desires et al. are concerned, motive force seems to be equivalent to felt strength or "psychic pull," i.e., the degree to which and the urgency with which an impulse imposes upon my attention. But we do not always act on our strongest desire construed in this way, and in those cases in which we exert our willpower to deny a particularly urgent or recurrent desire (e.g., for cigarettes) we typically feel deserving of praise for our fortitude. What we suppose to be the case where causality is concerned we do not expect in the case of desires and other motives for action, because it is not what we observe invariably to be the case. So, once again, the relation between ground and action in this case appears to be at best analogous to causation.

If we turn to the case of reasons for action construed as motives for action, we find ourselves even more perplexed. Of course, many philosophers deny that reasons have any motive force at all; but even if they do, we need to note that their motive force does not necessarily correlate with their degree of epistemic value in the circumstances. For, just as we do not always act on our strongest desires, neither do we always act on the strongest reasons, or even what we perceive to be the strongest reasons, under the circumstances. There are some occasions upon which we act against our better judgment; we can recognize the force of a reason or set of reasons without thereby automatically acting as those reasons dictate. So if reasons are causes, they are so in some fashion independent of their being reasons and this makes the appeal to reasons in the explanation of action problematic to say the least.[9]

The determinist can sidestep considerations of the foregoing type by proposing that the true causes of our actions, whether psychic, behavioral, genetic, or residing in our brain states, operate largely below the level of consciousness. On this sort of view, consciousness (if admitted at all) is viewed as at best an epiphenomenon, at worst an irrelevancy with vanishingly little to teach us about ourselves. Such a view makes us largely opaque to ourselves, converting nearly all that we recognize as self-knowledge into a sort of crepuscular rationalization. Such a view may be true, but we ought not accept it without compelling evidence. To adopt such a strategy, then, involves a significant shift in the burden of proof in the free will debate.

The Experience of Agency

Granted that our experience of the relation between the grounds of our actions and the actions themselves does not comport very well with the determinist's causal model of that relation, is there any positive evidence for free will to be garnered from experience? I believe that we can provide such evidence if we can show that there is an awareness of our agency that is part and parcel of the subjective point of view on action, i.e., action as we experience it when we are engaged in doing it, and that this agency is both necessary to and ineliminable from that point of view. I shall try to illustrate awareness of agency by reference to a particular case of action, i.e., deliberation, a fundamental preliminary to many instances of overt action.

In order to illustrate what I mean by agency, consider an account of deliberation from which this feature is conspicuously absent:

> When in the mind of man, appetites, and aversions, hopes, and fears, concerning one and the same thing, arise alternatively; and divers good and evil consequences of the doing, or omitting the thing propounded, come successively into our thoughts; so that sometimes we have an appetite to it; sometimes a aversion from it; sometimes hope to be able to do it, sometimes despair, or fear to attempt it; the whole sum of desires, aver-

sions, hopes, and fears, continued till the thing be either done, or thought impossible, is what we call deliberation.[10]

Thomas Hobbes goes on to avow that, on his account of deliberation, animals also deliberate, since they undergo the same sort of alternation in desire and aversion. He describes the will as merely the last appetite adhering to the action, which likewise must be attributed to the beasts.

What is remarkable about this account of deliberation is that it converts deliberation from something we do into something which happens to us. On the Hobbesian view, deliberation consists in my awareness of an alternating series of desires, aversions, and passions directed on a particular end. With regard to this alternating series I am at best a passive observer, at worst merely carried from pillar to post as each new impulse washes over me. These impulses he describes as contending among themselves for the right to produce my action; eventually, one of them wins out and becomes the last in the series, the one which attaches itself to my action and causes it to occur. Hobbes calls this will, since it is the psychological event which immediately precedes and gives rise to my action. But "will" here carries no implication of effort or direction on my part; in principle, at least, on Hobbes's view I ought to be able to sit back and wait to find out what I will decide and in consequence what I will do. I simply need to wait until the morass of conflicting impulses resolves itself and then observe what I find myself doing next.

Obviously, this is nothing like deliberation as I experience it from the inside. In the first place, deliberation is something that I undertake to do, not simply something that I happen to find myself doing; at any rate, I cannot recall ever having found myself deliberating in the way that I might find myself absentmindedly humming a popular melody. Secondly, far from being an automatic process which I could in principle simply observe myself undergoing, deliberation requires my sustained attention and direction. It continues only so long as I engage in it; if I sit back passively and wait for it to continue on its own, I cease to deliberate altogether.

Deliberation, in the third place, involves autonomy; it is no mere registering of the relative subjective weight of one's desires and aversions. Instead, it involves rational judgment; one notes the subjective weight of one's impulses but contrasts this with their objective weight in the circumstances. It is only because of this that the moral struggle is even possible. Fourthly and finally, there is nothing automatic about the transition from deliberation to overt action, no mere attachment of the last impulse directly to the action itself; deliberation and choice are distinct. I do not always do as deliberation suggests or requires that I act. I can take the counsel of judgment and yet act against that judgement and sometimes do, especially when the outcome of deliberation is different from what I anticipate it will be.

It is this awareness of myself as initiating, sustaining, and directing the course of deliberation which I identify with the experience of agency. It constitutes the attitude of directive engagement present in deliberation and in conscious action generally, and it makes all the difference, subjectively speaking, between what I do on the one hand and what merely happens to me on the other. I do not believe that this awareness can be grasped from or explained by the objective point of view. It is, however, endemic to the subjective point of view which, in turn, is a necessary condition for action since, as we have seen, if one passively waits to see what one will do, in most cases one will do nothing at all.

The foregoing helps explain why, as Farrer points out,[11] I cannot in the moment of action regard the act that I am contemplating as somehow prefigured in its causes. For action presupposes agency, and agency involves both my making an endeavor and (in all but the simplest cases) directing it towards its end. In the case of deliberation, for example, I must endeavor to sort out my conflicting motivations and direct my thoughts toward making a decision; in so doing, I cannot but act as though what I was doing was under my control or somehow "up to me"–and this regardless of whether I am a determinist or not.

The point of all this is that free will is a practical presupposition of the subjective point of view on action, which in turn is indispensable for action itself. Thus, regardless of my theoretical convictions, I cannot act without adopting a stance of which commitment to free will is an integral part. I may not believe in free will, but I must act as though I did in order to act at all. In my role as agent, I am (not surprisingly) committed to my own agency, and thus to contracausal freedom. The question is whether or not this practical fact has any theoretical significance.

The Presumption of Freedom

At first glance, one might suppose that it does not. After all, there is no logical contradiction in admitting that the subjective point of view on action presupposes free will while maintaining the truth of determinism. And the question at issue here is the truth of free will, not the phenomenlogy of action.

More importantly, however, there are considerations suggesting that the foregoing analysis is quite irrelevant to the question between free will and determinism. After all, someone acting under the aegis of a posthypnotic suggestion or a subconscious urge likely has the experience of agency, even though as a matter of fact what he or she does is causally pre-ordained and quite out of his or her control. Thus, no matter how seemingly pervasive and inseparable the experience of agency is from the subjective point of view on action, the fact remains that it is sometimes, and could perhaps always be, an illusion.

This possibility cannot be altogether discounted; still, it is hardly credible that it should turn out to be true. For, in the first place, the illusion will not go away; if I have shown anything, the assumption of free will is practically indispensable for action. Hence, it is not like the typical theoretical mistake, which, once exposed, can be discarded. If free will is an illusion, it is an illusion we are foredoomed to live, regardless of our philosophy. It seems strange that this should be the case if determinism is true.

One might question the significance of this, however. After all, where optical illusions are concerned, one's knowledge about the manner in which one is being imposed on does not necessarily alter the perceptual content; one arrow will continue to look longer than the other even after one has been persuaded by the ruler that despite appearances they are the same length. Perhaps, but the analogy does not quite go through. Optical illusions are parasitic on normal visual habits which lead us aright in most cases, and which are evoked only under highly unusual and for the most part artificial circumstances. But what the determinist is claiming is that our experience of ourselves as acting persons is somehow fundamentally illusory or delusive. Determinism as a hypothesis is more like Berkeley's account of perception than the more standard view which affirms the existence of the external world while admitting the possibility of illusion. And, like Berkeley's idealism, determinism may turn out to be true, though no doubt most of us would be frankly astounded if it did.

To put it another way, the simplest, most natural and straightforward explanation of something's appearing to be such-and-such is that it is such-and-such. This is not irrefutable proof, but it does create an initial presumption in favor of that most natural hypothesis. Thus, the fact that our ineluctable experience of ourselves in the context of action is precisely what we would expect it to be if we had free will, and not at all what we would expect it to be if determinism is true, is surely some reason for thinking that we have free will, and that determinism is false. By the same token, our experience of ourselves as agents is from the determinist point of view anomalous, and there is no ready explanation why this should be the case. For example, it cannot be explained, as Nagel proposes, simply as a misconstrual of the objective point of view of autonomy, since as I have shown agency is an ineliminable element of the subjective point of view on action.

Ironically, Farrer has suggested a way in which the determinist can square his hypothesis with the apparent facts. In *Freedom of the Will*,[12] he sketches a deterministic account of phenomenal liberty, which goes briefly as follows. Although my actions are determined, I cannot regard them as such prior to making a decision, because until that time the causal factors necessary to produce my act are not in place and my deliberative thought is a necessary link in the causal chain which produces my act. The purpose of deliberative thought is to evoke my subjective feelings about the various alternatives I consider, and I cannot evoke these feelings while viewing my responses clinically. The relation between alternatives considered and subjective response has to be direct; to intervene in the process by holding one's affective nature at a distance interrupts that process and prevents the occurrence of evocation, and hence of action itself. Thus, the attitude of calculation and prediction, of the clinical observer has to be left behind in the context of action, in order that the causal factors which determine behavior may be allowed to work.

Such an hypothesis may have the virtue of making determinism consistent with the fact of agency, but this does not by itself overcome the presumption in favor of free will. For there is no necessity, either theoretical or pragmatic, in the facts it postulates. The Hobbesian account of deliberation, however false, is not impossible. There is no reason in the nature of the case why external or internal causes ought not compel subjective reactions regardless of the attitude we adopt toward the process evoking them. Yet precisely what needs explaining is the apparent necessity of agency for action, which follows straight away on the assumption of free will.

Objections and Replies

If the foregoing is correct, there is no hope of reducing or eliminating the subjective point of view on action in favor of an objective point of view. Instead, human action, like consciousness itself, must always lie beyond the grasp of "the view from nowhere." Free will seems to leave our view of the world eternally bifurcated and one wants to ask whether anything untoward follows from this. For my part, I cannot see that it does.

That the world around us is largely deterministic is not a problem for the proponent of free will, since only if the world is largely regular is free will even possible. A structureless world in which anything could and did happen would make knowledge of the consequences of our actions impossible and hence much diminish the scope of free choice. The apparent uniqueness of free will in an otherwise deterministic world is a scandal and an anomaly crying out for an explanation only from the deterministic point of view; on the supposition that there is free will, it is what one would naturally expect.

But what of the actions of others? A determinist might contend that on this sort of reasoning, the same ought to hold of the actions of others, since unless human action is predictable the value of free will would be much diminished. But, of course, if human actions are predictable, then it is likely that human actions have causes and that there is no free will. So if a basic condition for free will is met in the case of human action, it appears to undermine that very possibility.

Fortunately, Farrer (among others) has shown how the predictability of human actions is in fact consistent with the freedom of the will. Since we ourselves are agents it is possible for us to interpret and understand the actions of others by reference to our own agency. All that is required for this sort of interpretation to be possible is that other agents be connatural to me, i.e., have roughly the same motivational structure as myself and hence a standard set of human responses to situations. Given this, plus imagination sufficient to conceive oneself exercising agency in someone else's situation, we can understand and predict the behavior of others without reliance on causes. Indeed, as Farrer points out, some of the predictions we make are inconsistent with the suggestion that we make such predictions from causes; e.g., when we predict that such-and-such a party guest will entertain us on account of his witty and unpredictable behavior.[13]

This does not exclude the possibility that we may sometimes be wrong about or mystified by what we ourselves or what others do, or even that there is no legitimate role for causal explanation in explaining some human actions. There is nothing to prevent a happy bridegroom from going out and hanging himself on his wedding day, except that neither he nor we can see any reason why he should. But if he does so, then it is typically then (and only then) that some sort of causal explanation seems required: the psychologist may speculate that he acted under the aegis of a sudden, irresistible impulse and the police that he was murdered.

It seems, then, that there is no significant cost, let alone necessity, in adopting the external or objective view with regard to human action whether in our own case or in that of others, at least in everyday circumstances. More than that, there seems nothing to be gained from doing so, no pressing theoretical demand requiring us to transcend our ordinary way of understanding human action. While free will (like consciousness itself) may appear to be extremely mysterious because it resists of its very nature explanation in causal terms, we may well at this point be able to rest content with that rather than deny what seems to be an obvious fact of experience.

What would overcome the presumption in favor of free will?

Nothing less, I think, than the establishment of a detailed and well-confirmed deterministic account of human action. If such a theory existed and the evidence for it was extremely persuasive, then to rest with experience would not be reasonable. But to the best of my knowledge no such theory has been concocted, nor am I aware of any likely candidates currently in the field. Of those which have been suggested, none is detailed enough or well-confirmed enough to count as a genuine threat to our ordinary conception of ourselves. At best we get general outlines of theories, used primarily to postdict our actions from the objective point of view. With regard to such views, we can point to numerous critiques (Farrer's among them) to which it seems unnecessary, on this occasion at least, to add further. So, for the moment, our experience of agency seems sufficient to ground a reasonable presumption in favor of the freedom of the will.

Notes

1. Thomas Nagel, *The View from Nowhere* (New York: Oxford University Press, 1986).
2. Reprinted in Thomas Nagel, *Mortal Questions* (New York: Cambridge University Press, 1979), 165-180.
3. Nagel, *The View from Nowhere*, 116-117.
4. Nagel, *The View from Nowhere*, 117-118.
5. According to the materialist, the mind is the brain and consciousness a physical process consisting only of brain states, which in turn possess only physical properties. However, consciousness as experienced, which consists of a wide variety of subjective internal states, is notoriously difficult to account for on materialist principles. As a result, materialists tend to discount or attempt to evade our direct experience of ourselves as conscious beings in their attempts to "explain," e.g., pain states in "scientific" terms. Nagel, by focusing our attention on the reality of our subjective mental lives, reminds us that the fundamental problem for materialist theories of mind remains unsolved.
6. Austin Farrer, *The Glass of Vision*, (Westminster: Dacre Press, 1948), 68-80.
7. For example, the humor in Willy Sutton's answer to the question why he robbed banks ("Because that's where the money is!") trades on the ambiguity inherent in the notion of the grounds of action. Sutton answers by referring to his motives, but this is both obvious and irrelevant, since the question clearly requires an answer in terms of justification or excuse.
8. In making these points, I am putting myself in opposition to the

popular account of intentional descriptions of human action as "folk psychology," i.e. as a crude, pre-scientific theory which postulates inner events as the causes of human behavior, competes on all fours with modern, scientific theories of human behavior and is easily blown away when confronted with the results of modern psychological research. Inner events are experienced, not postulated, and they are experienced not as causes, but as grounds, "inclining without necessitating" what we do.

9. Nagel, *The View from Nowhere*, 113-6.

10. Thomas Hobbes, *Leviathan* (Hammondsworth: Pelican Books, 1965), 127.

11. Austin Farrer, *The Freedom of the Will* (New York: Charles Scribner's Sons, 1958), 123-4.

12. Farrer, *The Freedom of the Will*, 128-129.

13. Farrer, *The Freedom of the Will*, 166.

14. I wish to thank Todd Currier, George Goodall, Rich Kang, Richard Kopczynski, Shawn Mintek, and Elizabeth Unger for many useful comments on an earlier draft of this paper.

Section III:
Freedom and Evil

Chapter 9

Evil, Human Freedom, and Divine Grace

Thomas F. Tracy

Theology and the Problem of Evil

The problem of evil constitutes perhaps the most widely felt and deeply troubling challenge to faith in the goodness and power of God. We live in a world that, for all its wonders and satisfactions, is also a place of horrifying miseries. Perhaps you and I will have the good fortune to be spared most of the worst that can befall human beings. But the cost of an open and empathetic heart is that one shares in the world's griefs, and there is in fact more grief in the world than any human heart can bear.

How can it be that this world exists by the will and under the watchful care of an all-powerful and perfectly good Creator? This is not merely a "philosopher's question," raised in the pleasant isolation of a classroom and pursued for the aesthetic satisfaction of generating a clever solution. It arises at the sickbed, in the disturbing presence of the ragged poor in the streets, in anguish over our incessant preparation for war, and at innumerable other points in our lives. Nor is the problem exclusively or primarily one raised by unsympathetic outsiders, the cultured despisers of the theistic faiths. Rather, it is first and foremost a matter internal to faith in God. If trust in God's benevolence and power is to be more than a pastel sentiment disconnected from our actual experience of the world, it must come to terms with the pervasive reality of undeserved suffering and be deepened by living with the tensions this engenders.

Although congregations gathered in church or synagogue do not often explicitly discuss "the problem of evil," the issue is deeply embedded in the theistic traditions, as the Book of Job makes abundantly clear. Job may be renowned for the patience of his faith, but he speaks with striking boldness in questioning God's justice.

> The poor, like herds of cattle,
>   wander across the plains,
> searching all day for food,
>   picking up scraps for their children.
> Naked, without a refuge,
>   they shiver in the bitter cold.
> When it rains, they are drenched to the bone;
>   they huddle together in caves.
> They carry grain for the wicked
>   and break their backs for the rich.
> They press olives and starve,
>   crush grapes and go thirsty.
> In the city the dying groan
>   and the wounded cry out for help;
>   but God sees nothing wrong.[1]

This is one of several passages that ends with an accusation about God's indifference to suffering. Job is caught between the conventional theology of retribution, reflected in the insistence of his "comforters" that he must somehow deserve his misfortune, and his experience of personal calamity out of all proportion to his misdeeds. Job tenaciously insists upon what he now knows in his own person and can see in the world around him–that the innocent suffer terribly. And from the vantage point of this hard-won knowledge, he decries what he may previously (as a wealthy and privileged man) have been hesitant to acknowledge–that injustice flourishes in the world and that the wicked grow powerful and arrogant in their evildoing. The world God has made is not organized as a system of retributive justice, and Job pours the passion of both his faith and his suffering into his questions about God's relation to evil.

The problem of evil is also raised, of course, as a challenge to belief in God by those who stand outside the theistic faiths. Here the skeptic can go on the offensive: beyond arguing (negatively) that there is insufficient evidence that God exists, he can contend (positively) that the quantity or distribution of evil in the world provides good reason to think that God cannot or does not exist. David Hume (echoing the Greek philosopher Epicurus) provides the classical formulation of this challenge:

> Is (God) willing to prevent evil, but not able? Then he is impotent. Is he able, but not willing? Then he is malevolent. Is he both able and willing?

Whence then is evil?[2]

This anti-theistic argument typically takes two more specific forms. First, one might argue that the existence of evil is incompatible with the affirmation that God is all-powerful and perfectly good. This is a very strong claim, viz., that if you think clearly about what is entailed by omnipotence and perfect goodness you will see that these attributes are logically inconsistent with creating a world that contains the evils we find around us. If that is so, then the believer's claims about God cannot be true. This is the logical form of the problem of evil. Second, one might argue that even if what theists say about God and evil is logically consistent, the presence of evil (or of this quantity or distribution of evil) gives us sufficient reason to believe that there is no God of the sort the theist affirms; although the theist's claims could be true, the evidence before us warrants the conclusion that they are in fact false. This is the evidential form of the problem of evil.

Modern philosophy of religion has generated a tremendous outpouring of reflection on these two forms of argument about God and evil. The focus of most of this activity has been on challenges posed by the skeptical "outsider" (like David Hume) rather than on difficulties faced by the troubled "insider" (like Job). Recent philosophical treatments of the problem of evil have contributed greatly to our ability to approach these issues with clarity and precision, and they have shown that powerful replies can be developed to anti-theistic arguments that had gained wide currency and considerable authority. But by turning toward the anti-theistic critic as its primary conversation partner, the philosophical discussion has tended to abstract the problem of evil from its religious and theological context. The resulting debate, while sometimes exquisitely clever, is often of dubious relevance to the religious traditions which spawned the problem in the first place.

For example, in answering those who claim that theistic beliefs about God and evil are logically inconsistent, you need only show that there is at least one set of circumstances (however peculiar it may be) under which it is morally acceptable for an omnipotent and perfectly good being to permit evil in the world.[3] When the philosophical discussion focuses strictly on this logical problem, the proposals it generates can be cut loose from worries about their truth or plausibility, much less their theological soundness. But while a response of this kind may suffice in answering a critic who has no stake in one of the theistic traditions, it will not be nearly enough for someone who is grappling with the problem as it arises within her tradition. The believer seeks an account of God's relation to evil that a) is coherent with a set of actual convictions about God's character and purposes and b) is offered as at least a candidate for being true.

Much remains to be done, therefore, in bringing the philosophical discussion back into fruitful relation to the characteristic concerns of the theological traditions within which the problem of evil initially arises. I want to make a modest effort in that direction here. I will look specifically at appeals to human free will in explaining the presence of evil in the world, noting some respects in which such arguments are morally and theologically problematic and suggesting modifications that hold promise of producing a theologically richer result.

The Free Will Reply

One familiar response to the problem of evil is to argue that much of the misery that afflicts human beings is the result of wrong human choices. Rather than turning indignantly toward God with the question, "How could you create such a world?," we direct this question back to the immediate makers of these evils–ourselves. Any developed version of this appeal to human freedom will need to include three key elements. First, it must be argued that if God creates free finite agents, then God must permit or produce certain evils. Second, it must be argued that free will is good in itself and/or is a necessary condition for realizing some intrinsic good. Third, it must be argued that the good that is achieved in or through human freedom is worth having even at the cost of the evils that actually occur. I want to make a few comments on all three of these elements in the free will reply; in each case, there are considerations that free will arguments typically overlook and which should be taken into account if the philosophical discussion of evil is to be theologically relevant.

Turning to the first element, the fundamental move in any free will reply is to turn aside the charge that God is the cause of evil by assigning immediate responsibility to the free actions of human beings; the strategy, in effect, is to vindicate God by convicting humanity. If this move is to be plausible, however, two important qualifications must be made.

First, we must make a distinction between moral evils and natural misfortune, or "natural evil" as it has come to be called. The appeal to free will obviously is helpful in dealing with the morally wrong actions of created agents, the awful history of human cruelty, selfishness, hatred, injustice, and so on. But it is less clearly relevant to the suffering that befalls us simply by virtue of being vulnerable creatures who must take our chances in an environment that presents many dangers to us. It must be granted that many of the natural evils we suffer reflect the interaction of our choices with the natural order; we build our cities on fault lines, we live in ways that increase our risk of this or that disease, and so on. At least sometimes, however, there is no wrongdoing involved in these actions, no recklessness or negligence or culpable ignorance. Generally speaking, we will be blameless in those cases in which we could not be expected to know in advance what the natural consequences of our actions would be.

Natural misfortunes of this sort cannot be ascribed to human moral failure unless we tell some further story about how they came about. Some theologians have held that natural suffering is inflicted on humanity as punishment for a primordial misuse of our freedom. Alvin Plantinga extends his elegant version of the free will defense to natural evils by supposing that sickness, famine, natural disasters, and so on, are the work of nonhuman free creatures, viz., fallen angels.[4] Apart from these or similar proposals, however, free will arguments are restricted in relevance to moral evils, though it is possible to argue quite powerfully that natural suffering (or the causal possibility of such suffering) is a necessary condition for moral life.

Second, given the conviction that God alone is the source of all finite things, it must be acknowledged that God bears the ultimate responsibility for there being free creatures who do evil. Even if we were fully successful in arguing that God cannot create free beings without permitting moral evil, we would still face the objections that a) it is not consistent with divine goodness for God knowingly to bring such beings into existence and b) it is not consistent with divine omniscience for God unwittingly to do so. These challenges hinge in part on subtle questions about divine goodness and knowledge, but the underlying point is clear enough: given the bloody history of the human race, it may look as though God has made a monster. This points to the importance of addressing the third (and most often neglected) element in free will replies, and I will turn to it below in the section, *Freedom and the Good*.

Even with these qualifications, free will arguments shift a great deal of the immediate responsibility for evil from God to human beings. Now, this division of responsibility requires that a particular account be given of the conditions for moral responsibility and the nature of human freedom. We will, on this account, be morally responsible only for those actions that we perform freely, and we will perform freely only those actions that we undertake without being causally determined to do so by the circumstances of action (i.e., by the laws of nature, the causal history of the universe, and the actions of any other agent, created or divine).[5]

This clearly is a very strong conception of freedom. It goes by various names among philosophers; I will refer to it here as "incompatibilist" freedom. It insists that freedom and determinism are not compatible; a free act will have necessary conditions in the events that precede it, but these will not constitute causally sufficient conditions. On this account, for example, when I raise my arm to vote at the town meeting, my action will have various biological, psychological, and social necessary conditions, but these do not causally necessitate my voting as I do.

This view stands in contrast to compatibilism, which holds that my action may (and on some views must) be causally determined; simply put, a free action just is one that is determined in the right way (e.g., by my desires and beliefs rather than by external coercion or constraint).[6] If my desires and beliefs are themselves determined by antecedent conditions, then an unbroken causal chain will be preserved. There are sophisticated versions of compatibilism, and many philosophers subscribe to some form of it. But whatever its merits, this position cannot serve the purposes of the free will reply to the problem of evil. For if our free actions can simultaneously be determined yet free, then it certainly appears that God could create free creatures but guarantee that they always do what is morally right. Appeal to human freedom, therefore, will be helpful in explaining why God permits evil in the world only if we understand freedom in the strong, incompatibilist sense.

Given this notion of incompatibilist freedom, we can then explain the ways in which the decisions of free creatures may limit God's control over (and therefore God's direct responsibility for) the balance of moral good and evil in the world. *Ex hypothesi*, it will be true of each of my evil free actions that I could have chosen to do otherwise under these causal conditions. So the responsibility for this moral evil is mine; God could not have left me free in a world with this causal history and guaranteed that I would do what is right.

It might be objected that God could have prevented this evil by not allowing these circumstances to occur or by not having brought me, as opposed to some other (morally better) finite person, into existence. The answer one gives to this objection will depend upon whether one thinks that God's omniscience can include knowledge of what each possible free creature would freely choose to do in each circumstance in which it might be placed. If God has this robust type of fore-knowledge, then it looks as though God can "survey" all the possible sets of free creatures and choose a set that includes only those who will always freely make morally right choices.

It will be easier to respond to the problem of evil if you conclude that God cannot have this kind of fore-knowledge. One might conclude, for example, there is no truth of the matter about what merely possible persons (who never actually exist) would freely choose to do (in circumstances that never occur).[7] In that case, even an omniscient being would not be in a position to know which possible world will, if actualized, turn out to be one in which free persons always do what is right.

If there are such truths for God to know, however, it may nonetheless be that *what* God knows is that there is no set of possible persons whose free choices would produce a better overall balance of moral good and moral evil than that found in the actual world.[8] This is not to say that this is the best of all possible worlds; morally preferable worlds are logically possible. But it is to say that this world (among those containing free creatures) may be as good a world as God can bring about, given God's knowledge of what every possible free creature would do if given the chance. In that case, God will not be able to improve the world by changing the circumstances of action or by switching agents. Rather, God must choose between a) creating a world in which there are free agents who are at least as wicked as we are or b) simply not creating free finite agents at all.

There is a tendency in presentations of the free will reply to focus on these questions about God's knowledge and power, and to leave the discussion of human freedom relatively undeveloped. The picture of free action at work here, however, is strikingly spare and abstract. All we have said so far is that the causal conditions under which a free choice is made do not determine the agent to act as she does. No attention has been given to the ways in which these conditions structure the agent's options and orient her choice. This positive relation of circumstance and action is not denied, of course, but neither is it examined for its bearing on human evil doing.

I want to argue that if we pay attention not only to the negative condition for freedom (i.e., causal non-determination) but also to its positive conditions (i.e., the various factors that make a causal or motivational contribution to action), then our account of human responsibility for evil must be qualified in certain ways and made more nuanced. The free will reply, as a result, becomes both more difficult and more interesting theologically.

Freedom in Context

If we deny that our free actions are determined by the circumstances within which they are initiated, we must immediately acknowledge that those circumstances limit our options and orient our choices. I do not possess a neutral power of choice ranging over an entirely open array of alternatives. I undertake each of my intentional actions in light of a complex web of perceptions and beliefs, memories and expectations, appetites and aversions, emotions and feelings, and so on. These action-guiding states of mind (which I will call "motivational states") reflect both my personal history and the relation I bear to my present physical and social environment. They are not entirely of my own making, nor are they all subject to direct intentional control or modification.

To be sure, I can bring about intentionally and directly (i.e., as a basic action) a great variety of mental states, e.g., I can call to mind scenes from childhood, say, when I think doing so would be helpful in deciding how to discipline my own child on some occasion. And I can bring about intentionally but indirectly (i.e., by using some means to my end) many additional mental states, e.g., I can try to remember more about my childhood by looking through an old photo album. Nonetheless, our free actions will always presuppose and work with a rich background of motivational states that we do not generate intentionally, but which are brought about in us through the operation of our cognitive, appetitive, and affective capacities. I will call these "elicited" motivational states.[9]

Our freedom, then, operates on the basis of motivational states that initially are elicited in us rather than enacted intentionally by us.[10] I certainly do not choose, for example, to be a member of the animal species homo sapiens and therefore a) to have the particular powers of sensation and action that this biological structure establishes and b) to be motivated by the agenda of needs, drives, and aversions that bodily life generates. The free human "will" (i.e., the person as intentional agent) is structured by the necessities of the body, and our agency is exercised by putting relatively fixed powers of bodily action to work in creatively addressing a prescribed, if flexible, array of interests.[11] Our interests, of course, extend well beyond the demands and satisfactions of bodily life. But the rest of our activity is woven around the agenda of bodily life, and if we ignore that agenda we undercut our capacity to act at all.

Further, our history as animals capable of free choice is lived out in a social world that is at work shaping our behavior long before that behavior becomes reflective and deliberate. We grow into the possession of our powers as agents in a network of relationships, most prominently with the members of our family of origin, but also with friends, teachers, coworkers, and so on. In these relationships, and through the wider culture they mediate to us, we learn how to describe the world, how to regard ourselves and our possibilities as agents, what activities are worthwhile or admirable, what we should expect of other persons and they of us, what sorts of persons we should aspire to become, and so on. As this developmental process unfolds, we grow in the capacity to reflect critically on our social world and on the norms it presents to us. But our much celebrated autonomy always operates against a background of socially embedded forms of thought and practice that we at least initially take for granted and that, having been internalized, shape the deepest sources of our decision making. My freedom, then, has a social history, and that history shapes the uses I make of my powers of self-determining choice.

In these ways and many others, motivational states are elicited in us which then provide the background conditions with which we work in making free choices. If some of our actions are free in the strong sense, then no set of needs, desires, beliefs, and so on, determine these choices. But it is clear that our freedom is always structured and oriented by factors outside its reach.

Responsibility for Evil

This point has a significant bearing on the free will reply to the problem of evil. In particular, it complicates the question of how responsibility should be assigned for moral evil. For even when an agent performs an act freely, she is only partially responsible for the orientation of her will, i.e., for recognizing just these options, for feeling this or that desire or aversion, for holding this or that belief (about herself, other persons, the likely consequences of action, etc.), and for having this or that conception of what is good.[12] Now, the elicited elements in the motivational background of a free choice may be morally neutral (or morally advantageous) in their contribution to the orientation of the will. But it is also possible that factors largely beyond the agent's control bring about desires, beliefs, and valuations that orient the agent toward (without determining her to perform) certain morally wrong actions.

Consider, for example, a story that appeared in the local newspaper. A boy was born into a poor family as his mother's fourth child, though the first with this father. The father deserted the family before the child was born, and shortly thereafter the mother took her third husband. The new man in the household was hostile and abusive to this youngest child, who he regarded as a problem left behind by someone else. The stepfather flew into rages against the child, beating him and shouting that he did not want him in the house, that it was a waste to have to feed him. Neighbors reported that the stepfather often awakened the child in the morning by slapping him and bellowing at him to get out of the house. As the child grew older his stepfather found a use for him, sending him out to steal whatever the stepfather thought could be turned into quick cash. Eventually, the boy was caught and spent some time in a detention center under harsh conditions. At the age of 11, he ran away from home and lived with an uncle in another town. When the child reached his teens, the uncle gave him a gun and told him to go make it on his own.[13]

None of us would be surprised to hear that this story does not get any better as it continues. We expect this person's history to be characterized by predatory behavior toward other persons and by indifference to their suffering. This expectation does not mean that we are committed to a thoroughgoing determinism which denies that this individual is ever in a position to make free choices in response to the circumstances of his life. But we do recognize that he has been shaped by those circumstances in ways that powerfully predispose him to certain kinds of behavior. He will make his free choices against a background of elicited beliefs (e.g., about the vicious self-interestedness of human beings) and desires (e.g., to have the power to intimidate and to enforce his will upon other persons) and emotions (e.g., of rage at his insignificance, and of compensatory grandiosity). These deeply rooted motivational states will orient and constrain the use he is able to make of his freedom. He may be free, but his freedom is biased toward destructiveness.

We need to make this picture a bit more complicated, however. In free action we exercise at least a limited power to determine the outcome of these motivational conditions, and so to determine the role they play in shaping our activity. This power can be used well or badly; there is the possibility of a deepening spiral of self-reinforcing deformation of character, but there is also the opportunity to moderate the bias of the will. Over time, we may become aware of our propensity for certain patterns of elicited emotion, desire, and belief, and we may recognize their role in our decision making. We may reflect critically on the ways they have shaped our past choices, and we may try to limit their role in our future actions. Further, we may seek to change these patterns themselves, struggling to reshape the motivational sources of our actions (e.g., as when someone tries to overcome a volatile temper or a prejudicial attitude or too avid a taste for expensive wine).

It is important to acknowledge, however, that we frequently encounter significant limits on how far we are able to go with this self-restoration of the will. Human beings most often find that certain patterns of elicited response are deeply entrenched and difficult if not impossible to root out completely. The troubling attitudes or valuations or emotional responses continue to be elicited, and while their role in shaping our actions can be diminished and counterbalanced, they may remain a source of suffering to us and perhaps to others. We are not helpless in the face of these elements within us; they are not compulsions that overwhelm our critical faculties. But we often find that we cannot have just the emotions, desires, operative (as opposed to professed) values, and attitudes that we want to have. Our choices remain free in the strong sense (i.e., they are not determined by the conditions under which they are made), but they continue to be constrained by motivational factors that lie beyond the reach of our (direct) intentional control.

In assessing an individual's responsibility for his wrongdoing, therefore, we must consider not only whether the action was done freely but also whether the conditions under which the choice was made biased him toward evil. If there is such a bias, then this may mitigate the agent's responsibility and partially distribute that responsibility to others.[14] In this case, the person who freely does evil, making others his victims, is also a victim himself. Indeed, victimization of this sort goes particularly deep. For here a person is not, as it were, wounded cleanly, with the damage having fixed boundaries. Rather the individuals very operation as a maker of free choices is distorted, and this perpetuates the harm, reproducing it in new forms. We can both be damaged in and do damage to the motivational sources from which human actions spring. Having had elicited within us motivational states that bias our freedom toward evil, we tend to act in ways that elicit such states in others, so that we are both victims and victimizers in a self-perpetuating cycle of wrongdoing.

As we think through the problem of evil, this is a particularly troubling aspect of our freedom. If human beings are in fact caught up in a cycle of misoriented freedom, then appeal to the individual's free moral choice will not, without the addition of some auxiliary hypotheses, be enough to explain the origin of evil and to affix responsibility for it. This "moral individualism" cannot capture our actual predicament. In the first place, responsibility for the evil I do must also be borne by those who have done evil to me. But no sooner is this said (with a sigh of relief) than the point turns back upon us. For, in the second place, I must share responsibility for the evil that is done by those to whom I have done evil.

Here is a remarkable, if perverse, human solidarity. We are harmed and do harm in an extended community of victimization. And our predicament is more poignant still, for it is apparent that the misoriented human will can do harm without intending to do so, indeed, while intending the opposite. We are enculturated into a biased freedom not only by those who are hostile or indifferent to us, but also (and perhaps most lastingly) by those who nurture us and seek our good as best they can. And of course we too, in our turn, pass along to those we love something of the defects of character with which we love them.

Theodicy and the Bound Will

A free will reply to the problem of evil, then, must go beyond explaining moral evil by appeal to free will and give some account of how it happens, in God's good creation, that freedom operates under conditions that bias it toward evil. One way to reply to this problem is to deny that the moral predicament of human beings is in fact as gloomy as I have suggested. It might be held that each of us could (whether or not we actually do) overcome enough of the misorientation of our will that we can be held individually responsible for the moral character of our lives. In this case, the cycle of misoriented freedom could be broken by each of us through our freedom, and if that cycle continues, we individually bear the responsibility for it doing so.

In addition to problems of plausibility that afflict this optimistic view (reflected in countless stories like the one I just related about the child), any such position faces deep opposition within the Christian theological tradition. That is no surprise; the good news Christianity proclaims is that we are redeemed by God's loving action in Jesus Christ, not that we are able to redeem ourselves through a sustained effort of free will. This insistence upon the primacy of God's action in redemption is tied to a corresponding insistence upon the depth of our involvement with evil. The problem is not simply that we perform sinful deeds but that we are embedded in a sinful condition which infects the deepest sources of our actions. The will is caught up in self-perpetuating patterns of evil from which we cannot free ourselves, so that our freedom itself needs to be set free.

Here we have an explicitly theological claim about the extent to which we are ensnared in the dynamics of misoriented freedom that I have described. The will is not only biased toward evil, but bound by it. If we take this claim seriously, as I think we should, then we cannot settle for versions of the free will reply that are sanguine about our powers of moral self-improvement.

So how might a free will theodicy take into account this biasing of the will? This is a question that deserves extended discussion, but it is enough for my purposes to introduce briefly two well-known families of views. First, it is possible to attribute this predicament to the free act of an initially unbiased will. This is Augustine's strategy in his reading of the early chapters of Genesis. Original humanity comes from God's hand with a free will oriented not toward evil but toward good, above all toward the highest good which is God. Because we are finite as well as free, it is possible for us to fall short of the good and to do what we know is morally wrong. Quite unaccountably, the first human beings actually choose to do evil, and they bequeathed to the rest of us a corrupted will.

Second, it is possible to understand the biasing of the will as a result of the exercise of freedom under the precarious conditions that are required if our freedom is to be morally and spiritually significant, e.g., we must be able to learn and develop as agents with some independence of action, we must have the opportunity to make choices that have important consequences, and so on. If we are indeed free, these conditions do not causally necessitate our evildoing, but they may make that evildoing likely, perhaps even inevitable.[15] On such a view, there was no actual state of original perfection from which humanity fell; rather human freedom has throughout its history been enmeshed in doing and suffering evil. Further, though we are responsible for our free actions, we do not bear the whole responsibility for our predicament, for we are by nature creatures who will be tempted to do what we believe to be wrong and whose moral lives will be full of peril.

These two stories about the origins of our entanglement in evil each face various objections, and they have somewhat different implications for the shape of the question about God's goodness and power. The point I want to make about them here is that they both leave us with important questions about why God would create creatures of this sort, creatures with a freedom that is fragile and can go wrong with such terrible consequences. Suppose we grant that, even though God is omnipotent, it is not within God's power to create free creatures who on balance would make any better use of their freedom than we have.[16] In that case, we may wonder whether it is consistent with God's wisdom and goodness to have created free creatures at all.

This brings us to the second and third elements that I initially identified as crucial to free will replies: it must be argued that free will is a good in itself and/or a necessary condition for some intrinsic good; and a case must be made that the good achieved through created freedom is worth having even though it comes at so great a cost in suffering and loss due to moral evils.

Freedom and the Good

What, then, is the good for the sake of which creaturely freedom is brought into existence and allowed to run its troubled course? Proponents of free will arguments ordinarily do not think that moral freedom *alone*, even if it is an intrinsic good, is a great enough good. It is safe to say that it would not be morally good to create a world of free creatures knowing that those creatures would, whenever they had the chance, freely inflict horrendous evils on one another.

Alvin Plantinga, in the best known contemporary version of the free will defense, offers the following suggestion: "A world containing creatures who are significantly free (and freely perform more good than evil actions) is more valuable, all else being equal, than a world containing no free creatures at all."[17] Here it is not just freedom that is valued, but the use of that freedom to perform morally good actions. Note two particular features of this specification of the good served by permitting human freedom. First, a minimum threshold is set for the attainment of this good: it will not be enough for the world merely to contain some morally good actions; rather moral good must outweigh moral evil. Second, no restriction is placed on how moral goods and evils are distributed in the world, and so we may assume that this balance may be struck over the course of the world's history (rather than, say, at each moment within it or in every individual life).

It is far from clear, however, that an overall preponderance of moral good in the world justifies permitting all of the evil that is also performed by free creatures.[18] The problem is that this net balance of good and evil may be achieved in a *way* that is morally unacceptable. Consider, for example, the lives of those who become the victims of other persons' morally wrong choices–say, the child I described earlier. Unless we are prepared to claim that the child somehow deserved (or needed) to suffer in these ways, we have to say that his good was sacrificed for the sake of permitting other persons to exercise their freedom.[19] Indeed, I argued earlier that he was harmed in his very capacity to exercise such freedom himself; so he suffers a particularly deep loss, namely, a diminishment of his ability to participate in the moral good for the sake of which freedom is permitted at all.

This is just the kind of problem that Dostoevski states so compellingly in *The Brothers Karamazov*. In a chapter titled "Rebellion," Ivan Karamazov spins out a series of horrifying tales of the destruction of childrens' lives, and he challenges his brother (who is about to enter a religious order) to say whether there is any good worth having at this price. Part of what appalls Ivan is the thought that the lives of the innocent are expended as "dung on the fields" of some good in which they have no share. I think he is right to be appalled by this, and it is difficult to see how a free will argument that appeals only to the overall balance of good and evil in the world can accommodate this powerful moral intuition. In reply to Ivan's challenge, it is not very promising to propose simply that the bottom line of the cosmic ledger will eventually show a net balance of moral good over moral evil.[20]

If we draw more fully upon the actual content of the Christian faith, however, we need not be left in this position. There are two centrally important considerations here, both of which bear on the nature of the good that is served by permitting persons to exercise moral freedom.

First, according to Christianity the good that God intends for free creatures is a great deal richer in content than simply the performance by them (whether collectively or individually) of a preponderance of morally good actions. We are made not simply for moral life but for the enjoyment of fellowship with God, a fellowship that is decisively enacted in Christ. In this relationship finite persons are given an inexhaustible good that exceeds all others in value. Indeed, this good, in its eschatological realization as fullness of life with God, is incomparably greater than any evil that might be suffered on the way to it. If our fragile and costly freedom is worth having, it is because it bears a relation to the good of fellowship with the God who is with and for us in Jesus Christ.

Second, the God who promises human fulfillment in Christ is concerned not just with overall outcomes in the world system, but also and
preeminently with the good of individual persons. It may be that one of
the necessary conditions for the exercise of human freedom is that God
permit evil to be done and innocent persons to be harmed[21] (and, more
pervasively, that God permit guilty persons to be harmed in ways that
are not explained simply by their guilt). But God's concern for the good
of each person is not compatible with abandoning the innocent, allowing them to be expended in a cosmic machinery that grinds along
toward some good in which they do not have the opportunity to share.
This is a point that we should concede to Ivan Karamazov. The faith
which proclaims that God raised Jesus from the dead must affirm that
victimization is never the last word on a person's life. If the good that
God intends for us requires that we be permitted to do and to suffer evil,
God can nonetheless assure that no one is excluded from sharing in the
good simply by virtue of what he or she undergoes as a victim of other
persons' misuse of their freedom.

At the heart of Christian reflection on evil, therefore, lies the promise
of redemption, the promise that God acts in response to evil so as to
restore us to the good that God intends. And because we are both doers
of evil and victims of evil, that promise is twofold. First, it is the
promise of forgiveness of sin and reconciliation, i.e., of being established in a new relation to God that is defined not by the wrongs we
have done but rather by God's freely given love. Second, it is the
promise of liberation and healing, of being returned to fullness of life in
a relation to God (and to one another) that is defined not by the wrongs
that have been done to us but rather by a divine love which shares our
sorrows (and teaches us to share one another's).[22] Insofar as our free
choices reflect a biasing of the will for which we are only partially
responsible, forgiveness and healing coincide in the freeing of our freedom from its bondage to evil.

This does not settle the question with Ivan Karamazov; he might
well say that forgiveness of victimizers is unjust and healing of victims
is insufficient. But in light of these Christian claims, Ivan's protest at
least loses its appearance of moral obviousness. The healing of the victim of evil, so that suffering does not remain an isolating and meaningless loss for the sufferer, has a crucial role to play in considering the
problem that Ivan raises, and more needs to be said about it. This is in
part a topic in christology, addressed in reflection upon God's own suffering in the world.

Evil, Freedom, and Grace
If we work with roughly this conception of the good, then we have

the makings of a theologically interesting free will theodicy. Some puzzling questions immediately arise, however.

We have seen that free will theodicies contend that God permits freedom, and therefore moral evil, because freedom is a necessary condition for the good that God seeks. Yet we acknowledge that human freedom has gone wrong, and that this has among its consequences not simply individual acts of wrongdoing, but also a shared human predicament of misoriented freedom. If we take a strong view of this misorientation (as much, but not all, of the Christian tradition does), then we will hold that we cannot entirely free ourselves from it, whatever we may be able to do to mitigate its effects. This leaves us in the apparently awkward position of contending that God makes free creatures because freedom is necessary to achieve an end which, given the actual state of our freedom, we cannot attain. If we say that God now bypasses human freedom to make the intended good available to us, then it would seem that the free will reply loses its point. For in that case it appears that God could have given creatures this good without bothering with freedom in the first place.

In order to avoid this result, we might say instead that God acts to restore our freedom, liberating us to give our free assent to the end for which we are intended. God might be understood to affect the motivating conditions of our actions, overcoming the bias of the will toward evil and drawing us toward the good. Without simply overriding our freedom, God progressively re-educates the will, setting our freedom free to embrace the good that God graciously makes available to us.

This view has much to recommend it, and it can be developed in conceptually powerful forms.[23] But it faces a theological objection that is likely to be raised to any free will theodicy, however carefully qualified, viz., the charge that it makes salvation conditional upon what *we* do and not just upon what God does. The simplest schemes of conditional salvation are straightforwardly Pelagian, i.e., they suppose that we are able freely to will and to do what is required for salvation. That cannot be said of the account I just sketched, however, since it insists not only that 1) it is solely God's free initiative that makes available to us the good of fulfillment in Christ, but also that 2) we cannot (by virtue of our entanglement in evil) freely choose to respond to this initiative in trust and love unless God prepares us to do so. Nonetheless, it is the case, on this account, that while God's grace is a decisively important necessary condition for salvation, it is not alone *sufficient*.

Many Christian thinkers (especially the classical Protestants, e.g., Luther and Calvin) have held that this is too weak a claim. It has been argued that if salvation depends upon something that we must do, then we may fall prey to the dual dangers of prideful self-congratulation (that

I have done what is necessary to secure right-relation with God) and anxious uncertainty (about whether I really have done what is necessary or have done it in the right spirit). Both of these attitudes reflect a self-preoccupation, a kind of religious self-centeredness, that seems out of keeping with the distinctive "freedom of a Christian," as Luther put it, which is rooted in the good news that *God* has secured our good where we cannot.[24] In addition, it has been argued that if we are free to turn away from God's solicitation of our good, then the creature has a veto power over the realization of the creator's purposes for us, and this is incompatible with God's sovereignty and providential governance of the world.

Powerful replies can be given to these objections, and the objections can be elaborated and extended in replies to the replies. All of this has kept theologians employed for generations, and it shows promise of continuing to do so, as long as anyone still cares about the issue. It is not my intention to try to settle these questions here. I do want to suggest, however, that the most familiar alternative positions do not exhaust the options.

It may look as though we must choose between saying that 1) human beings possess an incompatibilist freedom to affirm or reject the good that God offers them, and so must make a choice (or set of choices) upon which their salvation depends, and 2) that human beings possess at most a compatibilist freedom, and so choose for or against God's love only because they are determined to do so by God. The first position makes possible a free will response to the problem of evil, but it faces the theological objections we just noted. The second position avoids these theological objections, but it faces an intractable problem about God's relation to evil, since all events, including the choices in which human agents reject their own good, are determined by God. The prospect of choosing between these options is uncomfortable, and if weighty representatives of the tradition have opted for positions very close to the latter, contemporary theologians tend either to choose the former or they attempt to redraw the options.[25]

Let me venture a brief suggestion about a third alternative. It is worth entertaining the possibility that we might claim both that 1) human beings must possess incompatibilist freedom of will if we are to realize the good that God intends for us, and that 2) the actual attainment of this good is not conditional upon making an undetermined free choice (or series of choices) to accept what God offers rather than to reject it. It certainly appears to be logically possible to say both these things. The burden of argument lies in showing that they can be integrated into a theologically plausible position. The key to doing so, I think, is to reflect a bit further upon the nature of the good God seeks for created agents and its relation to freedom.

The first of these claims affirms that God makes us for a good that can be realized only by a creature with a certain sort of history: namely, a history as a genuinely free seeker of the good. God intends, on this view, that we be fulfilled as valuers, as lovers who are capable of loving many goods (both greater and lesser) and loving them to different degrees. It is precisely this which most deeply defines the personhood that God has given us. Our distinctive identities as persons are forged in the history of our attachments. If there is to be a particular individual personality that is fulfilled in relation to God, then there must a history of free choices in which we try out our intuitions about what is good, make commitments to what we take to be worthwhile, and see who we become in the process.

This history, I have contended, does not go altogether well for us. We love incompatible things (and so are pulled in contending directions), we love things more than they warrant being loved (and so are disappointed and destructive), and we find that what we actually love is not what we would like to love (and so we are at odds with ourselves). But in this uncertain history, this history of a restless heart, we generate the personal identity that finds its ultimate fulfillment in God.

It is important to recognize that God is not only the origin and the end of this life story; God is at work throughout the story as it unfolds, drawing the created agent toward the good for which we all are made. We can speak here of interaction and cooperation between the divine agent and human agents. For while God, in the creation and governance of the world, decisively sets the conditions under which we act, yet in those of our actions that are free, God does not determine our choices. Rather, God's activity can be variously described as guiding, influencing, inspiring, strengthening, chastening, and so on, in ways that best advance God's purposes for us without destroying our capacity to creatively determine our own purposes. By pervasively (though not exclusively) shaping the motivating conditions of free human action, God prepares us for the good that is the goal of God's creative activity.

This ultimate good for human beings is in one respect the same for all; it is the "vision" of God, the enjoyment of unobstructed relationship to an infinite Good.[26] In another respect, this good is different for each individual; it is the fulfillment of a particular personal history in a consummation that gathers up all that the person has been and done and suffered, and places this history in relation to a love that perfectly comprehends and completes it. So, the good that God intends for us can be realized in an infinite diversity of different particular ways, and the specific way in which a person enjoys the good depends upon who she has become in her freedom.

Having said all this, we need *not* conclude either that a) we bring about our own highest good through the exercise of our powers of incompatibilist free choice between alternative possibilities or, more cautiously, that b) the question of whether or not we attain this good is decided by any free action or set of free actions of ours. Rather, on this account, the finite agent is fulfilled precisely by being given what he cannot secure for himself, namely, the immediate presence of the ultimate Good. No doubt we assent to this relationship and willingly enter into it. But there is reason to think that this act is not appropriately described in terms of incompatibilist freedom, at least as it is most often characterized in free will arguments.[27] Here we are placed in a circumstance profoundly different than that of our ordinary choices between finite goods, each of which makes only a limited claim upon our interest and commitment. Rather, we are confronted directly with the Infinite Good which is our origin and highest end. In the immediate presence of this unique Good, our "freedom" for indifference or rejection would seem to be irrelevant. This Infinite Good will be unconditionally desirable, and if it discloses itself to us by making us able to recognize it as it is, then we will find it irresistible.

If a response of joyous affirmation is the only one available to us here, this does not represent a loss or diminishment of our agency. We do not cease to be agents, indeed, free agents. But the conditions under which we respond to the divine Good are such that an act of rejection is not an open option for us. Incompatibilist freedom, as an ability to choose for or against particular finite goods presented to us in this life, has served its purpose in the formation of the finite personal agent who enters into this final relationship with God. In the vision of God, the transcendent Good that we had at most glimpsed "through a glass darkly" is now manifest as the source and completion of all the goods to which we have aspired. This Good uniquely commands our love, and we cannot do otherwise than embrace it.

Note that in being captivated by this Good, the human will is not forced, coerced, or constrained, but rather is fulfilled by finding what the free agent has most deeply sought. No action of ours is more willing, more wholehearted, more undivided and unambiguous than this act of unconditional affirmation. Precisely for this reason, it expresses the fullest freedom.

In the immediate presence of God, on this account, our freedom reaches its end, i.e., its telos. This is not necessarily to say, however, that our freedom to make choices and direct our own lives is at an end. For while there can be no choice to reject the divine Good, we might imagine (and it is no more than that) that there is a freedom for alternative action even within beatitude, namely, a freedom to variously realize one's enjoyment of the divine life. Precisely because God is infinite, the creature cannot embrace the divine Good in any single act but must apprehend this Good in an unending exploration of an inexhaustible mystery. If something like this were the case, then the freedom exercised in this relationship (an "eschatological freedom") would be a heightened but reversed version of the freedom we presently possess. For where we are now biased toward evil, we would then be bound by the Good, unable to will anything else but able freely to choose how we shall delight in it.

With or without this notion of an eschatological freedom, we have here an alternative to the opposed positions on human freedom and divine grace that I initially identified. This third way depends upon distinguishing between two aspects of God's redemptive work in the lives of free creatures: 1) God's role in the history of the finite free agent, and 2) God's act of bringing the free agent into a final relation of fulfillment in God. With regard to the first, we can say that God grants and respects creaturely powers of undetermined choice, so that God's action is necessary but not sufficient for our realization of the fellowship with God which is available to us in this life. Here divine initiative and human response fit the pattern described by the more circumspect defenders of a "libertarian" position on grace and freedom. With regard to the second, God's action is sufficient and unconditional. Here divine initiative and human response might be understood to fit the pattern of a compatibilist position on grace and freedom.

On the account I have sketched, the human agent's history of freedom is for the sake of eschatological fulfillment, and that fulfillment is brought about by God's unobstructable action. Our salvation, then, is assured whatever the content or character of the free creature's history; salvation depends solely upon God's gracious decision. But there must be a history of free action if there is to be a personal agent to receive this good. Our free actions play a role in determining the particular character, but not the fact, of our fulfillment in God. Life with God in this life is both an integral part of God's ongoing creative work and, where we respond to God in love, an incipient appearance of the good that is to come, the first fruits of the kingdom of God.

Much remains to be done, of course, in developing this brief suggestion for a new approach to the ancient debate about human freedom and divine grace. A proposal of this kind, which tries to find a way between well-entrenched opposed alternatives, bears a special burden of argument. But perhaps enough has been said to show that there is some prospect of formulating a free will reply to the problem of evil that can accommodate even the strongest claims about the unconditional character of God's saving action. In any case, if free will arguments begin to incorporate a fuller understanding of the predicament and destiny of human freedom, then they inevitably will be led into the midst of these classical theological concerns.[28]

Notes

1. Stephen Mitchell, trans., *The Book of Job* (San Francisco: North Point Press, 1987), 60. Job 24: 5-12.

2. *Dialogues Concerning Natural Religion* (New York: The Bobbs-Merrill Company, 1947), Part. X.

3. This is Alvin Plantinga's strategy in distinguishing a "defense" from a "theodicy" in *God, Freedom, and Evil* (Grand Rapids: William B. Eerdmans, 1989), 27-28. A defense claims to provide only a logically possible reason for God's permission or production of evil. Unlike a theodicy, it does not claim that this is or might be (i.e., with some degree of epistemic probability) God's reason.

4. *God, Freedom, and Evil*, 57-59. Since Plantinga is responding to the logical version of the problem of evil, he is concerned only with whether his solution is logically possible, not with whether it is true or even plausible.

5. The absence of causal determination is a necessary but not sufficient condition for free action, on this account. Beyond this, it must be added that the agent intentionally undertakes the act. This claim has been expressed by contrasting agent-causation with event-causation. See, for example, Roderick Chisholm, *Person and Object* (La Salle, IL: Open Court, 1976), ch. II.

6. There are further conditions which must be added specifying the way in which the agent's desires and beliefs cause the action, since not just any causal route from desire/belief to action will generate an *intentional* action.

7. One can hold such a view only if one gives a particular account of how the law of the excluded middle applies to counterfactuals of freedom. For further discussion, see Robert Adams, "Middle Knowledge and the Problem of Evil," in *The Virtue of Faith and Other Essays* (Oxford: Oxford University Press, 1990) and Alfred Fredosso, "Introduction," *On Divine Foreknowledge (Part IV of the Concordia)* by Louis de Molina (Ithaca: Cornell University Press, 1988), 46-51.

8. This, of course, is what Alvin Plantinga argues with consummate skill. See *God, Freedom, and Evil*, 34-57.

9. We can include among elicited motivational states those which are the unintentional consequences of our intentional actions.

10. It has been suggested in discussion that it is odd to speak of

enacting a motivating state, since motives are not themselves actions but rather condition actions. Note, however, that various of the mental states that motivate an action A may be direct or indirect results of an action A' that is prior to A. In the example above, I intentionally recall scenes from childhood which then become part of the motivational conditions under which I decide how to act toward my own child. Here the relevant mental state is enacted directly, but there will be many motivational states that we can only indirectly bring about. Emotions and desires, for example, typically do not appear on command, though it is possible to use various means to cultivate and sustain them selectively.

11. Austin Farrer develops this point quite subtly in *Finite and Infinite* (London: Dacre Press, 1964), ch. 15.

12. It is worth emphasizing that I am not denying that we are, in various degrees, responsible for many of our motivational states. Motivational states may be the intended result of our intentional actions. And various elicited mental states may be foreseen consequences of intentional actions; these cases raise complex questions about responsibility. Beyond this, Robert Adams has argued that we are morally responsible for some states of mind whether or not they are subject to voluntary control: see Robert Adams, "Involuntary Sins," *Philosophical Review* 94, 1. Free-will replies to the problem of evil, however, typically suppose that we are morally responsible only for free intentional actions and omissions, along with certain of their consequences, and so for the purposes of my discussion I will maintain this link between voluntary control and moral responsibility.

13. Based upon Jack Anderson, "Saddam Was Abused as a Child," *Lewiston Sun-Journal*, 25 January 1991, p. 4.

14. If responsibility for wrongdoing is to be mitigated in this way, the motivational conditions that bias the agent's choice toward evil must not be attributable solely to prior actions by this agent which were themselves free from any bias toward evil. That is, the agent must not be the sole source of the conditions that now bias his will toward evil.

15. Reinhold Niebuhr famously contends that sin is the inevitable but not necessary result of our paradoxical situation of freedom and finiteness, *The Nature and Destiny of Man*, vol. I (New York: Charles Scribner's Sons, 1964), 182. Niebuhr acknowledges his indebtedness for this idea to Soren Kierkegaard, *The Concept of Dread*.

16. There are several ways one might develop such an account, spelling out the relevant conditions and their bearing on human freedom. The best known modern attempt to develop a position of this general type is John Hick's "soul-making" theodicy, the roots of which he finds in the pre-Augustinian theologian, Irenaeus. See *Evil and the God of Love* (New York: Harper and Row, 1978), 201ff. It is worth noting,

however, that Hick does not in the end hold a strong view of the mis-orientation of the will, but rather affirms that each of us is able, given sufficient opportunity, to work our way out of this predicament and freely embrace the highest good.

17. This is the line of argument sketched in Section II above.

18. Plantinga, *God, Freedom, and Evil*, 30.

19. This objection retains its force even if God could not create a world containing free creatures whose actions produce a better balance of moral good over moral evil.

20. On the suggestion that each individual needs to suffer just what he or she does, see Eleonore Stump, "The Problem of Evil," *Faith and Philosophy* 2, no. 4 (October 1984): 409ff.

21. In fairness to Plantinga, it is important to note that his free will defense does not claim to provide a morally sufficient reason for God's permission of evil, but only to identify a set of conditions compatible both with theistic affirmations about God's power, knowledge, and goodness and with the existence of a world containing evil. It may be that certain additional conditions must be added to those he states in order to meet the requirements of moral sufficiency. Plantinga need not spell out what these are; but if the conditions he states are not them-selves sufficient, it must be clear that there is some set of further condi-tions that, conjoined with his, are sufficient.

22. I have argued elsewhere that God's perfect goodness is compati-ble with permitting persons to suffer involuntary and undeserved sacri-fices of their interests. See "Victimization and the Problem of Evil: A Reply to Ivan Karamazov," *Faith and Philosophy* 9, no. 3 (July 1992).

23. Michael Root offers a very helpful analysis of the subtle interplay of images in the New Testament of evil as a) an oppression, or victim-ization, from which we need liberation and b) habitual misdoing for which we need forgiveness. "Dying He Lives: Biblical Image, Biblical Narrative and the Redemptive Jesus," *Semeia* 30 (1984).

24. Eleonore Stump has developed a particularly interesting and sub-tle form of this general type of view. She makes use of Harry Frankfurt's distinction between first-order and second-order desires, and suggests that the corrupted human will is unable to make itself have the desires it wants to have. We can think of the repentant human agent as freely asking that God reform the will, so that the agent's first-order desires conform more closely to her second-order desires. If God then intervenes in the will, God has not violated the human agent's freedom, but rather has acted (in accordance with a free petition) to liberate it. See, for example, "Justification By Faith and the Atonement," in *Trinity, Incarnation, and Atonement* ed. Ronald Feenstra and Cornelius Plantinga (Notre Dame: Notre Dame Press, 1988).

25. Martin Luther, *The Freedom of a Christian*, in John Dillenberger, ed., *Martin Luther: Selections From His Writings* (Garden City: Doubleday, 1961).

26. For contrasting contemporary accounts see J.R. Lucas, "Freedom and Grace," in *Freedom and Grace* (Grand Rapids: Wm. B. Eerdmans, 1976) and Robert Jenson, "Pneumatological Soteriology," in Carl Braaten and Robert Jenson, eds., *Christian Dogmatics*, Vol. Two (Philadelphia: Fortress Press, 1984), 125-142. Lucas opts for an account that preserves incompatibilist freedom and so treats God's action as the decisively significant necessary, but not sufficient, causal condition of our salvation. Robert Jenson, in a brief and remarkably rich discussion of these issues, initially sets out to avoid both of the classical alternatives, arguing that they trade upon the same error, viz., they attempt to offer a "third-person" and "causal" account of the relation of divine and human agency in salvation. In contrast, he proposes a "hermeneutical" account, i.e., that talk about God's work of salvation should function performatively to declare and enact the divine promises. Jenson also vigorously repudiates incompatibilist freedom, however, and insists that the unconditional character of God's promise of salvation entails that God's will must determine every event in the world's history. This certainly looks like a third-person and causal description that embraces the second of the two classical alternatives, and he candidly acknowledges the split this generates between "God revealed in the gospel as absolute love and God revealed in all history as merely absolute" (p. 138).

27. It is important to distinguish here between the infinite Good that God *is* and the finite good of the creature's fulfillment in God. The latter is the greatest possible good for any free creature, but it is not an infinite good, since the creature is a finite value. The greatest possible good for the creature is its fulfillment in relation to the infinite Good, i.e., God.

28. I noted above that free will arguments typically link moral responsibility to a conception of freedom according to which our free actions have necessary but not sufficient causal conditions in antecedent events. One of the motivations for this position is the intuition that an action can be free and responsible only if the agent could have done otherwise. This claim, often referred to as the "principle of alternate possibilities," has been variously interpreted and attacked by compatibilists, notably by Harry Frankfurt. It is worth noting that Eleonore Stump has recently argued that incompatibilists should also reject this principle ("Intellect, Will, and the Principle of Alternate Possibilities," in Michael Beaty, ed., *Christian Theism and the Problems of Philosophy*, [Notre Dame: Univ. of Notre Dame Press, 1990]).

Whether or not one embraces the particular position Stump develops, it is worth examining whether and in what sense(s) incompatiblist freedom entails an ability to do otherwise. Consider, for example, cases in which an agent is presented with an option for action that he finds truly repellent, say, a parent is offered a large sum to sell his child on the black market. The parent might say, "It would be impossible for me to do such a thing!" Here the impossibility is not metaphysical (there is a possible world in which the parent sells his child), and it need not be causal. An incompatibilist could affirm that this parent was the agent-cause of his emphatic refusal, and was not determined in this decision by antecedent events and the laws of nature. Nonetheless, it may be that, given the agent's character and commitments, it is correct to say that he could not do otherwise than refuse this offer. This requires distinguishing between determination within an unbroken series of event-causes and determination by overwhelming reasons for acting, where the latter cannot be exhaustively analyzed in terms of the former. We could then say that the human agent, in embracing life with God, both possesses incompatibilist freedom and cannot do otherwise.

29. For helpful comment on this paper I am indebted to Michael McLain, Mark Richardson, Philip Clayton, Steve Duncan, Timothy Jackson, and audiences who have heard this paper at Hendrix College and the Farrer conference. I am particularly grateful for vigorous and extended discussion with members of the Theology Group. This paper was initially drafted during the term of a fellowship from the National Endowment for the Humanities.

Chapter 10

Aquinas on the Sufferings of Job

Eleonore Stump

Aquinas wrote commentaries on five books of the Old Testament (Psalms, Job, Isaiah, Jeremiah, Lamentations), two Gospels (Matthew and John), and the Pauline epistles. These biblical commentaries have not received the same sort of attention as some of his other works, such as the *Summa theologiae* or the *Summa contra gentiles*, but they are a treasure trove of philosophy and theology.[1] The commentary on Job in particular is one of Aquinas's more mature and polished commentaries. Unlike many of them, which are preserved in the form of a *reportatio*, a transcription of Aquinas's lecturers by someone who attended them, the commentary on Job is an *expositio*, material reworked and revised by Aquinas himself.[2] The commentary sheds light on Aquinas's understanding of God's providence and especially of the relation between God's providence and human suffering. Aquinas does discuss providence in other works as well, most notably in book 3 of the *Summa contra gentiles*, which is roughly contemporary with the commentary on Job; and he considers problems involving suffering in many of the biblical commentaries, especially those on the Pauline epistles.[3] But the book of Job is the paradigmatic presentation of the problem of evil for anyone trying to reconcile the existence of God with the presence of evil in the world, and it is therefore particularly interesting to see how Aquinas interprets this book. So, although I turn to the *Summa contra gentiles* and the commentaries on the Pauline epistles when appropriate, my focus is on Aquinas's commentary on Job.

Aquinas's Approach to Job

Contemporary readers tend to think of the subject of the book of Job as the problem of evil. Since the book itself says that Job was innocent and since the book is equally clear about the fact that Job's suffering is (indirectly) caused by God, who grants Satan permission to afflict him, it seems to contemporary readers that the story of Job's suffering is hard to reconcile with the claim that there is an omnipotent, omniscient, perfectly good God. How could such a being allow an innocent person to suffer the loss of his property, the death of his children, a painful and disfiguring disease, and the other sufferings Job endured? And so the story of innocent Job, horribly afflicted with undeserved suffering, seems to many people representative of the kind of evil with which any theodicy must come to grips. But Aquinas sees the problems in the book of Job differently. He seems not to recognize that suffering in the world, of the quantity and quality of Job's, calls into question God's goodness, let alone God's existence. Instead Aquinas understands the book as an attempt to come to grips with the nature and operations of divine providence. How does God direct his creatures? Does the suffering of the just require us to say that divine providence is not extended to human affairs? Of course, this question is clearly connected to the one we today generally find in the book of Job. But the difference between the contemporary approach to Job and the one Aquinas adopts is instructive for understanding Aquinas's view of the relation between God and evil.

On Aquinas's account, the problem with Job's friends is that they have a wrong view of the way providence operates. They suppose that providence assigns adversities in this life as a punishment for sins and earthly prosperity as a reward for virtue. Job, however, has a more correct view of providence, according to Aquinas, because he recognizes that a good and loving God will nonetheless allow the worst sorts of adversities to befall a virtuous person also. The disputation constituted by the speeches of Job and his friends is a disputation concerning the correct understanding of this aspect of the operations of providence. What is of more interest to us here than the details of this disputation, as Aquinas understands it, is his analysis of the reasons the friends take such a wrong view of providence. In connection with one of Eliphaz's speeches, Aquinas says, "If in this life human beings are rewarded by God for good deeds and punished for bad, as Eliphaz was endeavoring to establish, it apparently follows that the ultimate goal for human beings is in this life. But Job intends to rebut this opinion, and he wants to show that the present life of human beings doesn't contain [that] ultimate goal, but is related to it as motion is related to rest and the road to its end."[4]

Constraints on Theodicy

Aquinas's idea, then, is that the things that happen to a person in this life can be justified only by reference to her or his state in the afterlife. That a medieval Christian thinker should have an other-worldly view comes as no surprise, but it is at first glance perplexing to see that Aquinas thinks taking the other world into account will settle questions about how providence operates. For we might suppose that even if all that happens in a person's life is simply a prolegomenon to her state in the afterlife, nothing in this claim allays the concerns raised by seeing that in this world bad things happen to good people. Job's comforters take the line they do, that suffering is punishment for sins, just because they see no other way to maintain God's goodness and justice. It's hard to see how indicating the existence of an afterlife would change their minds. Because Aquinas has always in mind the thought that the days of our lives here are short while the afterlife is unending,[5] he naturally supposes that things having to do with the afterlife are more important than the things having to do with this life. But nothing in this attitude of his is incompatible with supposing that if God is good, things in this life ought to go well, at least for the just, if not for everybody.

We might suppose that Aquinas is here presupposing a view familiar to us from contemporary discussions of the problem of evil: God's reasons for allowing suffering are mysterious, and we do not know what sort of justification, if any, there is for God's allowing evil; but the immeasurable good of union with God in heaven recompenses all the finite evils we suffer here.[6] The benefits of the afterlife do not justify God's allowing evil, but they do make up for the suffering of people who experience evil, in the sense that in union with God such people find their sufferings more than compensated. But Aquinas adopts a line different from this. His line makes constructing an adequate theodicy more difficult but also (to my mind) more satisfying if successful. He supposes that we can know, at least in general, the good that justifies God's allowing evil. And he accepts basically the same constraints as those some contemporary philosophers insist on: if a good God allows evil, it can only be because the evil in question produces a benefit for the sufferer and one that God could not provide without the suffering.[7]

In his commentary on Romans, Aquinas distinguishes between the way providence works with respect to persons, on the one hand, and the rest of creation, on the other hand. As part of his defense of the line that all things work together for good for those who love God, Aquinas says this:

> Whatever happens on earth, even if it is evil, turns out for the good of the whole world. Because as Augustine says in the *Enchiridion*, God is so

good that he would never permit any evil if he were not also so powerful
that from any evil he could draw out a good. But the evil does not always
turn out for the good of the thing in connection with which the evil
occurs, because although the corruption of one animal turns out for the
good of the whole world–insofar as one animal is generated from the corruption of another–nonetheless it doesn't turn out for the good of the animal which is corrupted. The reason for this is that the good of the whole
world is willed by God for its own sake, and all the parts of the world are
ordered to this [end]. The same reasoning appears to apply with regard to
the order of the noblest parts [of the world] with respect to the other parts,
because the evil of the other parts is ordered to the good of the noblest
parts. But whatever happens with regard to the noblest parts is ordered
only to the good of those parts themselves, because care is taken of them
for their own sake, and for their sake care is taken of other things...But
among the best of all the parts of the world are God's saints...He takes
care of them in such a way that he doesn't allow any evil for them which
he doesn't turn into their good.[8]

In discussing providence in the *Summa contra gentiles*, he takes the
same line. In a chapter headed "Rational creatures are governed for their
own sake but others are governed in subordination to them," Aquinas
repeatedly argues for the conclusion that "by divine providence, for
creatures with intellects provision is made for their own sake, but for
other creatures provision is made for the sake of those with intellects."[9]
In fact, Aquinas not only accepts the biblical line that (by divine
providence) all things work together for good for those (rational creatures) who love God, but he has a particularly strong interpretation of it.
How are we to understand the expression "all things" in this line?, he
asks in his commentary on Romans. The general claim that for created
persons God permits only those evils he can turn into goods for them is,
Aquinas says, "plainly true when it comes to the painful evils that [cre-
ated persons] suffer. That is why it says in the gloss that the humility [of
those who love God] is stimulated by their weakness, their patience by
affliction, their wisdom by opposition, and their benevolence by ani-
mosity."[10] But what about the evils that are sins? Are they also among
the things which work together for good for those who love God?
"Some people say that sins are not included under 'all things' [in the
biblical passage]...But against this is the passage in the gloss: ...if some
among the saints go astray and turn aside, even this God makes efficacious for good for them...(S)uch people rise again [from their fall] with
greater charity, since the good of human beings is charity...They return
more humble and better instructed."[11]
So Aquinas adopts a line different from the one some contemporary
philosophers argue for. He apparently believes that we can and in some

cases do know the goods which justify suffering. On the other hand, like some contemporary philosophers, Aquinas feels that (at least for creatures with minds) suffering is justified only in case it is a means to good for the sufferer herself. And Aquinas's examples of such good all have at least a natural, if not a necessary, connection with the evil in question: patience brought about by affliction, humility brought about by the experience of sin and repentance.

What shall we say then about Aquinas's approach to Job? Given his understanding of the constraints governing theodicy, how shall we explain Aquinas's view that the perplexities of the story and the inadequacies of the comforters can all be satisfactorily accounted for by the recognition that there is an afterlife and that rewards and punishments are distributed there rather than in this life? The first part of the explanation comes from Aquinas's attitude toward happiness; the second part stems from his account of suffering.

Aquinas's Attitude toward Human Happiness

That human beings naturally desire their own happiness is a commonplace of Western philosophy. And we also suppose that any good person, but especially a perfectly good divine person, will desire the happiness of other persons. What raises the problem of evil for us is watching cases in which, it seems to us, God is not doing enough to promote the happiness of his creatures, or is permitting their unhappiness or even, as in Job's case, actively conniving at the unhappiness of one of his creatures. But then in order to investigate the problem of evil we need first to be reflective about the nature of human happiness. It is noteworthy that in his long treatment of providence in the *Summa contra gentiles* Aquinas has virtually no discussion of what we would consider the problem of evil but fifteen chapters on the nature of human happiness.

What exactly happens to Job that makes us wonder about God's goodness? (We might also ask about what happens to Job's animals, Job's children, or Job's wife, because questions about God's goodness obviously arise in connection with them, too; but I will focus here just on Job.) He loses his animals, the basis of wealth in his society. Afflicted with a miserable skin disease, he loses his health. And he loses his children, all of whom are killed in one day. We might term these losses Job's first-order afflictions. These first-order afflictions are the cause of further, second-order afflictions for him, the most notable of which is his disgrace in his own society. In consequence of the way in which his society interprets his troubles, he becomes a pariah among those who once honored him. And, finally, because Job's friends react very negatively to his insistence that he is innocent, their response to the way in which Job sees his first- and second-order afflictions provides yet more suffering for him, a third-order suffering. Because his reactions to his first-and second-order suffering differ radically from theirs, he finds himself deeply at odds with the very people who might have been a source of comfort to him–first his wife and then the men closest to him. (His conflict with God, to which Aquinas is oblivious, seems to me the most important part of this third-order affliction, but I will leave it to one side here, and not only because Aquinas is insensitive to it. Since this part of Job's misery stems from his inability to understand how the God he trusted could let such things happen to him, the enterprise of theodicy is itself an attempt to explain this part of Job's suffering.)

We naturally take Job's losses to constitute the destruction of his happiness. But if we look at the chapters on happiness in the *Summa Contra Gentiles*, we find Aquinas arguing the following claims: happiness does not consist in wealth,[12] happiness does not consist in the goods of the body, such as health,[13] and happiness does not consist in honors.[14] Happiness is the greatest of goods, on Aquinas's account, but any good that is not by nature completely shareable, that is, which is such that in giving it to others one has less of it, is only a small good. Most, if not all, the gifts of fortune will therefore count just as small goods, on Aquinas's view. There is enough of medieval Christianity left in twentieth-century Western culture that many of us can read such claims and vaguely affirm them without paying much attention to what they mean. But on this view of Aquinas's, if happiness does not consist in health, honor, or riches, then it does not follow that a person who does not have these things is without happiness. It is therefore not immediately clear, contrary to what we unreflectively assume, that Job's happiness is destroyed in consequence of not having these things.

Two things are worth noticing here. First, Aquinas, even with all his otherworldly focus, is not a Stoic. Among the many chapters in *Summa Contra Gentiles* saying what happiness does not consist in, there is no chapter saying that happiness does not consist in loving relations with other persons. Unlike some ancient philosophers, Aquinas does not understand happiness as a matter of self-sufficiency. So Aquinas's arguments about what happiness does not consist in are apparently not relevant to one of Job's losses, the loss of his children, or to the third-order afflictions of discord with his wife and friends. Second, even if health, honor, riches, and the other things on Aquinas's list do not constitute happiness, it might nonetheless be the case that the loss of them or the presence of their opposites–sickness, disgrace, impoverishment–produces so much pain as to make happiness impossible. On Aquinas's view, human happiness consists in the contemplation of God. Apart from worries over whether human cognitive faculties are capable of contemplating God in this life, one might wonder whether pain and suffering do not interfere with such contemplation. And, in fact, as part of the evidence for the conclusion that true happiness cannot be achieved in this life, Aquinas himself says that weaknesses and misfortunes can impede the functions which must be exercised for happiness.[15] Consequently, even if, as Aquinas thinks, happiness consists in contemplation of God, rather than in the gifts of fortune, so that the loss of health or honor or riches does not by itself entail the loss of happiness, Aquinas apparently recognizes that it is possible for misfortune in any of its varieties to be an obstacle to happiness. So although it is helpful to understand Aquinas's views of happiness, we also need to consider his account of suffering in order to understand his approach to the book of Job.

Aquinas's Attitude toward Pain and Suffering

When from the standpoint of religion we reflect on the many evils of the world—murder, rape, torture, the oppression of apartheid, the evils of nuclear armament, the horrors of Auschwitz and Treblinka—we can hardly avoid wondering how a good God could let such things occur. But another thing to wonder about is the nature of human beings, who in all cultures and all ages can be so vicious to one another. On Aquinas's view, all human beings have a terminal cancer of soul, a proneness to evil which invariably eventuates in sin and which in the right circumstances blows up into monstrosity. On his view, even "our senses and our thoughts are prone to evil."[16] The pure and innocent among human beings are no exception to this claim. When the biblical text says that Job was righteous, Aquinas takes the text to mean that Job was pure by human standards. By the objective, uncurved standards of God, even Job was infected with the radical human tendencies toward evil.[17] No human being who remains uncured of this disease can see God. On Aquinas's view, then, the primary obstacle to contemplation of God, in which human happiness consists, is the sinful character of human beings.

Aquinas thinks that pain and suffering of all sorts are God's medicine for this spiritual cancer, and he emphasizes this view repeatedly. In his commentary on the Apostles' Creed he says, "If all the pain a human being suffers is from God, then he ought to bear it patiently, both because it is from God and because it is ordered toward good; for pains purge sins, bring evildoers to humility, and stimulate good people to love of God."[18] In his commentary on Thessalonians he says, "As water extinguishes a burning fire, so tribulations extinguish the force of concupiscent desires, so that human beings don't follow them at will...Therefore, [the Church] is not destroyed [by tribulations] but lifted up by them, and in the first place by the lifting up of the mind to God, as Gregory says: the evils which bear us down here drive us to go to God."[19] He comments in great detail on the line in Hebrews: "whom the Lord loves he chastens."[20] "All the saints who have pleased God have gone through many tribulations by which they were made the sons of God."[21] "Since pains are a sort of medicine, we should apparently judge correction and medicine the same way. Now medicine in the taking of it is bitter and loathsome, but its end is desirable and intensely sweet. So discipline is also. It is hard to bear, but it blossoms into the best outcome."[22]

The same general point appears recurrently in the commentary on Job. Arguing that temporal goods such as those Job lost are given and taken away according to God's will, Aquinas says "someone's suffering adversity would not be pleasing to God except for the sake of some good coming from the adversity. And so although adversity is in itself bitter and gives rise to sadness, it should nonetheless be agreeable [to us] when we consider its usefulness, on account of which it is pleasing to God...For in his reason a person rejoices over the taking of bitter medicine because of the hope of health, even though in his senses he is troubled."[23] Even the dreadful suffering Job experiences at the death of his good and virtuous children becomes transformed on this account from the unbearable awfulness of total loss to the bitter but temporary pain of separation. In being united to God in love, a person is also united with others. The ultimate good of union with God, like any great good, is by nature shareable.

In commenting on a line in Job containing the complaint that God sometimes does not hear a needy person's prayers, Aquinas says, "Now it sometimes happens that God hearkens not to a person's pleas but rather to his advantage. A doctor does not hearken to the pleas of the sick person who requests that the bitter medicine be taken away (supposing that the doctor doesn't take it away because he knows that it contributes to health); instead he hearkens to [the patient's] advantage, because by doing so he produces health, which the sick person wants most of all. In the same way, God does not remove tribulations from the person stuck in them, even though he prays earnestly for God to do so, because God knows these tribulations help him forward to final salvation. And so although God truly does hearken, the person stuck in afflictions believes that God hasn't hearkened to him."[24]

In fact, on Aquinas's view, the better the person, the more likely it is that he will experience suffering. In explicating two metaphors of Job's,[25] comparing human beings in this life to soldiers on a military campaign and to employees, Aquinas makes the point in this way. "It is plain that the general of an army does not spare [his] more active soldiers dangers or exertions, but as the plan of battle requires, he sometimes lays them open to greater dangers and greater exertions. But after the attainment of victory, he bestows greater honor on the more active soldiers. So also the head of a household assigns greater exertions to his better servants, but when it is time to reward them, he lavishes greater gifts on them. And so neither is it characteristic of divine providence that it should exempt good people more from the adversities and exertions of the present life, but rather that it reward them more at the end."[26]

In his commentary on Thessalonians, Aquinas makes the same sort of point: "Many who are alive [in the eschaton] will be tried in the persecution of Antichrist, and they will surpass in greatness the many who had previously died."[27] And in his commentary on Philippians, he makes the point more generally: "from sufferings borne here a person attains to glory."[28]

With this background, we should not be surprised to find Aquinas affirming Paul's line in Romans that we should be glad of suffering: "It is a sign of the ardent hope which we have on account of Christ that we glory not only because of [our] hope of the glory to come, but we glory even regarding the evils which we suffer for it. And so [Paul] says that we not only glory (that is, in our hope of glory), but we glory even in tribulations, by which we attain to glory."[29]

The Oddness of Aquinas's Views

In Plato's *Gorgias* Callicles accuses Socrates of turning the world upside down; if Socrates' views are correct, Callicles says, "Everything we do is the exact opposite of what we ought to do."[30] Aquinas's views here also seem upside down. If he is right, everything we typically think about what counts as evil in the world is the exact opposite of what we ought to think. The topsy-turvy nature of this view of evil in the world is made vivid by a passage in a much earlier commentary on Job by Gregory the Great, whose views on this score are similar to Aquinas's. The ways of providence are often hard to understand, Gregory says, but they are

> still more mysterious when things go *well* with good people here, and *ill* with bad people...When things go well with good people here, and ill with bad people, a great uncertainty arises whether good people receive good so that they might be stimulated to grow into something (even) better or whether by a just and secret judgment they see the rewards of their deeds here so that they may be void of the rewards of the life to come...Therefore since the human mind is hemmed in by the thick fog of its uncertainty among the divine judgments, when holy people see the *prosperity* of this world coming to them, they are troubled with a frightening suspicion. For they are afraid that they might receive the fruits of their labors here; they are afraid that divine justice detects a secret wound

in them and, heaping external rewards on them, drives them away from
internal ones...Consequently, holy people are more fearful of prosperity
in this world than of adversity."[31]

In other words, since it is in Gregory's view so difficult to understand
how a just and benevolent providence could allow *good* things to happen to good people, when good people see that there is no adversity in
their lives, they cannot help but wonder whether they are not after all to
be counted among the wicked. For that reason, prosperity is more
frightening to them than adversity.

This upside-down view of evil is the foreseeable conclusion of
Aquinas's twin accounts of happiness and suffering. True happiness
consists in the contemplation of God, shared and enjoyed together by all
the redeemed in heaven. But the spiritual cancer which infects all
human beings, even those who count as pure and innocent by human
standards, makes it impossible for them to be united with God (or with
each other) in heaven. Suffering is a kind of medicine for that disease.[32]
Furthermore, at least for those who assent to the process and are eventually saved from their sinfulness, there is a direct connection between
the amount of suffering in this life and the degree of glory in the life to
come. Given such views, the sort of topsy-turvy thought represented by
the passage from Gregory the Great is less surprising. If suffering is the
chemotherapy for spiritual cancer, the patients whose regimen does not
include any are the only ones for whom the prognosis is really bad.

This attitude on Aquinas's part also helps to explain his reaction to
the book of Job. Like Aquinas, we take the attitude we do toward Job
because of the values, the metaphysics, the general worldview we bring
to the book. Because *we* assume, unreflectively, that temporal well-
being is a necessary constituent of happiness (or even the whole of it),
we also suppose that Job's losses undermine or destroy his happiness.
Consequently, we wonder how God could count as good if he allowed
these things to happen to a good person such as a Job, or we take stories of undeserved suffering to constitute evidence for thinking there is
no God. Aquinas, on the other hand, begins with the conviction that neither God's goodness nor his existence are in doubt, either for the characters in the story of Job or for the readers of that story. Therefore, on
his view, those who go astray in considering sufferings such as Job's do
so because, like Job's comforters, they mistakenly suppose that happiness and unhappiness are functions just of things in this life. And so
Aquinas takes the book of Job to be trying to instill in us the conviction
that there is another life after this one, that our happiness lies there
rather than here, and that we attain to that happiness only through suffering.[33] On Aquinas's view, Job has more suffering than ordinary peo-

ple not because he is morally worse than ordinary, as the comforters assume, but just because he is better. Because he is a better soldier in the war against his own evil and a better servant of God's, God can give him more to bear here; and when this period of earthly life is over, his glory will also be surpassing.

Concerns about Aquinas's View

For many of us, the reaction to this view of Aquinas's will be indignation. If we take it not as piously platitudinous but as a serious expression of otherworldliness, we are likely to find it so alien to our own sensitivities that we reject it as outrageous. I think that there are two primary forms such a reaction will take.

Our more articulate reaction is likely to center on the thought that this view constitutes a reprehensible callousness toward human affliction and misfortune and a disgusting willingness to accept evil.[34] Concern for others is a good part of what prompts this reaction; the asceticism and otherworldliness of Aquinas's sort of attitude seem to rule out all attempts to alleviate the suffering of other people. And, of course, an emphasis on otherworldliness has in the past been used in abominable ways as a basis for exploiting and oppressing the poor and defenseless. When the labor movement in this country was trying to protect workers through unionization, part of its strategy was to cast opprobrium on hope in an afterlife. Instead of offering decent conditions and fair wages, union organizers said, the exploitative bosses held out to their workers the hope of "pie in the sky when we die."

In fact, if what we take away from Aquinas's text is just the general conclusion that on his view pain and adversity are good things, then his view will yield results worthy not only of vituperation but of ridicule as well. We might suppose, for example, that his views entail the claim that anesthetics are to be eschewed[35] or, more generally, that any attempt to palliate or end anyone's pain is a bad thing.

One thing worth noticing at the outset here is that it is perhaps not quite so obvious as we might suppose where callousness lies in this discussion. If, contrary to what Aquinas supposes, human happiness requires the gifts of fortune, then people in contemporary wealthy and developed countries, or just the middle and upper classes in them, will have a vastly greater share of happiness, and the bulk of the world's population will be ruled out of that state. Aquinas's alien otherworldliness at least has the implication that the highest human good of happiness is not another monopoly of the industrialized nations.

But the more detailed and appropriate response to our emotive reaction in both its altruistic and its more general forms consists in seeing that on Aquinas's view suffering is good *not simpliciter* but only *secun-*

dum quid. That is, suffering is not good in itself but only conditionally, insofar as it is a means to an end. "The evils which are in this world," Aquinas says, "aren't to be desired for their own sake but insofar as they are ordered to some good."[36] In itself suffering is a bad thing; it acquires positive value only when it contributes to spiritual well-being. We have no trouble seeing this sort of point when it comes to chemotherapy. In chemotherapy toxic drugs are administered to the patient, and the patient's friends and family are grateful for the treatments; but no one gets confused and supposes that it is then all right to allow the patient to ingest any sort of poisonous substance or that the medical personnel who administer the drugs are as a result in favor of administering poison generally.

It is sometimes easy to confuse conditional goods with nonconditional ones. The development of muscles is a conditional good, to be valued insofar as it contributes to health and strength and their accompanying attractiveness, but steroid users can mistakenly value it as a good in its own right. No doubt, even those steroid users who are not ignorant of the dangers of steroids would claim that they took the drugs to enhance their bodies. But their behavior belies their explanation and suggests that they have lost sight of the purported purpose; bulking up of muscles appears to have become a good in itself in their eyes, even if it is harmful to health in the long run. Similarly, not eating is good only *secundum quid*, insofar as it leads to a healthier and more attractive body, but anorexics misprogram themselves to value it even when it leads to an ugly destruction of health. An anorexic might believe of herself that she was continuing to diet because dieting is a good means to a more attractive body; but in face of her distressing skeletal appearance, it would be hard not to suppose that she had lost sight of the goal she professed to want in her obsessed valuing of the means. It is clear from the stories of ascetic excesses in the patristic and medieval periods that it is possible to become confused in the same sort of way about the conditional good of suffering. Simeon Stylites spent thirty-seven years living on top of pillars, the last of which was sixty feet high and only six feet wide. He is reputed to have come close to death on one occasion as a result of wearing next to his skin an abrasive material which grew into the skin and infected it.[37] It seems not unreasonable to take him as a spiritual anorexic, mistaking a conditional good for a nonconditional one. Perhaps he believed of himself that his purpose for self-denial was spiritual progress, but like the anorexic he appears to have become obsessed with the means at the expense of the goal. No doubt, part of what the Renaissance found so repulsive about the Middle Ages was a certain tendency on the part of medievals to engage in prolonged and pointless bouts of self-destructive asceticism.

But how do we know that Simeon Stylites, or one of the other over-rigorous ascetics of the patristic period, is the medieval analogue to a neurotic and unstoppable dieter? It is not so hard to know the difference between healthy dieting and anorexia, but how would we know with regard to suffering when it was serving the function of spiritual health and so was good rather than destructive? The answer, I think, is that we cannot know. Sometimes in dealing with conditional goods we have to rely on experts. The steroids which some misguided athletes take to their misfortune are also important therapeutic drugs for certain sorts of cancers; but we learn this fact from medical experts, and we have to rely on them to administer the drugs in such a way that they contribute to health rather than destruction. In the case of suffering and its role in redemption, it seems clear that at least in the great majority of cases we do not know enough to turn suffering into a help toward spiritual health. We have to rely, therefore, on God's expertise instead.[38]

How do we avail ourselves of that expertise? How do we know in any given case whether God intends some suffering as a cure for evil or whether a particular degree of suffering will not produce spiritual toxicosis instead? When we see someone suffer as a result of human injustice, then on Aquinas's view (other things being equal) we have a clear obligation to do what is in our power to stop the suffering. Injustice is a mortal sin which separates a person from God; in intervening we help to rescue not only the victim of the injustice but also the perpetrator, whose condition on Aquinas's view is otherwise apparently terminal. Job, in arguing for his innocence, points not just to the fact that he has not exploited any of those dependent on him but that he has even been particularly attentive to the needs of the poor and downtrodden,[39] and Aquinas comments on these passages with evident approval.[40] There is nothing in Aquinas's attitude toward suffering which is incompatible with a robust program of social justice. More generally, one way (though not the only way) to tell if any particular suffering on the part of a given individual is ordained by God to spiritual health is if we try to alleviate that suffering and it turns out not to be possible to do so. Part of what makes Simeon Stylites repulsive to us is that he not only does not try to avoid suffering but even deliberately seeks it out for its own sake.[41] Gregory the Great's line, on the other hand, implies that redemptive suffering cannot be instigated by us but has to be received from God's hand. Otherwise, the good men who tremble at their prosperity could stop trembling and just flagellate themselves to put a stop to their worrisome lack of adversity.

For these reasons the concern that Aquinas's account prompts indifference to suffering is mistaken; and if our indignation at his views is based on this concern, it is misplaced. But perhaps our negative reaction to Aquinas's account of evil stems from attitudes more complicated and less amenable to crisp articulation. Renaissance attitudes toward the Middle Ages were something like Callicles' reaction to Socrates. The Renaissance thought the Middle Ages had turned human values upside down, and it found medieval worldviews repellent because it saw them as inhuman. As intellectual descendants of the Renaissance (more nearly than of the Middle Ages), we might feel somewhat the same way about Aquinas's view of the world: any life really lived in accordance with this worldview would be wretched, inhumanly repudiating all the loveliness and goodness of this world, unnaturally withdrawing from all that makes life worthwhile.

Aquinas is not oblivious to this problem. For that matter, neither is the apostle Paul. "If in this life only we have hope in Christ," he says, "we are of all people most miserable."[42] In commenting on this passage, Aquinas says, "If there is no resurrection of the dead, it follows that there is no good for human beings other than in this life. And if this is the case, then those people are more miserable who suffer many evils and tribulations in this life. Therefore, since the apostles and Christians [generally] suffer more tribulations, it follows that they, who enjoy less of the goods of this world, would be more miserable than other people." The very fact that Aquinas feels he needs to explicate this point in some detail highlights the difference between our worldview and his; no one has to explain to us that those who suffer more evils in this world are more miserable than others. But what Aquinas goes on to say spells out explicitly the difference between the worldview of his culture and our own. "If there were no resurrection of the dead," he continues, "people wouldn't think it was a power and a glory to abandon all that can give pleasure and to bear the pains of death and dishonor; instead they would think it was stupid." He assumes that Christians are people who do glory in tribulations, and so he ends his commentary on this passage in Corinthians by saying, "And so it is clear that [if there were no resurrection of the dead,], [Christians] would be more miserable than other people."[43]

So Aquinas's account of evil has inherent in it a response to objections of the Renaissance variety. If you suppose that fast-food-munching couch potatoes are just as healthy or healthier than nutrition-conscious physical-fitness advocates, you will of course find all the emphasis of the exercisers on diet and physical training perplexing or neurotic or worse. Denying oneself appealing foods and forcing oneself to sweat and strain in exercise are conditional goods only. Unless you share the view that these things do lead to desirable ends, you will not find them good in any sense. Similarly, if we do not share the worldview that holds that there is an afterlife, that true happiness consists in union with God in the afterlife, and that suffering helps us to attain that happiness, we will naturally find Aquinas's valuing suffering even as a conditional good appalling or crazy.

Consolation

Even those who share with Aquinas the conviction that there is an afterlife and that the truest or deepest happiness is be found in it might nonetheless feel queasy about or alienated from his account of evil. For many people, the supposition that suffering has the therapeutic value Aquinas claims for it will not be enough; they will still feel that there is something frighteningly inhuman in a worldview that tells us not only that the whole of our life on earth will be one prolonged spiritual analogue to chemotherapy but also that we ought to rejoice in that state of affairs. And so they are likely to side with the Renaissance humanist repudiation of such a worldview. I, too, think the Renaissance humanists were right to reject this worldview, but I think it would be a mistake to take it as the correct description of Aquinas's account. There is a more humane side to the medieval view of suffering which the Renaissance humanists missed. As Aquinas explains it, this part of his account applies primarily to the suffering of fully functional adults who are Christians. (I think it is possible to see in Aquinas's thought a way in which to transpose his line so that it applies also to the suffering of children and non-Christian adults.[44] For the sake of brevity, however, I will consider it here only in the form he gives it, in which it applies to Christian adults with normally functioning faculties.)

The missing element has to do with the work of the Holy Spirit. On Aquinas's view, the Holy Spirit works in the hearts of those who believe in God and produces spiritual consolation. The Holy Spirit, Aquinas says, "purges us from sin," "illumines the intellect," "brings us to keep the commandments," "confirms our hope in eternal life," "counsels us in our perplexities about the will of God," and "brings us to love God."[45] The Holy Spirit guides toward truth those whom it fills and helps them to conquer their weaknesses[46] so that they can become the sort of people they are glad to be. Most importantly, the Holy Spirit fills a person with a sense of the love of God and his nearness, so that one of the principal effects of the Holy Spirit is joy.[47]

The Holy Spirit perfects us, both inwardly and outwardly, Aquinas says; and "the ultimate perfection, by which a person is made perfect inwardly, is joy, which stems from the presence of what is loved. Whoever has the love of God, however, already has what he loves, as is said in 1 John 4:16: 'whoever abides in the love of God abides in God, and God abides in him.' And joy wells up from this."[48] "When [Paul] says 'the Lord is near,' he points out the cause of joy, because a person rejoices at the nearness of his friend."[49]

Perhaps there is no greater joy than the presence of the person you love when that person loves you to the fulfillment of your heart's desire.[50] Joy of that sort, Aquinas says, is not destroyed by either pain or tribulation. In order to keep joy whole, even in the adversities of this life, the Holy Spirit protects people against the evils they encounter: "and first against the evil which disturbs peace, since peace is disturbed by adversities. But with regard to adversities the Holy Spirit perfects [us] through patience, which enables [us] to bear adversities patiently...Second, against the evil which arrests joy, namely, the wait for what is loved. To this evil, the Spirit opposes long-suffering, which is not broken by the waiting." In this way and others, Aquinas says, the Holy Spirit makes human joy whole, even in the midst of pain.[51]

But what about Job?, we might think at this point. Was he not someone who faced his troubles without consolation from God? Aquinas thinks, after all, that God sometimes heeds a suffering person's advantage, rather than his prayer, and it is in connection with Job that Aquinas develops that line. If the sufferer cannot see that advantage, then, as even Aquinas recognizes, the sufferer may not be consoled but rather be afflicted in spirit also.[52] But I think Aquinas would be inclined to deny our characterization of Job as someone who suffers without divine consolation. One of the longest speeches attributed to God in the Bible is the speech he makes to Job; and when God's speech is finished, what does Job say? "I had heard of you before with the hearing of the ear, but now my eye sees you."[53] Whatever else we need to say about the complicated relations between God and Job, and that is no doubt a great deal, it is clear that with his views of happiness Aquinas would certainly attribute deep, sweet consolation to anyone who could truly claim to be seeing God. Furthermore, part of the point of Christianity, on Aquinas's account, is to make it clear to people that there is a point to suffering, so as to ward off the kind of theological perplexity and anguish many of us think we see in Job. In his passion, Christ not only makes atonement for sinners but also sets them an example, so that they will understand that the path to redemption goes through suffering.[54] The lesson learned for us by Job and the example presented by Christ make it easier for others afterwards, Aquinas thinks, to endure suffering without losing spiritual consolation during the period of pain.[55]

In fact, Aquinas thinks that for Christians the inner sweetness of God's consolation increases directly with the troubles of this life. At the start of his commentary on 1 Thessalonians he quotes with approval the line in 2 Corinthians which says that "as the sufferings of Christ abound in us, so our consolation also abounds by Christ." And in explaining that line, in his commentary on 2 Corinthians, he describes spiritual consolation in this way:

> People need to be supported in the evils that happen to them. And this is
> what consolation is, strictly speaking. Because if a person didn't have
> something in which his heart could rest when he is overcome with evils,
> he couldn't bear up under them. And so one person consoles another
> when he offers him some relief, in which he can rest in the midst of evils.
> Now there are some evils in which one human being can console us in all
> [our] evils."[56]

Even in our sins, which from Aquinas's point of view are more
frightening than adversity, because unlike adversity they separate us
from God, even then, Aquinas holds, we are consoled by God; that is
why, Aquinas says, Paul calls him the God of all consolation.[57]

The Renaissance saw the Middle Ages as inhuman in part because it
no longer shared the medieval worldview and in part because it had
missed this side of the medieval story. On Aquinas's account,
Christianity does not call people to a life of self-denying wretchedness,
but to a life of joy, even in the midst of pain and trouble. Without joy,
Aquinas says, no progress is possible in the Christian life.[58]

Conclusion

Aquinas's attitude toward evil is clearly as different from our own
as Socrates' attitude toward the good life is different from Callicles'.
Aquinas's analysis of the reaction of Job's comforters would also, I
think, be his analysis of the reaction to evil on the part of those of us
concerned with the problem of evil in this culture:

> Human beings are made up of a spiritual nature and of earthly flesh.
> Consequently, evil for human beings consists in their abandoning spiri-
> tual goods, to which they are directed in virtue of [having] rational
> minds, and their cleaving to earthly goods, which suit them in virtue of
> [having] earthly flesh.[59]

Job's loquacious friends did not understand the spiritual consolation
of Job, and so he adds, "You have put their heart far from learning–that
is, from the spiritual learning [which comes from] you, by which you
teach [human beings] to disdain temporal goods and to hope for spiritual ones. And because they put their hope only in things low and temporal, they could not reach a spiritual plane to be placed next to God."[60]

It certainly does seem true, at any rate, that there is a correlation
between the degree to which we associate human good with things in
this world and the extent to which we see the problem of evil in its contemporary form. The story of the metamorphosis from the medieval

worldview to our own is, of course, in large part a matter of a shift from a religious to a secular outlook. But even among Christians we can chart the change from the otherworldly approach of the medievals to the more common contemporary attitudes. We can see this change in its beginnings in, for example, the pious Christian adherents of the *devotio moderna*, a religious movement important in the Netherlands, particularly in the fifteenth century. There was a distinctly non-medieval attitude in the devotio moderna in its tendency to conflate temporal and spiritual goods and in its emphasis on the religious importance of temporal concerns. Commenting on the death of a recently appointed principal of a school for religious instruction, an anonymous adherent of this movement raises the problem of evil in a way which is devout but altogether different from Aquinas's approach. He says,

> Permit me to take a moment here to allude to the wondrous and secret judgments of our Lord God, not as if scrutinizing them in a reproachful way but rather as humbly venerating the inscrutable. It is quite amazing that our fathers and brothers had set out with a single will and labored at their own expense, to the honor of God and for the salvation of souls, to erect a school here in Emmerich to do exercises with boys and clerics... And now after much care and trouble, everything had been brought to a good state: we had a learned and suitable man for rector, the venerable Master Arnold of Hildesheim...Then, behold,...our Lord God, as if totally unconcerned with all that we had in hand, which had just begun to flower, suddenly and unexpectedly threw it all into confusion and decline, nearly reducing it to nothing. For just as the sheep are dispersed when the shepherd is struck down, so when our beloved brother [Master Arnold] died the whole school was thrown into confusion. The youths left in swarms...not, it is to be feared, without some danger to their souls... Nonetheless, to [him] be the honor and the glory now and through the ages, to him whose judgments, though hidden, are yet never unjust.[61]

Between the attitude of this author, who finds adversity for God's people fundamentally inexplicable, and the attitude of such medievals as Aquinas or Gregory the Great there is a world of difference.

In this paper I have only expounded Aquinas's views of evil; I have not sought to argue for them, although they seem to me impressive and admirable in many ways. (No doubt, a thorough philosophical defense or refutation of his views would require book-length treatment.) But what Aquinas's interpretation of Job and general account of evil show us, whether we are inclined to accept or reject them, is that our approach to the problem of evil is a consequence of our attitude toward much larger issues, such as the nature of human happiness and the goal of human life. To make progress on the problem of evil, in my view, we need to face up to these larger issues in a reflective way. One of the benefits of the history of philosophy, especially the history of philosophy from periods such as the Middle Ages whose cultures are so different from our own, is that it helps us to see the otherwise unnoticed and unexamined assumptions we bring to philosophical issues such as the problem of evil. Aquinas's worldview, characterized by a renunciation of the things of this world and a rush toward heaven, is a particularly good one to juxtapose to the worldview of our culture, steeped in comforts and seeking pleasure. "[T]heodicies," says Terrence Tilley in his passionate denunciation of them, "construct consoling dreams to distract our gaze from real evils."⁶² What reflection on Aquinas's account helps us to see is that in evaluating this claim and others like it, hostile to theodicy, everything depends on what you take to be dream and what you take to be reality.⁶³

Notes

1. Norman Kretzmann has discussed some of the issues raised in Aquinas's commentary on Romans in a recent paper; see his "Warring against the Law of My Mind: Aquinas on Romans 7," in *Philosophy and the Christian Faith*, ed. Thomas Morris (Notre Dame, Ind.: University of Notre Dame Press, 1988), 172-95.

2. This commentary, *Expositio super Job ad litteram*, is available in the Leonine edition of Aquinas's works, vol. 26, and in an English translation: *Thomas Aquinas, The Literal Exposition on Job: A Scriptural Commentary Concerning Providence*, trans. Anthony Damico and Martin Yaffe, The American Academy of Religion. *Classics in Religious Studies* (Atlanta: Scholars Press, 1989). The commentary was probably written while Aquinas was at Orvieto, in the period 1261-1264. See James Weisheipl, *Friar Thomas D'Aquino: His Life, Thought, and Works*, 2d ed. (Washington, D.C.: Catholic University of America Press, 1983), 153; see also *Albert and Thomas: Selected Writings*, ed. Simon Tugwell, *Classics of Western Spirituality* (Mahwah, N.J.: Paulist Press, 1988), 223.

3. The commentaries on the Pauline epistles were probably written during Aquinas's second Parisian regency, 1269-1272, and during his subsequent stay in Naples. See Tugwell, *Albert and Thomas*, 248; Weisheipl, *Friar Thomas D'Aquino*, 373.

4. Aquinas, *Expositio super Job*, chap. 7, secs. 1-4, Damico and Yaffe, p.145. Although I have preferred to give my own translations, I have found the Damico and Yaffe translation very helpful, and I will give references to this work both to the Latin and to Damico and Yaffe

translation.

5. See, for example, Thomas Aquinas, *Super ad Romanos*, chap. 12, lec. 2.

6. See, for example, Marilyn Adams, "Redemptive Suffering: A Christian Solution to the Problem of Evil," in *Rationality, Religious Belief, and Moral Commitment: New Essays in the Philosophy of Religion*, ed. Robert Audi and William Wainwright, (Ithaca, NY: Cornell University Press, 1986), 248-267.

7. See, for example, William Rowe, "The Empirical Argument from Evil," in *Rationality, Religious Belief, and Moral Commitment*, op.cit.

8. Aquinas, *Super ad Romanos*, chap. 8, lec. 6.

9. SCG III, 112. See also *Expositio super Job*, chap. 7, secs. 10-18; Damico and Yaffe, pp.151, 153.

10. Aquinas, *Super ad Romanos*, chap. 8, lec. 6.

11. Ibid.

12. SCG III, 30.

13. SCG III, 32.

14. SCG III, 28.

15. SCG III, 48.

16. Thomas Aquinas, *Super ad Hebraeos*, chap. 12, lec. 2.

17. Aquinas, *Expositio super Job*, chap. 9, secs. 24-30; Damico and Yaffe, p.179.

18. For an excellent annotated translation of the text, see Nicholas Ayo, *The Sermon-Conferences of St. Thomas Aquinas on the Apostles' Creed* (Notre Dame, Ind.: University of Notre Dame Press, 1988). Although I have preferred to use my own translation, I found Ayo's quite helpful, and for this work I give citations both to the Latin and to Ayo's translation. Thomas Aquinas, *Collationes Credo in Deum*, sec. III; Ayo, pp.40-42. For some reasons for thinking that Aquinas's approach to the problem of evil is right, see my "The Problem of Evil," *Faith and Philosophy* 2 (1985) 392-424 and "Providence and the Problem of Evil," in *Christian Philosophy*, ed. Thomas Flint, (Notre Dame, IN: University of Notre Dame Press, 1990), 51-91. In those papers I discuss reasons for supposing that a good God would create a world in which human beings have such a cancer of the soul, that suffering is the best available means to cure the cancer in the soul, and that God can justifiably allow suffering even though it sometimes eventuates in the opposite of moral goodness or love of God.

19. There is a translation of this commentary: *Commentary on Saint Paul's First Letter to the Thessalonians and the Letter to the Philippians by St. Thomas Aquinas*, trans. F. R. Larcher and Michael Duffy (Albany: Magi Books, 1969). Although I have preferred to use my own translations, I found the Larcher and Duffy translation helpful, and I will give

citations for this work and for the commentary on Phillippians both to the Latin and to this translation. Thomas Aquinas, *Super ad Thessalonicenses I*, prologue; Larcher and Duffy, p.3.

20. Thomas Aquinas, *Super ad Hebraeos*, chap. 12, lec. 1.

21. Ibid., lec. 2.

22. Ibid.

23. Aquinas, *Expositio super Job*, chap. 1, secs. 20-21; Damico and Yaffe, p.89.

24. Aquinas, *Expositio super Job*, chap. 9, secs. 15-21; Damico and Yaffe, p.174.

25. Only one of the two metaphors is in the Revised Standard Version, the King James, and the Anchor Bible.

26. Aquinas, *Expositio super Job*, chap. 7 sec. 1; Damico and Yaffe, p.146. The idea here seems to be that there are degrees of glory or degrees of reward in heaven, and those persons who are better are given more suffering for the sake of the concomitant greater glory. Presumably, part of what makes such persons better is that they would be willing to accept greater suffering for the sake of greater glory; see the section on martyrs in "Providence and the Problem of Evil," op. cit. Someone might suppose that on Aquinas's views he ought to say not that better people suffer more but rather that worse people, who need more suffering, suffer more. But here I think the analogy with chemotherapy is again helpful. Sometimes the most effective kinds of chemotherapy cannot be used on those who need it most because their systems are too weak to bear the treatments, and so the strongest kinds of treatment tend to be reserved for those who are not too old or too advanced in the disease or too riddled with secondary complications—in other words, for those who are (besides the particular cancer) strong and robust.

27. Thomas Aquinas, *Super ad Thessalonicenses I*, chap. 4, lec. 2; Larcher and Duffy, p.39.

28. Thomas Aquinas, *Super ad Philippenses*, chap. 3, lec. 2; Larcher and Duffy, p.102.

29. Thomas Aquinas, *Super ad Romanos*, chap. 5, lec. 1.

30. Plato, *Gorgias* 481C.

31. There is a nineteenth-century translation of this work: *Morals on the Book of Job by Gregory the Great, the First Pope of that Name* (Oxford, 1844). Although I have preferred to use my own translations, I give the reference both to the Latin and to this translation: *Gregory the Great, Moralia in Job*, book 5, introduction; *Morals*, pp. 241-42. The line taken by Gregory has the result that if we come across saintly people who do not suffer much, we should be inclined to wonder whether they really are as saintly as they seem. The implausibility of this line is significantly reduced if we remember that it is possible, Mother Teresa fashion, to be

afflicted for the suffering of others as well as for one's own.

32. One should not misunderstand this claim and suppose Aquinas to be claiming that human beings can earn their way to heaven by the merit badges of suffering. Aquinas is quite explicit that salvation is through Christ only. His claim here is not about what causes salvation but only about what is efficacious in the process of salvation. It would take us too far afield here to consider Aquinas's view of the relation between Christ's work of redemption and the role of human suffering in that process. What is important for my purposes is just to see that on Aquinas's account suffering is an indispensable element in the course of human salvation, initiated and merited by Christ.

33. See, for example, *Expositio super Job*, chap. 7, sec. 1, Damico and Yaffe, p.145; and chap. 19:23-29, Damico and Yaffe, pp.268-71, where Aquinas makes these points clear and maintains that Job was already among the redeemed awaiting the resurrection and union with God. Someone might wonder whether it is possible to maintain this approach to suffering when the suffering consists in madness, mental retardation, or some form of dementia. This doubt is based on the unreflective assumption that those suffering from these afflictions have lost all the mental faculties needed for moral or spiritual development. For some suggestions to the contrary, see the sensitive and insightful discussion of retarded and autistic patients in Oliver Sacks, *The Man Who Mistook His Wife for a Hat* (New York: Summit books, 1985).

34. For a vigorous response of this sort to all kinds of theodicy, see Terrence W. Tilley, *The Evils of Theodicy* (Washington, D.C.: Georgetown University Press, 1991).

35. As late as the end of the nineteenth century, even *Scientific American* was publishing diatribes against anesthetics (see the quotation in *Scientific American* [August 1991]: 14), and the lamentable nineteenth-century animus against anesthetics, particularly in connection with childbirth, often had a religious basis. For a detailed discussion of nineteenth-century attitudes toward anesthetics, see Martin S. Pernick, *A Calculus of Suffering: Pain, Professionalism, and Anesthesia in Nineteenth-Century America* (New York: Columbia University Press, 1985).

36. Thomas Aquinas, *Super I ad Corinthios*, chap. 15, lec. 2.

37. David Hugh Farmer, *The Oxford Dictionary of Saints* (Oxford: Oxford University Press, 1988).

38. Clearly sometimes we do know, or at least have a pretty good idea, as when loving parents deliberately inflict some suffering on their children in response to intolerable behavior on the children's part.

39. Job 31. In supporting Aquinas's line here, I am assuming that sins of thought and deed are worse than the analogous sins of thought alone.

That is, I am assuming that someone who is murderous but who is prevented by his friends from acting on his intentions is morally better off than he would be if he had been allowed to go ahead and commit murder. This assumption is widely, though not universally, shared.

40. See also ST II-II, 32, 5 and 6, where Aquinas argues that not giving alms, or keeping for oneself more than one needs, can be punished with damnation.

41. Two caveats are perhaps necessary here. (1) Nothing in these remarks should be taken as denigrating asceticism as a whole. Rigorous training, of body or mind, does take self-discipline and, by implication, self-denial. But it is possible to become obsessed with the self-denial itself, so that it effaces the goal for which it was originally intended as a means. There is a difference between anorexia and dieting, and one can see the problems in anorexia without thereby eschewing discipline as regards eating. (2) By saying that Simeon sought suffering for its own sake, I do not mean to deny that he might have believed of himself that the purpose of the ascetic suffering he engaged in was spiritual progress. It seems nonetheless true that many of his actions focus just on inflicting suffering on himself, rather than on the goal to which the suffering was supposed to be a means. It certainly appears as if he lost sight of the professed goal of spiritual well-being in his fixation on mortifying the flesh. I am grateful to Marilyn Adams for comments on this point.

42. 1 Cor. 15:19.

43. Aquinas, *Super I ad Corinthios*, chap. 15, lec. 2.

44. I have discussed ways in which this sort of approach to the problem of evil might be applied to those who are not adults or to those who are not Christian in "The Problem of Evil," op. cit.

45. Thomas Aquinas, *Collationes Credo in Deum*, sec. 11; *Ayo*, pp.116-18.

46. Thomas Aquinas, *Super ad Philippenses*, chap. 1, lec. 2; Larcher and Duffy, p.63; also, chap. 1, lec. 3; Larcher and Duffy, p.68.

47. See, for example, *Super ad Romanos*, chap. 5, lec. 1.

48. There is an English translation of this work: *Commentary on Saint Paul's Epistle to the Galations by St. Thomas Aquinas*, trans. F. R. Larcher and Richard Murphy (Albany: Magi Books, 1966). Although I have preferred to use my own translations, I found the Larcher and Murphy translation helpful, and I will give citations for this work both to the Latin and to the Larcher and Murphy translation. *Super ad Galatas*, chap. 5, lec. 6; Larcher and Murphy, pp.179-80.

49. *Super ad Philippenses*, chap. 4, lec. 1; Larcher and Duffy, p.113.

50. Someone might suppose that this line is false, on the grounds that sometimes pain or sickness makes us just irritable and unable to find

any joy or even relief in the presence of a person we love. The mistake in this view can be seen by considering cases of childbirth. In the painful, humiliating, or embarrassing circumstances which sometimes arise in childbirth, a woman may get irritable enough at the father of her child to lash out at him, verbally or even physically. That she wants him there anyway, that his presence is a great comfort to her underneath and around the irritation, is made manifest by the fact that she still wants him in the delivery room, that she would find his leaving intolerable. Being irritable under pain in the presence of someone you love is compatible with finding great comfort in his presence at another level. It should perhaps also be said, as an additional consideration in this connection, that the degree of joy or comfort one person has at the presence of another will be proportional to the intensity of the love between them.

51. Aquinas, *Super ad Galatas*, chap. 5, lec. 6; Larcher and Murphy, p.180: Also, *Super ad Galatas*, chap. 5, lec. 6; Larcher and Murphy, p.179; and *Super ad Hebraeos*, chap. 12, lec. 2.

52. Aquinas, *Expositio super Job*, chap. 9, secs. 15-21, Damico and Yaffe, p.174.

53. Job 42:5.

54. See, for example, Aquinas, *Collationes Credo in Deum*, sec. 6; Ayo, pp.69, 73.

55. Aquinas therefore supposes that Job's later return to worldly prosperity is at least in part a divine concession to the fact that Job is part of a pre-Christian culture. "And [Job's return to prosperity] was appropriate to the time, because of the position of the Old Testament in which temporal goods are promised, so that in this way by the prosperity which he recovered an example was given to others, to turn them to God." *Expositio super Job*, chap. 42, secs. 10-16; Damico and Yaffe, p.472. It should be said that nothing in Aquinas's position requires him to hold that all Christian adults experience divine consolation in their suffering. For some people, the point of the suffering might be to bring them to the stage where they are able to experience consolation; and even for those people who are well advanced in spiritual or moral progress, consolation can always be warded off by a spirit which refuses it.

56. Aquinas, *Super II ad Corinthios*, chap. 1, lec. 2.

57. Ibid. See also *Super ad Romanos*, chap. 8, lec. 7.

58. *Super ad Philippenses*, chap. 4, lec. 1; Larcher and Duffy, p.112.

59. Aquinas, *Expositio super Job*, chap. 1, secs. 6-7; Damico and Yaffe, p.79.

60. Aquinas, *Expositio super Job*, chap. 17, secs. 2-9: Damico and Yaffe, p.252.

61. *Devotio Moderna: Basic Writings*, trans. John van Engen (New York: Paulist Press, 1988), p.151. I am grateful to John van Engen for calling my attention to the intriguing material in this book.
62. Terrence Tilley, *The Evils of Theodicy*, (Washington, D.C.: Georgetown University Press, 1991), 219.
63. I am grateful to the referees for this volume for useful questions and suggestions. I am especially indebted to Norman Kretzmann for many helpful comments on earlier drafts of this paper.

Chapter 11

Must Job Live Forever?: A Reply to Aquinas on Providence and Freedom, Evil and Immortality

Timothy P. Jackson

Introduction

"If God is so good, why isn't God's creation more so?" This is the problem of evil *in nuce*, and it trades on the fear that perhaps God is not so good after all–indeed, that God may not exist. To assuage this fear we moderns cast about for either (a) convincing empirical evidence of God's real benevolence or (b) imaginative scenarios in which God and evil are logically compossible. Finding (a) would suggest that we are rationally justified, if not compelled, in believing in God's goodness (a theodicy proper), while finding (b) would suggest that we are not necessarily *un*justified in doing so (a more modest defense of religious faith).[1]

In contrast to our post-Enlightenment concerns, the problem of evil does not centrally occupy Thomas Aquinas. As we will see, this is true even in Thomas's *Literal Exposition on Job*, the place where theodicy questions would seem most pressing.[2] This does not mean that Thomas is oblivious to the relevant issues, for he is clearly aware of the apparent incompatibility of worldy evils and an all-good God (see ST, I, Q. 2, art. 3, ad 1).[3] But the vector of his commentary runs in the opposite direction from that of most modern theodicists: again, moderns tend to reason from the world even with its palpable evil to a real (or at least possible) God, whereas Thomas tends to reason from a palpable God to a defeated (or at least eschatologically defeasible) evil.[4]

Just as Thomas is aware of the Argument *from* Design in the world *to* the existence of God (the fifth of the the "five ways" in ST, I, Q. 2, art. 3) yet focuses more on the Argument *to* Design *from* the existence of God,[5] so he is aware of the Argument *from* the Defeasibily of Evil but focuses more on the Argument *to* the Defeasibilty of Evil. One can overdraw the contrast here, but first of all and most of the time Aquinas begins with trust in God's providence and asks what follows with respect to the nature and final disposition of evil, rather than the other way round. Aquinas's concern is not so much with "intellectual obstacles" to justified belief in God as with practical obstacles to the profitable contemplation of God.[6] His primary purpose is not to defend believers' rationality, as several commentators have reminded us, but rather to promote their happiness.[7]

I want to explore here in a limited way the relation between divine providence and human history, especially the experience of freedom and evil. I first examine three alternative conceptions of the meaning of temporal life and how it relates to "the love of God,"[8] all of which are discussed or alluded to by Thomas in his *Expositio super Job ad litteram*. I call them: (1) impersonal fatalism, (2) Deuteronomic retributivism, and (3) eschatological perfectionism. I am deeply indebted to Aquinas's views, but in opposition to his considered opinion, I next elaborate and defend a fourth vision, dubbed (4) strong agape. My aim is not to solve the modern theodicy problem but rather to understand a religious faith that flows from being touched by divine love.

I applaud Aquinas's distancing of the problem of evil, as well as his denial of impersonal fatalism[9] and this-worldly retributivism. These moves allow him to avoid many of what Terrence Tilley calls "the evils of theodicy"[10] (e.g., explaining away temporal suffering). Thomas does offer cosmological arguments for the existence of God,[11] but I want to emulate his typical pattern of beginning primarily with God and then reasoning to order in the world. It is my thesis, however, that this pattern in fact leads to some nonThomistic conclusions. More specifically, affirming the transcendent goodness of God counts against (a) a compatibilist doctrine of irresistible grace, (b) an exclusively pedagogical account of human suffering, and (c) an emphatic insistence on personal immortality.

The lesson of Job, I argue, is that God's love is an utterly gratuitous personal presence, the possibility of tenderness even in the face of extreme suffering and death. It is an ineffably kind visitation that is its own reward, as well as a source of the obligation to be kind to others. The more maximal our appreciation of divine charity, including its permission of human freedom, the more minimal can be our bother over theodicy and longevity. We are rightly moved by human (and animal) suffering, and "longevity has its place" (King), but abstract theodicies tend to inure us to others' pain and to make an idol of an afterlife. The more we admit that the problem of evil remains mysterious and that physical death may be the end of one's personal existence, the more constructive is our response to tragedy and mortality.

Impersonal Fatalism

By "impersonal fatalism" I mean any perspective on the meaning of life that denies divine attention to and promotion of the well-being of individual finite agents. This denial may involve construing human history as the more or less chance upshot of random forces (the priority of contingency) or the more or less fixed upshot of predetermined forces (the priority of necessity). Beyond this, on my definition even the Aristotelian-Averroist denial of particular providence counts as impersonal fatalism, since on this account God is not (indeed, cannot be) concerned with individual human beings but only with the species. In our personal lives, we must be resigned to a sort of divine indifference, and this rules out, among other things, the possibility of a personal relation with the ultimate Power in the universe. At the theological level, our fate simply bears down on us; to hold otherwise is to embrace a crude anthropocentrism.[12]

Aquinas takes a rejection of fatalism to be a central lesson of the "Book of Job." The various versions of fatalism are mistaken about divine providence and lead, in turn, to private despair and public immorality. Whether or not some form of "fatalistic virtue" is conceivable (cf. Stoicism), one can readily agree with Thomas that it would be a far cry from traditional Christian faith as well as from the foundational beliefs of Job. Impersonal fatalism amounts to a denial of God's omniscience and omnipotence, but more significantly for Christians it slanders God's love. If God created human beings such that the hairs on their heads are numbered, then God can and does care for them as individuals. In short, Thomas's siding with Job on the particularity of providence (see also ST, I, Q. 22, art. 2) seems convincing to most believers, though the question of how this providence operates (whether it leaves room for human freedom, whether it orchestrates an afterlife for believers, etc.) remains open.

Deuteronomic Retributivism

An alternative view of divine providence is Deuteronomic retributivism. A weak version of such retributivism holds that God often punishes the wicked and rewards the virtuous in this life, but Zophar, Eliphaz, and Bildad embrace a much stronger version in their accusations against Job. In an effort to explain Job's suffering while preserving God's limitless power and discriminating justice, they endorse two related theses: (i) that God provides earthly rewards for good individuals and earthly punishments for wicked individuals, and (ii) that *everything* that happens in human history is *always* explicable as part of this retributivist system. If Job suffers, they reason, it *must* be due to his past sins.

Aquinas takes exception with the friends' strong retributivism. The "comforters" subscribe to the this-worldly, divine retributivism outlined in "Deuteronomy" and challenged by "Job," as well as by Biblical Wisdom literature generally. Like Zophar, Eliphaz, and Bildad, Thomas thinks that God is just and that God rewards and punishes individuals; but Thomas also holds two related beliefs that separate him from both impersonalists and Deuteronomists. According to Aquinas, (i) divine rewards and punishments are not (usually) in the form of material goods and ills or physical pleasures and pains, and (ii) they are not meted out in time (at least not uniformly or decisively).[13] God's providence is at work in history, but it is only in eternity that the means and ends of that providence are finally realized for, and fully evident to, finite persons. In this life, the righteous suffer injustices and the wicked often flourish, at least in material terms.

To the extent that religion is identifiable with Deuteronomic theology, therefore, "Job" is an irreligious book. Aquinas is similarly irreligious, however, and would have us (like Job) "repudiate and repent of dust and ashes."[14] He encourages us, that is, to reject all rituals that presume earthly ills always or even usually to be punishments for personal guilt. Worldly losses are genuine ills: we are communal creatures who are vulnerable to real harms, and virtue is not the only good thing.[15] Nevertheless, given Thomas's equation of human happiness with the contemplation of God, even those who (like Job) are physically and emotionally afflicted in this life may still, to a degree, be called "happy"–though they cannot, of course, enjoy the "ultimate felicity" of an entirely stable relation to God.[16]

I consider virtue and happiness to be still more vulnerable, more separable, than Thomas at times allows. Though not a Stoic, Aquinas comes uncomfortably close to what I have elsewhere called, playing off of Martha Nussbaum, "the facility of goodness."[17] For Thomas, happiness is "nothing else than the right order of the will to the last end (God)" (ST, I-II, Q 5, art. 7), and this implies that the good are happy by definition (see ST, I-II, Q. 2, art. 2, ad 1). But does the Holy Spirit always protect the peace and joy of those who remain faithful in affliction, and may we call someone "happy" who is without peace and joy, however morally upright? Here we must recur to *Summa Contra Gentiles* and remind ourselves, in Thomas's own words, that "freedom from death (and accompanying sorrow) is something man cannot achieve in this life. Therefore, it is not possible for man in this life to be (entirely) happy."[18] Thomas holds that "no man can of himself be the sufficient cause of another's spiritual death, because no man dies spiritually except by sinning of his own will" (ST, Q. 73, art. 8, ad 3). But even if no one can be compelled by another to sin, what of those who are so abused as to be kept from virtue, from moral agency itself, through no fault of their own? These are challenging questions, and the heart of Thomas's answer is an eschatological perfectionism that presumes personal immortality, as well as compatibilist freedom.[19] These are precisely the premises I wish to probe, however.

Eschatological Perfectionism

Perhaps the key difference between Job and his friends, on Thomas's view, is that Job believes in bodily resurrection, while they do not.[20] For it is Beatitude in the afterlife that makes evil and suffering defeasible.[21] This commitment to personal fulfillment in an afterlife, when specifically coupled with the claim that there *must* be an afterlife for there to be fulfillment, is definitive of eschatological perfectionism. As Thomas writes in *Summa Contra Gentiles*:

> ... it is impossible for natural desire to be unfulfilled, since "nature does nothing in vain." Now, natural desire would be in vain if it could never be fulfilled. Therefore, man's natural desire (for felicity) is capable of fulfillment, but not in this life, as we have shown. So, it must be fulfilled after this life. Therefore, man's ultimate felicity comes after this life. (SCG, Bk. III, Ch. 48, 11)

As with impersonal fatalism and Deuteronomic retributivism, there are two major versions of eschatological perfectionism: that which emphasizes divine justice and that which emphasizes divine compensation. Whereas Thomas highlights God's eschatological justice in rewarding the virtuous with eternal joy and punishing the wicked with eternal torment, many contemporary philosophers of religion (e.g., Robert and Marilyn Adams) highlight God's eschatological charity in compensating people for the ills suffered (either unfairly or merely unfortunately) during their temporal lives. The difference here is between construing the perfection of God's providence as God's giving finite individuals their spiritual due and construing it as God's giving them a joy that outstrips all moral merit and demerit.

Unlike Job's accusers, Aquinas rejects this-worldly retributivism, but he is a firm believer in *eschatological* retributivism. For all of his accent on the gratuitousness of God's love, Thomas still speaks of a just God who ordains heaven for some and hell for others "in that life to which man is restored by resurrection."[22] Yet is there sufficient warrant to say, as Thomas does, that God damns some to eternal torment without chance of mercy (ST, Suppl. Q. 99, arts. 1 & 2)?[23] Compensationalists do not try to justify suffering (either in this life or a next) with reference to divine retribution.[24] Nevertheless, there are two related theses common to both versions of eschatological perfectionism: (i) that God's providence comes to consummation only beyond the end of time, and (ii) that without an afterlife involving some form of resurrection, God cannot be either just or loving.[25] If God is to be God, so to speak, there must be personal immortality, at least for believers.

Strong Agape Defined

Strong agape is an alternative to the three visions considered thus far. As I define it, strong agape affirms: (1) that the reality of agapic love is not merely the greatest good but also a metavalue: that virtue which makes other human virtues possible and that good without which no other human good can be substantively enjoyed, and (2) that the possibility of loving and being loved, freely, may be a sufficient reason to justify creation of the world in spite of its liability to sin and natural evil. Ideally, the love in question is directed toward and received from both God and other human beings. To emphasize that it be given and taken "freely" does not imply, however, that agape must always be a matter of self-conscious deliberation and/or struggle against inclination; pace Kant, spontaneous dispositions count.

In elaborating these affirmations, strong agapists side with compensationalists in one key respect and depart from both Thomas and the compensationalists in another.[26] They believe, that is, that God's goodness entails that whatever salvation there is is offered to all creatures independently of merit or demerit (either pre- or postmortem) and is accepted (if accepted) freely. Yet they also believe that there is no way of knowing whether God's goodness requires our immortality for its perfection and no way of knowing whether the world will eventually be good overall. Like most compensationalists, strong agapists hold that incompatibilist human freedom is essential if we are to escape impersonal fatalism; but they also hold that putting charity first among the virtues does not require God either to reward us for goodness, to punish us for evil, or to compensate us for ills, in either this life or an afterlife. Charity as participation in the life of God is its own reward, and this is possible here and now (as Thomas reminds us elsewhere)[27]; hatred as willing harm for another is its own punishment, and this is all too actual here and now.

What is the basis for such a strong position? Is any counterevidence entertainable?[28] Answers must be largely biographical and autobiographical. The example of Job himself suggests that death need not be known to be defeated before goodness can be realized, any more than evil need be known to be defeated before faith can be realized. Job celebrates God in spite of temporal pain and doubt. The presence of an infinitely loving Person makes existence worthwhile, if trying; indeed, the power to care that flows from that presence suggests to strong agapists that Love is the generating source of one's very being. Were virtues like empathy and hope, justice and mercy, creativity and patience, thwarted rather than enhanced by agape, this would offer grounds for rejecting the view. But the opposite seems to be the case. Strong agape reflects a leap of faith, more a matter of trust in the Creator than of calculations about creation, but it is not arbitrary.

Strong Agape, Human Suffering, and Incompatibilist Freedom

Aquinas need not be insensitive to human pain or utterly dismissive of the import of the temporal world, because it is in this world that (some) people are prepared for eternal joy. Such joy, in turn, justifies the pain experienced in acquiring it. Commentators like Eleonore Stump rightly emphasize that Aquinas is no masochist: individuals are schooled in patience by affliction, according to Thomas, yet the suffering in question is not judged good *simpliciter* but only *secundum quid*, i.e., as a means to an end (cf. ST, I, Q. 21, art. 4, ad 3).[29] Temporal suffering is like a harsh (spiritual) medicine administered by a benevolent physician. Yet Stump asks the crucial question: "...how would we know with regard to suffering when it was serving the function of spiritual health and so was good rather than destructive?" She answers that "we can't know"[30] and thus must rely on the expertise of God. I want to contend, however, that both Stump's question and her answer are virtually impossible for Thomas to formulate, given his account of divine providence and human freedom.

Aquinas's views on freedom, a form of compatibilism, render the modern problem of evil *unintelligible*, not merely secondary or uninteresting. I have emphasized and even applauded the fact that Thomas wants to reject impersonal fatalism, but at the end of the day his own conception of grace undercuts any significant human agency, I believe. His compatibilism (cf. ST, I-II, Q. 13, art. 6) is untenable: this life and God's love lose their import when we factor in Thomas's mature claim that God is the sufficient cause of all objects, actions, and events (what Bernard Lonergan calls the "universal instrumentality" thesis[31]). Thomas insists that God respects inferior causes, giving creatures "the dignity of causality" (ST, I Q. 22, art. 3), but he nevertheless holds that God (irresistibly) moves the human will:

God moves man to act, not only by proposing the appetible to the senses,

or by effecting a change in his body, but also by moving the will itself;
because every movement either of the will or of nature, proceeds from God
as the First Mover. And just as it is not incompatible with nature that the
natural movement be from God as the First Mover, inasmuch as nature is
an instrument of God moving it: so it is not contrary to the essence of a voluntary act, that it proceed from God, inasmuch as the will is moved by
God. Nevertheless both natural and voluntary movements have this in
common, that it is essential that they should proceed from a principle within the agent. (ST, I-II, Q. 6, art. 1, ad 3; see also art. 4, esp. ad 1)

As the Creator of the world, God brings about necessary things necessarily and contingent things contingently, according to Thomas (ST, I-
II, Q. 10, art. 4; and I, Q. 22, art. 4). It is paramount to recognize that
God's moving an individual's will is not like a thug's violently coercing
another to do something. God is not like one more finite agent (especially powerful or ruthless) competing for causal efficacy. God acts
"within us, without us," in the stock phrase, such that we cannot but
realize our divinely ordained end according to our rational nature.
When a person is moved by God to virtuous action, this is the *perfection* of finite agency, not its *violation*, in Thomas's estimation. The
action remains "voluntary" in the literal sense that it flows from the person's will (*voluntas*) and is accompanied by knowledge of the action's
end (ST, I-II, Q. 6, arts. 2 and 3).

But does it really make sense to speak of God's irresistibly moving
the will in such a way that genuine creaturely freedom is preserved?
Can God as omnipotent Creator be the sufficient reason for everything
that happens without having providence collapse into a determinism in
which God is directly responsible for evil?[32] If freedom entails the ability to do otherwise, then no one can render ineluctable a free act, not
even the Deity, for this would be a contradiction in terms. (Someone
can, of course, necessitate the *absence* of a free act–by killing me, for
instance.) But Harry Frankfurt has argued that meaningful freedom of
the will does not require the sort of liberty of indifference (*liberum arbitrium*) commonly associated with the ability to do otherwise.
Frankfurt's is the best recent defense of compatibilism, so I want now
to ask whether it might be enlisted in support of Thomas's views on
providence and freedom. I hope eventually to show that Frankfurt's
ingenious argument is flawed.

Frankfurt maintains that it is enough for personal agency that one
have second-order volitions, that one care normatively about what first-
order desires move one to action. Personal freedom, in turn, is a matter
of one's second-order volitions effectively governing one's first-order
dispositions. "(T)he statement that a person enjoys freedom of the will

means (...roughly) that he is free to want what he wants to want. More precisely, it means that he is free to will what he wants to will, or to have the will he wants."[33] Moral responsibility does not require the ability to do other than what one does, in brief, only the ability to want to do what one in fact does. One may be accountable for an action even though one could not have done otherwise—as in the case of a willing addict who could not resist taking a drug if he wanted to, but who does not want to resist and who takes the drug "by choice."

Frankfurt illustrates his thesis with a famous example, the complexity of which requires that I quote it at some length:

> Suppose someone—Black, let us say—wants Jones to perform a certain action. Black is prepared to go to considerable lengths to get his way, but he prefers to avoid showing his hand unnecessarily. So he waits until Jones is about to make up his mind what to do, and he does nothing unless it is clear to him (Black is an excellent judge of such things) that Jones is going to decide to do something *other* than what he wants him to do. If it does become clear that Jones is going to decide to do something else, Black takes effective steps (e.g., pronounces a threat, gives him a potion, hypnotizes him, or manipulates his brain) to ensure that Jones decides to do, and that he does do, what he wants him to do. Whatever Jones's initial preferences and inclinations, then, Black will have his way.
>
> . . .
>
> In this example there are sufficient conditions for Jones's performing the action in question. What action he performs is not up to him. Of course it is in a way up to him whether he acts on his own or as a result of Black's intervention. That depends upon what action he himself is inclined to perform. But whether he finally acts on his own or as a result of Black's intervention, he performs the same action. He has no alternative but to do what Black wants him to do. If he does it on his own, however, his moral responsibility for doing it is not affected by the fact that Black was lurking in the background with sinister intent, since this intent never comes into play.[34]

Frankfurt's analysis of "responsibility" is akin to Thomas's analysis of "voluntariness." In both cases it is self-conscious action in accordance with an internal principle, rather than the ability to do otherwise, that is key. Indeed, it is tempting to think of Frankfurt's Black as analogous to Thomas's God, though the Angelic Doctor's Deity is waiting ubiquitously with prevenient grace rather than "lurking in the background with sinister intent." The parallel is not exact, of course, since Thomas's God (unlike Black) is the First Mover who *always* moves the will of rational creatures to the universal object of their will, the good, even if God only "sometimes" moves their will to "something determinate" (ST, I-II, Q. 9, art. 6, ad 3).

For all its subtlety, in any case, Frankfurt's example does not prove the compatibility of moral responsibility and determinism (whether natural or supernatural, human or divine). The fallacy lies in thinking that Jones "performs the same action" come what may, regardless of the causal etiology involved. The identity of an action is inseparable from the casual chain that brought it about. If I lift my arm because I consciously willed to do so, this is a different "action" from what I do when a threat, potion, hypnotic suggestion, or neural manipulation causes me to raise my arm involuntarily. Indeed, the last three scenarios seem more like events than actions. Motives matter when denumerating actions, not just gross external movements or effects, and only a narrowly utilitarian theory of agency tempts us to forget this. The question is whether an action performed due to divine agency can also be one and the same action performed due to human freedom.

Consider how "the-action-performed-by-consciously-willing-to-move-one's-arm" cannot be substituted in many sentences, *salva veritate*, for expressions like "the-action-performed-by-hypnotic-suggestion." Take the following two examples:

(1) "The-action-performed-by-consciously-willing-to-move-his-arm constituted Jones's voting for Johnson."
(2) "The-action-performed-by-hypnotic-suggestion constituted Jones's voting for Johnson."

The first sentence might be true, but the second never could be. The genesis of the "action" in (2) would mean that no legitimate vote had been cast, the illegitimacy stemming from the sense that a hypnotized individual has no alternatives while a consciously willing individual does. This failure of substitutability suggests absence of identity in the referents of the hyphenated expressions. Jones does not "perform the same action" in both cases. At the very least, the lines quoted from Franfurt present us with what Willard Quine calls the problem of "referential opacity."[35] We don't know what it would mean to speak of "the same action" or "a different action" given Jones's conditions, thus the point of Frankfurt's inventive example is blunted.

Consider another flight into science fiction: what if Chipper Jones, the third baseman for the Atlanta Braves, were to hit a game ball over the outfield fence by virtue of manager Bobby Cox's having hypnotized him to swing in a particular way upon seeing a certain pitch?[36] Wouldn't this be "hitting a home run," even though the "action" might be considered less "voluntary" than normal? I grant that the run would count in this case. At what point, however, would "novel management" give way to charges of "cheating?" What if Cox had planted electrodes in Jones's head and literally caused him to swing by throwing a switch in the dugout? (One might imagine Cox secretly picking up the opposing catcher's signs and moving his own batter like a Nintendo figure in response.) I presume that now we would be inclined to say that Jones had not "hit a home run," he only seemed to. Once again, how we specify the action (and agent) depends on history and context, not merely external results.

In spite of Frankfurt-like scenarios, the incompatibilist intuition remains intact that if God is the sufficient reason for everything that happens, if there are no "alternate possibilities" open to human agents as proximate causes, then God is indeed responsible for evil. For then meaningful human freedom vanishes and God's providence is indistinguishable from fate. All historical truths are *de dicto* (if not *de re*) necessary, on this reading of providence. Since God's predestination is irresistible, history could not be other than it is and is exactly as God planned–wars, famines, tyrannies, diseases, etc. notwithstanding. Even if human beings are the secondary causes through which divine determination partially operates, they are more like pawns than moral agents. As Thomas himself writes, "there is no distinction between what flows from free will, and what is of predestination...For the providence of God produces effects through the operation of secondary causes..." (ST, I, Q. 23, art. 5). Rather than embracing such a view, I prefer instead to reject Thomas's compatibilist account of "freedom" and with it the "consolation" he offers for human suffering and its "ordainment" by divine providence. I prefer, that is, to allow a place for genuinely fortuitous events and genuinely free actions that are undetermined (or at least underdetermined) by both nature and grace. Saints and sinners are both subject to blind chances and both capable of willing and doing other than they in fact will and do.[37]

It may be argued that I have underestimated the sublimity of God's causality as Thomas conceives it, thus that I have after all treated God like one more finite agent subject to (or subjecting others to) fate. In *De Malo*, Q. 16, art. 7, ad 15, for instance, Thomas reminds us that

> from the fact that God sees in themselves all the things that take place, the contingency of things is not done away with. And as regards the will we must take into account that the divine will is universally the cause of being and universally of all the things that follow on this, hence even of necessity and contingency; but His will itself is above the order of the necessary or contingent just as it is above all created being.[38]

This is a powerful statement of what it means to be Creator rather than creature. But even if God is above necessity and contingency on the finite plane, the horizontal axis of causality, it still remains a question whether God is above necessity on the infinite plane, the vertical axis of causality.[39] It is common for theologians to claim that God is necessarily existent, necessarily perfect, etc., and it would seem that (for Thomas) God necessarily brings about necessary things necessarily and contingent things contingently. It would seem, that is, that God's vertical causality is infallibly and ubiquitously efficacious in the world, thus that God may rightly be called the "necessary and sufficient" reason for everything that happens. This result is what threatens human freedom and/or indicts God for directly bringing about evil. It does little good to say that human beings are not utterly determined by the realities of the created world (physical forces, desirable goods, psychological habits, etc.), if humans beings are nonetheless fully determined by the Reality of the Creator God. For God "does it all" in either case.

In opposition to Thomas's claims about God's universal instrumentality, stands an Arminian vision of God's creative fidelity. To speak of "creative fidelity" is to accent God's redemptive love for creatures rather than God's controlling power over them; it is to allow for the kind of covenantal *relation* between Creator and creature that Thomas himself describes so eloquently at times. Evidence for God's redemptive love takes its most graphic form in the cross of Christ (see ST, III, Q. 1, art. 2); more accurately, Christ's sacrificial death on the cross is Love Incarnate calling most poignantly for a response. Only an omnipotent Deity could freely create, then redeem, responsible creatures.

This is not a sentimental vision of being "close confreres with the Almighty." In as much as God creates them *ex nihilo*, judges them *ab extra*, and finally saves them *sola gratia*, human beings remain absolutely dependent on God for their existence, self-awareness, and salvation. Nevertheless, their being made in the Image of God implies that human beings are capable of real (if minimal) responsiveness to grace. However finite, creatures retain their ontological otherness to God; they are neither mere nothings nor simple appendages to the Deity. However fallen, human beings retain a modicum of freedom that permits them to accept or decline the gratuitous offer of redemption. They cannot earn their salvation, nor even prepare for it on their own–here is neither Pelagianism nor semi-Pelagianism–but they can say "Yes" or "No" to God's indispensable gift of it (cf. ST, I, Q. 23, art. 5).

Aquinas's commitment to God's universal instrumentality precludes him from acknowledging the extent to which the goodness of the world depends on creatures and is still open-ended. God has "immediate provision over everything" (ST, I, Q. 22, art. 3, ad 2) and "(t)he order of divine providence is unchangeable and certain" (ST, I, Q. 22, art. 4, ad

2). If the love for which we are made by God is a passive potential that must be freely realized, in contrast, then the instrumental value of suffering is up to us in part. If suffering does not elicit love, then the former may be deeply harmful, as Stump allows. Indeed, Thomas seems to have no room for utterly fortuitous and radically maiming suffering that completely unmakes a person—what Stump calls "spiritual toxicosis."⁴⁰ When a strong accent on *agape* is combined with an incompatibilist view of human freedom, however, there is no *need* to insure *a priori* the goodness of the world. The effort only leads to such abortive doctrines as universal instrumentality, election and reprobation, etc. The world's goodness can remain an open question even if the goodness of God is taken for granted.

Putting charity first flows from the belief that the possibility of our freely loving and being loved by God and neighbors, in this life, may be sufficient ground for God to have created the finite world. This is so even though such creation also opens up the possibility of evil, both moral and nonmoral varieties. Love may be construed as either an action or a disposition to act or both, but in any case it requires freedom. Without freedom, actions would be events, dispositions would be fates. Freedom, however, entails the possibility of evil, even radical evil wherein creatures perversely reject salvation.

The priority of charity is not a solution to the problem of evil, but rather implies a recognition of the problem's temporal insolubility. This is so for two reasons. To begin with, the strong agapist's putting charity first *presumes* the existence of a benevolent God as the source of *agape* instead of proving it. The operative intuition is that our love has a transcendent source; we experience charity as a good and perfect gift, and we wish simply to respond in gratitude. Second, because freedom is held to be internal to human virtue as well as vice, the final goodness of the world is yet to be determined. Goodness awaits our responsible choices, if only our free consent to grace, thus there is no guarantee of the defeat of evil. To believe in the possibility of good free choices is, in a limited sense, to believe in the defeas*ibility* of evil. But love's priority constitutes neither a strict theodicy nor a strict anthropodicy.⁴¹

God has taken a risk in creating the world that Thomas could not acknowledge, but it is not the case that if the experiment turns out badly God is somehow culpable. A modest defense of the goodness of God despite the present reality of evil turns on distinguishing between God's dispositional goodness and God's utilitarian efficacy. Biblical faith holds that God's love is forever disposed to offer creatures relation with Deity, the greatest good; but love's unwillingness to coerce such a relation means that there is no way to guarantee that the greatest good for the greatest number will actually be brought about as a consequence. I agree with any number of people (e.g., Alvin Plantinga) that humanity's having significant free will is not a morally sufficient reason for God to allow evil. If my developing free agency depends on God's permitting the extreme affliction of the innocent (or even of the guilty), and if free agency as such is the highest good, then I am inclined to say (with Ivan Karamazov) that it is not worth it. This leaves open, however, the possibility that *agape* may be such a morally sufficient reason.

Professor Stump performs a very great service in suggesting that any account of Aquinas on the meaning of life and the place of suffering in it must begin (or at least end) with charity, "*quia bonum hominis in caritate consistit*."[42] But we must freely love through suffering in spite of it. Even God must bring good out of evil for which God is not responsible, not via evil that God irresistibly ordains, or else the Deity is reduced to doing evil that good might come. God may have no obligation to intervene to prevent human sin, but God would be unworthy of worship were She to necessitate or pander to it.

Strong agapists believe that God was (or at least may be) justified in creating the world for the sake of the possibility of love, but one can only judge such things in the first person. There will be no universally convincing arguments on this head. And even if one does judge the question affirmatively, one might still favor saying that evil (especially natural evil) is a "mystery" that constitutes *prima facie* evidence against the existence of an omnipotent, omniscient, and omnibenevolent Deity. There is indeed evidence against God, if one is looking for it, but the personal experience by creatures of the love of God remains a source of joy and hope. The experience is constitutive of, not merely epistemic warrant for, belief in God. And one defends religious faith by testifying to and acting out of love, however difficult this may be, rather than by trying to explain away evil and its impact or by trying to prove God's reality at one remove.

In fact, reference to God's suffering presence with human beings in the midst of physical affliction and moral corruption seems to me the only Christian response to the problem of evil–an "incarnational" response, but not an answer in any final sense. Such Love, and the attendant human joy, is the substance of divine providence as we know it.[43] Stump herself writes: "Perhaps there is no greater joy than the presence of the person you love when that person loves you to the fulfillment of your heart's desire. Joy of that sort, Aquinas says, is not destroyed by either pain or tribulation." She goes on to add: "On Aquinas's account, Christianity does not call people to a life of self-denying wretchedness, but to a life of joy, even in the midst of pain and trouble. Without joy, Aquinas says, no progress is possible in the Christian life."[44] In light of these emphases, I can only ask again: why the Thomistic *requirement* of an afterlife?

Is the possibility of temporal joy not enough? Must earthly existence be a fleeting school of virtue for the Creator to be good and creatures fulfilled? I turn to these questions in earnest in the next section, but I can anticipate by stressing that I do not claim to resolve the problem of evil without recourse to immortality. Rather, I indicate that others cannot resolve the problem even with such recourse, for the meaning of immortality itself is elusive.

The Pedagogy of Love: Agape Without an Afterlife?

Thomas's understanding of God's providential goodness leads him to construe human suffering as instrumentally valuable, orchestrated by God for humanity's spiritual edification.[45] Two corollaries to this view are worth noting, then interrogating. (1) If we accept Aquinas's account of God's universal instrumentality, it is too weak to say that God merely "permits" evil for the sake of positive ends. Even if God is thought to be beyond both necessity and contingency in some sense, God is the universal and sufficient reason for whatever happens, according to Thomas, thus God must be seen to prepare persons for heaven by actively prescribing temporal woes that remind them of their true home. But what of the possibility that suffering can become so destructive as to "unmake"[46] (rather than school) an individual's identity, through no fault of her own?

It is standard to suggest that natural evil is necessary to bring out such virtues as courage and self-sacrifice, even as moral evil is necessary to elicit such goods as retributive justice and forgiveness. There is considerable plausibility in these claims: as Thomas avers, "there would be no patience of martyrs if there were no tyrannical persecution" (ST, I, Q. 22, art. 2, ad 2). It is also standard, however, to point to the problem of *excess* suffering: there is more pain in the world than seems warranted for pedagogical purposes, and sometimes this pain utterly destroys innocent parties. Surely a loving God would not actively ordain affliction, if this meant that some were innocently undone by it, even if the overall goodness of the world were thereby maximized. Aquinas contends that "it belongs to (God's) providence to permit certain defects in particular effects, that the perfect good of the universe may not be hindered, for if all evil were prevented, much good would be absent from the universe" (ST, I, Q. 22, art. 2, ad 2). But if God loves us as individuals, God cannot be a pure utilitarian, for this entails sacrificing the legitimate interests of the few in the name of the many.[47]

A defender of Thomas might point out a second corollary of his view of providence: (2) God does not will eternal life for all; some persons are reprobated, in the sense of "permitted" to fall into sin and thus into the punishment of damnation (ST, I, Q. 23, art. 3). We should conclude, the defender might reason, that when someone is broken by suffering this indicates they are not among the elect whom God intends for heaven. God cannot be faulted for ordaining catastrophic suffering because, with respect to membership in eternity, not everyone "counts as one and no more than one." (Indeed, Christ died only for some, those happy few chosen to benefit from his Atonement.) In sum, Thomas's God is not unjust because creatures who go under have no claim on any other fate.[48]

The problem with this defense is twofold. First, given that immortality is a supernatural end "which exceeds all proportion and faculty of created nature" (ST, I, Q. 23, art. 1), heaven is the true home of no one. If "our happiness lies there," this happiness is as alien and imponderable to the worst sinner as to the greatest saint. Speaking naturally, *nobody counts as much as one when it comes to life eternal*, nobody has a claim on it. If heaven is a reality, it is a pure gift. So we are left with an ancient question. An all-powerful and all-loving Creator may not be obliged to give immortality to any creatures, but why would She offer it to some and not all, even as a matter of Her "consequent" will? This implies, as Thomas grants (ST, I, Q. 23, art. 3, ad 1; see also art. 4), that God does not love all equally. If God elects some and reprobates others because, in Thomas's words, "the completion of the universe" requires "different grades of being(,) some of which hold a high and some a low place in the universe" (ST, I, Q. 23, art 5, ad 3), then God seems an objectionable utilitarian after all. It is not unjust to give persons more than they strictly deserve; it is not unjust even to give this more to some persons and not all (cf. Jesus' parable of the vineyard, Mt. 20:1-16); but it *is* unjust to use the innocent pain of some as a *means* to the undeserved glory of others. This is to give *less* than is due to creatures made in God's Image.[49]

God's "permitting" the abominable misery and death of some in order to "edify" others as to their immortality appears especially farcical. The "edified elect" (my phrase) could only be arbitrarily predestined for a reality about which they can know nothing and do nothing. To attest, with Thomas, that God's mercy spares the elect and God's justice punishes the reprobate is to set God at odds with Himself. Rather than "manifest His goodness" (ST, I, Q. 23, art. 5, ad 3), it would make God schizophrenic; it is unloving, indeed perverse, to punish individuals for doing what you yourself have engineered they could not but do.

This brings me to the second major problem with my projected defense of Thomas on providence. Given God's universal instrumentality, the distinction between election for heaven and reprobation for hell is actually a distinction without a difference. Again, it is misleading to say that God merely "permits" something, including sin.[50] As the sufficient reason for everything that happens, God controls all. Without prevenient grace providing the power to avoid sin, moreover, all creatures must fall into damnation. It simply does not make sense for the Deity to punish individuals for not doing something which they could not but fail to do on their own. This is rather like a parent spanking her newborn baby for not feeding itself. It is the very picture of abuse to induce a dependency in others, unbidden, and then to condemn them for being needy. A God who would do this would be unworthy of worship.

Rather than defending the instrumental value for the elect of natural and moral evil, it seems better to admit that evil (like immortality) remains largely a surd. The radicality of evil, its power to stifle moral personality, is opaque. Modern believers struggle to square *some* moral evil with the goodness of God by referring to humanity's abuse of liberty, but such "explanations" *of* evil will always be secondary to cleaving in faith to God's free decision to be with creatures *amid* evil. If the pious did not first sense God's presence, they would not be so concerned to defend God's (or the world's) goodness. The destructive nadir of evil (abomination) can only be contrasted with the kenotic apex of good (Incarnation). Yet it is just here, in the face of evil, that Thomas, for all his massive astuteness, oversteps the epistemic limits he himself regularly sets. Although he maintains in the *Secunda Secundae of the Summa Theologiae* that "those things are in themselves of faith, which order us directly to eternal life" (ST, II-II, Q. 1, art. 6, ad 1), he argues more forcefully in the *Supplementary Question on the Resurrection*: "it is clear that if man cannot be happy in this life, we must of necessity hold the resurrection" (ST, Suppl. Q. 75, art. 1) or else humanity's natural end would be unrealizable. The word "necessity" is potentially misleading, however, and difficult to square with Thomas's own insistence that "resurrection, strictly speaking, is miraculous" (ST, Suppl. Q. 75, art. 3). In spite of his distinction between faith and science, that is, and in spite of his contention that "nature cannot be the principle of resurrection" (ST, Suppl. Q. 75, art. 3), Thomas relies at times on the ace in the hole of life after death as though it is something rationally demonstrable rather than a blessed hope (see SCG, Bk. III, Ch. 48).

To reiterate, Aquinas reads the "Book of Job" as demonstrating the inseparabilty of divine providence and human immortality: since God is good, Job must live forever. But is immortality so clearly required for Job (or us) to avoid meaninglessness and/or malice? Does insisting on an afterlife necessarily follow from affirming that God is Love? In the spirit of Thomas's distancing of the Argument from Design, I maintain that we cannot reason from temporal exigencies to the fact (much less the necessity) of God's granting human beings eternity. Such an argument would presume to tie God's hands on the basis of ambiguous empirical evidences: we cannot know that earthly suffering must be

234 *Human and Divine Agency*

compensated for in heaven. But can we reverse the argumentative direction and reason from the omnibenevolence of God to the perdurability of (faithful) human beings? My thesis is that communion with the living God, together with scriptural revelation, gives believers cause for *hope* for immortality, but this hope is distinct from dogmatic *certitude*.

Aquinas overstates the case in this regard, even by his own best lights. He writes: "man always desires the future as if he is not content with the present; hence, it is *manifest* that the ultimate end is not in this life but that this life is ordered toward another end."[51] That this other end is resurrection is made clear when he contends: "if there were no other life of man except that life on earth, man would not seem worthy of such great concern about him on God's part; therefore, the very concern which God has especially for man *demonstrates* that there is another life of man after the death of the body."[52] These arguments too readily explain away death and are typical of the certitude I oppose. *Pace* Thomas, they are not attributable to Job, even if they approximate the position of other biblical figures.

I do not wish to play the Sadducee to Thomas's Pharisee. In considering personal immortality the object of a blessed hope, I entertain the *possibility* of resurrection and thus do not repeat the Sadducees' dogmatic denial of same. But I do reject Thomas's eschatological perfectionism in which postmortem resurrection of the righteous becomes at times a *clear and indispensable* part of divine providence, if not an answer to Job's affliction. Such a picture is a threat to compassion, I fear, for two reasons. First, eschatological perfectionism may unintentionally corrupt motivation by encouraging individuals to act compassionately in order to guarantee heaven; second, it may make us blind to suffering in the present, imperfect world by accenting Beatitude in the next. So I opt instead for strong agape. Strong agape, as adumbrated by the "Book of Job," makes freedom an internal element of charity but lets go of immortality as an inevitable upshot of that love.

Putting charity first among the virtues is not a philosophical answer to the problem of evil, to repeat, and neither is it a theological guarantee of everlasting life. Job demands that we be disconsoled away from any such answer or guarantee. Why some people are unmade by suffering, we do not know. Job supports the belief, nonetheless, that it is possible to know the God who is Love even amid extraordinary doubt and pain. Joban faith says "neither/nor" to the Pharisee/Sadducee debate, neither affirming nor denying an afterlife, because it considers God's *hesed* here and now the primary good. The possibility of knowing God's *agape* in this life is key: sufficient unto the day is the good thereof.

Aquinas (and apparently Stump) disagrees. Stump quotes Aquinas's "Commentary on I Corinthians:" "If there were no resurrection of the dead, people wouldn't think that it was a power and a glory to abandon all that can give pleasure and to bear the pains of death and dishonor; instead they would think it was stupid." And Stump herself concludes that

> if we don't share the worldview which holds that there is an afterlife, that true happiness consists in union with God in the afterlife, and that suffering helps us to attain that happiness, we will naturally find Aquinas's valuing suffering even as a conditional good appalling or crazy.[53]

If we accept God's universal instrumentality, however, then an afterlife loses much of its point: it cannot be a perfection of our finite freedom, and it cannot be the eternal context of condign reward or punishment. Everything has been unalterably prescribed. More importantly, the remarks quoted from Aquinas and Stump wrongly suggest, I believe, that if there is no immortality then the discipleship of love in this life is meaningless or wrong-headed. This proposition I dispute, taking my lead from Job himself.

Aquinas rightly claims that Job does not deny resurrection,[54] but nowhere does he affirm it either. Thomas repeatedly attributes to Job a desire for and a belief in an afterlife.[55] In fact, however, the desire is muted and the belief nonexistent. Job says:

> "... there is hope for a tree,
> if it be cut down, that it will sprout again,
> and that its shoots will not cease.
>   . . .
> But man dies, and is laid low;
> man breathes his last, and where is he?" (14:7-10)

In the end, Job seems to accept his mortality as a sad matter of course, even as he struggles to hold on to some hope and sense of meaning. He asks "If a man die, shall he live again?" (14:14), but the implicit answer seems to be either "No" or "I have no idea." Job does want God to "remember" him (14:13), but Thomas's insistence that this "is nothing else than to appoint a time for resurrection"[56] seems strained eisegesis. Edwin Good is much truer to the text when he comments:

> The Hebrew Bible has no expectation of a pleasant afterlife, and the analogy to the tree has a rueful tone. Job goes on to wish (vv. 13-15) that, as a special case, he might have an afterlife, that God might conceal him among the dead ("in Sheol," v. 13) until he is ready to deal with him. He would wait eagerly for a positive outcome (v. 15). But it is for nothing. The idea is raised only to be dropped. The physical world wears away,

"and you destroy a man's hope" (vv. 18-19). Nothing is there for Job except "his flesh's pain" and a lamenting soul (v. 22).[57]

Thomas notwithstanding, Job requires not bodily resurrection followed by endless life but rather relief from pain and a just recognition of his state before he dies. Above all, perhaps, Job wants and needs to love God, and to be loved by God. If Job gets any relief from suffering, it comes with God's presence to him in time–their mutual seeing and hearing–not with "plausible reasons"[58] for confidence in a future eternity. The Catholic premise of immortality is simply read by Thomas into the Hebrew text,[59] thereby blurring the fact that theophany (not immortality) is what gives Job his ineffable consolation *in extremis*.

Exegeting "Job," Responding to Jobs

The section of the "Book of Job" in which God speaks out of the whirlwind is the dramatic climax of the story, though it provides a relational theophany rather than a rational theodicy. God appeals to superior power and knowledge–things which Job never denied–and thereby challenges Job's right to question the divine. Unlike the comforters, however, God does not call Job guilty; and unlike Aquinas, God does not promise Job an afterlife. The personal presence of a Deity who cares enough to respond moves Job to cease to question and to "repent in (or of) dust and ashes" (see footnote #13 above). The questioning was essential, one imagines, but the reality of God evoked by the questioning finally renders the questions secondary. Job is thus able to move from despair to faith: the mystery of God's justice is not penetrated intellectually but there is a peace that comes through trust.

The Epilogue is a return to the original framing story–how else could one end?–but Job's getting property and children back double and living happily ever after is a betrayal of the main point of the central composition. It is an ersatz immortality even more troubling than heavenly perdurability. Children are not interchangeable and the Deuteronomic theory of the Prologue and Epilogue are exactly what Job has refuted in his own case against the Comforters. How are we to explain this slippage between the heart of the work and its retributivist and utilitarian packaging?

The history and authorship of the "Book of Job" are exceedingly difficult to determine with any confidence, but on the basis of archaeological, theological, linguistic, and literary evidences (many of which were unavailable to Aquinas) the following account seems likely. The Prologue and Epilogue were taken from an already existing story of a patient sufferer Job, a story perhaps as ancient as the second millenium BCE. This is suggested by the fact that the Prologue and Epilogue are in prose, while the central Dialogue is in poetry, and by the fact that the theology is markedly different. The character of Job is fundamentally at odds in the middle parts with that described in the Prologue and Epilogue that frames them. The Job of the Dialogue is more like Ecclesiastes than the patient sufferer we may think of when we think of Job independently of the actual work. The Dialogue and Theophany were probably written during the sixth or seventh century BCE, though given that the hero is an Edomite sheik from the land of Uz, it is unclear whether the author was an Israelite. Some have argued that the concern with justice and injustice marks the book as "Jewish 100%," but others are not so sure.[60]

Even if this exegesis of "Job" is accurate, of course, we are still left with the normative issue of whether Job-like sufferers require an after-life. Maybe Thomas saw something that even the author(s) of the biblical text(s) missed. Let me amplify "Job," therefore, to make the strongest case I can for the theological indispensability of an afterlife, and then respond to it. Imagine that innocent Job were entirely broken by his suffering, driven mad or even rendered sociopathic. At a point of excruciating sadness and alienation, he can only howl with pain, evidently insensate to the moral presence of other human beings and of God. This is a Job, then, who does not see God and who does not receive back his health and children. Would we not say that such a life had become a burden to Job? And would we not say that the only way to avoid faulting God for having made a world where this could happen, is to postulate an afterlife in which Job is compensated for his earthly affliction? The fact that some persons are unmade by suffering through no fault of their own—a fact neglected by Thomas because of his emphasis on the pedagogy of pain—is actually the most powerful support for Thomas's insistence on eternal life. There are real individuals like my imagined Job, the argument runs, and if they do not experience the rectifying joys of heaven, then God has created a universe full of undeserved and unredeemable evil.

How might a strong agapist respond to this forceful claim? A first step is to observe that pure arbitrariness, in which individuals are forever free to do just anything without qualification, is not the only alternative to hard determinism, in which they are never free to choose among various possibilities. Our reality lies in between these extremes. We are extensively products of our environments; gravity, genes, parental knees, and social mores limit our options and tailor our dispositions. "The experience of freedom" (Kant) continues to convince many, however, that environmental causation is not the full story. Indeed, our situatedness in concrete contexts is the germ of both necessity and liberty; our identities as moral agents presuppose tastes and talents that have been both circumscribed and empowered by experience. Present spontaneity grows out of past history.

The reality of freedom means that, for all the dull facticity of matter and all the sad ubiquity of sin, neither other persons nor even God can necessitate a particular moral act. Within a finite range, discrete choices can be made for which persons are accountable. Even a coerced act may be called "intentional," in the sense that it is willed by the agent, though under duress. Beyond a certain level of coercion, of course, the agent will not be deemed blame- (or praise-) worthy: it would have been too difficult to make another choice. A literally "necessitated act," however, is a contradiction in terms. Unavoidable determination precludes responsibility, as I have argued above, so being unmade by fate is distinct from being rendered ineluctably culpable.[61]

A second step is to grant that, although we are substantially free and responsible, we are nonetheless also deeply vulnerable. It is empirically undeniable that some lives are undone either by the malevolence of others or by sheer bad luck. Some infants are so stunted early in life, for instance, as never to be able to love or even to achieve the threshold of personal agency.[62] Others, like my imagined Job, are victimized as adults to the point of despair, "spiritual toxicosis." Even though innocence cannot be taken from without, happiness can.

A third and final step is to maintain that all human lives are, nevertheless, good creations since all are given the *potential* of loving and being loved by God. Again, this potential is thwarted in some, through no fault of their own, by natural or moral evil. But the potential granted to all may be enough to justify God's creating a world where some fall into actual despair. No creature is wronged by God when he or she is unmade by suffering, the strong agapist presumes, so long as allowing suffering is the only way that God can simultaneously allow for love, the greatest good. But God must only *permit*, not cause, human misery. Creatures morally wrong other creatures when they torture the innocent, abuse the weak, fail to protect the vulnerable, etc., but this does not indict God. For, *ex hypothesi*, God has made it possible for all to experience charity, though not all actually do.

The most plausible Christian response to Job, then, even an amplified version—a response implicit in the "Book of Job" itself—is that the partial reality of the kingdom here and now, experienced by those who love God and neighbor with the aid of the Holy Spirit, is of surpassing worth independently of the possible immortality of persons. Joban love is disinterested, fearing God "for nought" (1:9).[63] In addition, it is precisely in living agapically that one both discerns human suffering and freely acts to remedy it, without falling into hopelessness over its tragic dimensions. (Job will always have friends who do not love him and

enemies whom he loves.) *Agape* might see some suffering as a conditional good, regardless of an afterlife, if that suffering prompts sympathy for others or clarity about oneself. Yet this vision of human pain is
dangerous and needs to be highly qualified; it is nowhere near enough
for a full-blown theodicy, and it may contribute to a masochistic acquiescence in evil. For those unmade by it, innocent suffering is purely and
simply bad.

It is always risky for an ethicist to say what Yahweh can and cannot
do–"Where were you when I laid the foundation of the earth?...Will you
even put me in the wrong?" (Job 38:4 and 40:8)–but if speaking of God
as "just" and "loving" is to be meaningful, some things must be ruled
out. God would be unworthy of worship, for example, if He directly
used the innocent suffering of some as a means to the greater utility of
many, or even of the elect few. (Recall that the reprobate *both* suffer *and*
are damned, according to Thomas; they never taste the sweetness of
heaven toward which human suffering putatively points, so their pain is
not instrumental to *their* saving edification.) Yet God does not directly
cause innocent suffering, as the strong agapist sees things, at least not
unto the unmaking of human identity. Innocent suffering may be merely permitted by God as a double effect.

The possibility of innocent suffering may be inseparable from the
possibility, initially open to all, of achieving the highest good: loving
union with God and the neighbor. I understand why some suspect that
even divine permission would be enough to render God unjust, assuming that there is no compensating afterlife, since innocent suffering
sometimes completely undoes individuals in this life. The strong agapist
trusts in an alternative, however. Because the possibility of all persons
loving and being loved is such an overwhelming good, the strong
agapist speculates, it could outweigh *even in the minds of the afflicted*
the tragic losses they experience in reality. To echo Rawls, impartial
contractors could consent to life with no immortality for any, even the
least well-off, if this were required to open the possibility of life with
love for all. Allowing the possibility of suffering might be to the greatest benefit of the least well-off, if the alternative is either nonexistence
or existence without the metavalue of charity.

This is not a prescription for callousness. One hopes for a compensating afterlife for the afflicted, a final convergence of happiness and
virtue, and affliction-unto-despair remains a painful mystery to the
pious. But divine proportionality does not seem straightforwardly to
mandate immortality. (Though immortality may require God, the
reverse proposition does not appear to be true.⁶⁴) After all, the most dev-
astating failures of love are first of all and most of the time the fault of
human beings. Immortality would be required by divine justice were

God to have promised an afterlife to some or all persons. But no such promise is evident in the "Book of Job," and New Testament revelation on this score is moot.

Saint Paul is adamant in I Corinthians 15:12-19: "if there is no res-urrection of the dead, then Christ has not been raised; if Christ has not been raised, then our preaching is in vain and your faith is in vain... If for this life only we have hoped in Christ, we are of all men most to be pitied." But it is unclear if Christ himself saw eternal life in this way. Although he speaks of the faithful having "treasure(s)" and "reward" in heaven (e.g., Mt. 6:20 and 19:21, Luke 6:23), Jesus seems not to make immortality-as-endless-life a *sine qua non* for purity of heart. Christ evidently believed that the just will be resurrected and that the pure in heart "shall see God" (Mt. 5:8), but this assumption of faith is not a theodical proof of or insistence upon immortality. Jesus clearly rejected Deuteronomic retributivism (see John 9:1-5), and it is in the spirit of such a rejection that one lets go of dogmatic versions of eschatological perfectionism. It is surely a less than pure intention, a less than Christlike obedience, to dwell on whether or to what degree virtue must win an afterlife. It is the gratuitous and demanding reality of the king-dom that matters to the Redeemer. Even the "eternal life" promised in John 3:16—"For God so loved the world that he gave his only Son, that whoever believes in him should not perish but have eternal life"—can be read as present "participation in God's life" (RSV note) rather than trans- or supra-temporal perdurability.[65]

Misgivings about being ethically motivated by immortality extend beyond concern for the characters of agents; one fears for the patients of deathless actors as well. Focus on heavenly torment or ecstasy may warp one's own personality, but it can also lead to blindness to the tem-poral suffering of others, if not to active cruelty. Judith Shklar states the qualm energetically:

> The pursuit of eternal salvation may function just like the aristocratic quest for self-perfection in shunting the victim of injustice aside. In Augustine's *City of God* we are told that the victim of political injustice, the slave in particular, is ultimately less of a victim than the owner because the victim is not exposed to nearly as many temptations...In a Christian view, the powerful are the real victims, while the poorest and most miserable people stand the best chance of avoiding sin. Any picture of the Last Judgment will tell us what an advantage they have.[66]

The familiar challenge for Christian ethics is not to allow ideas of eschatological retribution to undercut attention to the plight of the Jobs of this world. The seriousness of Last Judgment doctrines—vivid portrayals of the final *effects* of different ways of life–must be augmented by insouciance about immortality as an ethical *motive*. Even if all virtuous actions are performed in part for God's sake because at base at God's command, obedience as such wills the Good rather than its own endless survival. Charity's dying to the self entails, in other words, a dying to both death and deathlessness as springs for love of God or neighbor. Desire for eternity *for oneself* ought not usually to move one; desire for eternity for *others* is more admirable, especially when it springs from their need for compensation for temporal ills.

There may be an afterlife (who knows?), but an accent on its pure graciousness and unpredictability is characteristic of the best of biblical religion and foreign to much of modern theodicy.[67] Certainly any talk of "necessary evolution" between this life and a next will erode a piety that would be grateful to, and responsible before, God for earthly existence and its potential for love. Whatever the place of attrition in ethics, one can no more preserve genuine charity when motivated by fear of death or coveting of life than one can reconcile significant human freedom with irresistible grace. Thus just as Aquinas encourages a faith that distances the problem of evil, so the strong agapist encourages a love that distances the problem of immortality. If love "bears all things" (I Cor. 13:7), this must include love's own finitude and possible extinction. (Again, Job nowhere appeals to deathlessness as a requirement for meaning or as a viable remedy for suffering.) The best of Thomistic faith is not blind to the religious implications of undeserved suffering, but the antecedent concern is with how to be a faithful minister to those now in pain. Similarly, rather than postulating the necessity of an afterlife, the strong agapist stops with the realization that, in Thomas's words, "(w)hoever has the love of God ...already has what he loves."[68]

Conclusion

Job may not live forever, for he is now free to live for and with God. By Job's own lights, it is not essential that he be given an afterlife in order to avoid despair or immorality.[69] For one who is personally touched by the living God, the experience of perfect Goodness may make existence bearable even in the midst of great anguish and uncertainty. (For one *not* touched, through no fault of her own, the story is admittedly less clear.) This is not to say that one becomes blind to human vulnerability or, more generally, that one champions *amor fati*. Just the opposite. The strong agapist would not be guilty of "marginalizing suffering;"[70] she is, therefore, neither Stoic nor Nietzschean. Like Jonah, she "does well to be angry" over injustice (especially her own, but including others' and even what appears to be God's); unlike Job's "friends," she does best to be uncritically compassionate before affliction (especially other people's, but including her own). The strong agapist simply believes that her pity for the world is itself God working with her, consensually. If there were no God, she feels, one would not give a damn about innocent suffering so long as it spared one's house; but since there is a God, one can and must care. (Hence the theodicy problem is partially self-dissolving: if one feels the itch, one has already been scratched by grace, so to speak.) One loves not because all is well or one "finds the world enough" (Auden), but because one would participate in a charity that is supernaturally present to the finite world in all its woe.[71] This is not immanentizing the eschaton but humbling epistemology, not theodicy but theism.

Supernatural charity is nothing less, and nothing more, than steadfast love of the particular by the particular. And since providence makes such love possible (even mandatory) for individuals in time, the standard problems of evil and immortality may be left to the philosopher's study, on weekends, in a dry season. Or perhaps we can stop preoccupying ourselves with them altogether, finally dismissing them as temptations to abstraction–as (in Aquinas's famous expression from another context) just so much "straw." A realistic practical goal, in any event, is to avoid the extremes of what Shklar calls an "unreasoning fatalism" and a "scapegoating" fanaticism. Fatalism often amounts to an "ideologically convenient" complacency before others' victimization, while fanaticism would always rather blame people than accept the legitimate distinction between misfortune (what just happens to us) and injustice (for which someone is culpable).[72] Strong agape, as I have described it, seems more likely to generate a proper balance here than Thomas's eschatological perfectionism.

A closing example from a well-known Holocaust memoir may illuminate what remains at this juncture a rather abstract thesis. In the most moving scene from Elie Wiesel's *Night*, SS guards hang a young boy and two adults accused of sabotage "in front of thousands of spectators." The boy, "being so light," struggles literally at the end of his rope for more than half an hour, "dying in slow agony." Forced to pass by and witness the pathetic figure, Wiesel (himself only a child at the time) recalls that

Behind me, I heard (a) man asking:
"Where is God now?"
And I heard a voice within me answer him:
"Where is He? Here He is–He is hanging here on this gallows...."

This is a very Jewish answer to a very Joban question with a very humane wisdom for anyone with eyes to see and ears to hear. The narrator has previously described a loss of religious "faith," but what's in a name? I can only believe that Wiesel's courage and compassion–his resolution, e.g., "Never shall I forget the little faces of the children, whose bodies I saw turned into wreaths of smoke beneath a silent blue sky"–*is* the Spirit of God incarnate amid monstrous evil.[73] As Christians sing in Taize services, "*Ubi caritas, Deus ibi est.*"[74]

Notes

1. I take the distinction between a theodicy proper and a defense of faith from Terrence Tilley's *The Evils of Theodicy* (Washington, D.C.: Georgetown University Press, 1991), 130-133.
2. As Eleonore Stump has noted:

> ... the story of innocent Job, horribly afflicted with undeserved suffering, seems to many people representative of the kind of evil with which any theodicy must come to grips. But Aquinas sees the problem in the book of Job differently. He seems not to recognize that suffering in the world, of the quantity and quality of Job's, calls into question God's goodness, let alone God's existence. Instead Aquinas understands the book as an attempt to come to grips with the nature and operations of divine providence.

See Stump, "Aquinas on the Sufferings of Job," in *Reasoned Faith*, ed. by herself (Ithaca and London: Cornell University Press, 1993), 333. This essay also appears in this volume.
3. See Aquinas, *Summa Theologiae* (ST), trans. by the Fathers of the English Dominican Province (Westminster, Maryland: Christian Classics, 1981); all of my subsequent references to and quotations from ST rely on this five-volume edition.
4. Call evil "defeasible" if it can be shown by argument (either *a priori* or *a posteriori*) not to undermine the overall goodness of human lives, either individually or collectively. Present-day theists tend to argue from the defeasibility of evil to the (possible) existence of an omnipotent and omnibenevolent God who created and governs those lives (cf. Richard Swinburne); atheists and agnostics tend to argue from the indefeasibility of evil to the (probable) nonexistence of such a God (cf. J.L. Mackie and William Rowe); Aquinas, in contrast, tends to argue from the reality of God's eternal love and providential power to the defeasibilty of temporal evil.
5. I take this terminology from Jonathan Wells, *Charles Hodge's Critique of Darwinism: An Historical-critical Analysis of Concepts Basic to the 19th Century Debate* (Lewiston, N.Y.: Edwin Mellen Press, 1988), 9, 93-101, and 215-223.

6. John Hick writes: "... the challenge of evil to religious conviction seems to have been felt in the early Christian centuries and in the medieval period as acutely as it is today." He goes on to observe that "in the thirteenth century Thomas Aquinas listed as the two chief intellectual obstacles to Christian theism, first, that constituted by the reality of evil and, second, the difficulty of establishing the existence of God in view of the apparent explicability of the world without reference to a Creator." See Hick, *Evil and the God of Love* (New York: Harper and Row, 1978), 3-4.

7. See Eleonore Stump's "Aquinas on the Sufferings of Job," Op. cit. As Martin Yaffe has maintained, Thomas's commentary is more "protreptic" than "dialectical" or "scientific;" it points out the limits on philosophical argumentation concerning the nature of divine providence even while exhorting readers/listeners to faith. See Yaffe, "Interpretive Essay" accompanying Anthony Damico's translation of *The Literal Exposition on Job: A Scriptural Commentary Concerning Providence* (Atlanta: Scholars Press, 1989), 6-7. In a similar vein, Nicholas Wolterstorff has argued that Aquinas generally does not offer an "evidentialist apologetics" in which traditional dogmas are grounded in certitude; he provides, instead, a natural theology which clarifies humanity's ultimate felicity as a union with God that is orchestrated by God. See Wolterstorff, "The Migration of the Theistic Arguments: From Natural Theology to Evidentialist Apologetics," in *Rationality, Religious Belief, & Moral Commitment*, ed. by Audi and Wainwright (Ithaca: Cornell University Press, 1986).

8. I mean the phrase "the love of God" to play on both the objective and the subjective genitive, i.e., God's love of creatures as well as creatures' love of God.

9. As I argue below, I do not believe that Thomas completely escapes a sophisticated version of providential fatalism. He explicitly *wants* to preserve meaningful human freedom (e.g., ST, I, Q. 23, art. 6), but his embracing of unalterable predestination undercuts this.

10. "Certainly one can construct a Thomistic resolution to the problem of evil...," Tilley concedes, "but 'the problem of evil' was not Thomas's problem." According to Tilley, in fact, "constructing theodicies is not a Christian discourse practice before the Enlightenment." Tilley, *The Evils of Theodicy*, 227 and 229.

11. Victor Preller exaggerates an important insight when he intimates that the "five ways" to prove God's existence, discussed in the *Summa Theologiae*, are not Thomas's ways. See Preller, *Divine Science and the Science of God* (Princeton: Princeton University Press, 1967), 109. It is momentous to realize how little work the cosmological arguments do in Thomas's apophatic project, but he does endorse them as sound. He

sees the existence of God as one of the "preambles" of faith that can be "proved" by natural reason *ab effectu*, beginning with (God's) sensible effects (see ST, I, Q. 2, arts. 2 and 3).

12. For a highly nuanced attempt to defend a theocentric emphasis in ethics, one that also uncouples belief in personal immortality from genuine piety, see James Gustafson, *Ethics from a Theocentric Perspective*, Vols. 1 and 2 (Chicago: University of Chicago Press, 1981 and 1984). Gustafson does not deny human freedom, but he does make the faithful individual's relation to God less personal than is traditionally assumed. He is the most cogent Stoic Christian writing today.

13. As Eleonore Stump points out:

> On Aquinas's account, the problem with Job's friends is that they have a wrong view of the way providence operates. They suppose that providence assigns adversities in this life as a punishment for sins and earthly prosperity as a reward for virtue. Job, however, has a more correct view of providence, according to Aquinas, because he recognizes that a good and loving God will nonetheless allow the worst sorts of adversities to befall a virtuous person also.

See Stump, "Aquinas on the Sufferings of Job," 333-334.

14. This translation of 42:6 follows that of Dale Patrick, as cited by Gustavo Gutierrez in *On Job: God-talk and the Suffering of the Innocent* (Maryknoll, New York: Orbis Press, 1987), 83. Gutierrez reads Job as at last being so moved by God's loving presence as to change his mind about his previous lamentation. Job comes to see that, although he is innocent, "he cannot go on complaining" (87). Edwin Good agrees that Job's final "repudiation" or "repentance" does not negate his claim to innocence, but Good emphasizes even more than Gutierrez that verse 6 can be read as Job's rejection of the Deuteronomic obsession with guilt and innocence and its self-mortifying ritual symbolized by "dust and ashes." "Job takes a religious action to foreswear religion... He repents of repentance," according to Good. Good, "Job," in *Harper's Bible Commentary*, ed. by James L. Mays (San Francisco: Harper and Row, 1988), 431; see also Good, *In Turns of Tempest: A Reading of Job, with a translation* (Stanford: Stanford University Press, 1990), 170. For a criticism of Gutierrez, see Tilley, *The Evils of Theodicy*, 99-102.

15. Stump demonstrates that Thomas is no Stoic who insists on radical self-sufficiency or simply denies the reality of temporal evil. See "Aquinas on the Sufferings of Job," 339.

16. See Aquinas, *Summa Contra Gentiles*, Bk. III, ch. 48, trans. by Vernon J. Bourke (Notre Dame: Notre Dame University Press, 1956), 162-167.

17. Jackson, "The Disconsolation of Theology: Irony, Cruelty, and Putting Charity First," in *The Journal of Religious Ethics*, vol. 20, no. 1 (Spring 1992): 2.

18. Aquinas, *Summa Contra Gentiles*, Bk. III, ch. 48, p. 164. I add the qualifier "entirely" because Thomas himself does so in his next paragraph.

19. In theological contexts, compatibilism is the view that creaturely responsibility is not undermined by the Creator's determination of all actions and events as their sufficient reason; human freedom and divine determinism are "compatible." Incompatibilism, by contrast, contends that such freedom and determinism are not reconcilable; not even God can "necessitate" a finite free act. "Compatibilist freedom," then, is had by a human agent the actions of whom can, in theory, be causally guaranteed by God–e.g., by God's irresistibly moving the agent's will. While "incompatibilist freedom" is a liberty that admits of no such divine determination.

20. Yaffe repeatedly makes this point; see "Interpretive Essay," *passim*.

21. As Stump puts it: "Aquinas's idea... is that the things that happen to a person in this life can be justified only by reference to her or his state in the afterlife." "Aquinas takes the book of Job to be trying to instill in us the conviction that there is another life after this one, that our happiness lies there rather than here, and that we attain to that happiness only through suffering." See Stump, "Aquinas on the Sufferings of Job," 334 and 345.

22. Aquinas, *The Literal Exposition on Job*, 225.

23. For a contrasting Catholic perspective, see Hans Urs von Balthasar, *Dare We Hope "That All Men Be Saved"?, With a Short Discourse on Hell* (San Francisco: Ignatius Press, 1988).

24. Again, Eleonore Stump makes this abundantly clear.

25. Marilyn Adams, as Stump underscores, merely insists that the presence of God experienced by creatures after death will be of such surpassing value that it will make up for the evils of this life. The reasons for evil remain a mystery for us in time, but eschatologically the overall goodness of the world is guaranteed. See Adams, "Redemptive Suffering: A Christian Solution to the Problem of Evil," in Audi and Wainwright, eds., *Rationality, Religious Belief, & Moral Commitment* (Ithaca: Cornell University Press, 1986), and "The Problem of Hell: A Problem of Evil for Christians," in *Reasoned Faith*, 301-327.

26. In "Aquinas on the Sufferings of Job," Stump expounds Thomas's views on evil rather than argues for them; still, she finds them "impressive and admirable in many ways" (356).

27. See, e.g., ST, II-II, Q. 27, art. 4, ad 3.

28. James Gustafson has pressed these questions, in conversation.

29. Stump, "Aquinas on the Sufferings of Job," 347.
30. Ibid., 348.
31. See Lonergan, *Grace and Freedom: Operative Grace in the Thought of St. Thomas Aquinas*, ed. by J. Patout Burns (London: Darton, Longman, & Todd, 1971). Lonergan notes that in his *Commentary on the Sentences of Peter the Lombard* and parts of *De Veritate*, Aquinas has not yet embraced providential determinism. The divine attributes do not yet translate into irresistible grace. Beginning consistently with *Summa Contra Gentiles*, however, Thomas thinks that he must bring God's omnipotence into line with His omniscience, thus he construes God's will as all-effecting even as he had been construing His intellect as all-knowing. This "universal instrumentality" doctrine is fully developed in *Summa Theologiae*.
32. For a useful glimpse at the contemporary debate concerning divine grace and human freedom, see Thomas F. Tracy, ed., *The God Who Acts: Philosophical and Theological Explorations* (University Park, PA: Penn State University Press, 1994). Kathryn Tanner and David Burrell defend here a form of compatibilism similar to Aquinas's own, while Tracy and William Hasker argue that such "compatibilism" is in fact a form of determinism that undoes genuine human freedom and/or makes God the direct cause of evil. I side with Tracy and Hasker, for reasons indicated below.
33. Harry Frankfurt, "Freedom of the Will and the Concept of a Person," in *The Importance of What We Care About* (Cambridge: Cambridge University Press, 1988), 20.
34. Frankfurt, "Alternate Possibilities and Moral Responsibility," in *Importance*, 6-8. Throughout the quotation, I have dropped the subscript from "Jones4" for the sake of clarity.
35. See Quine, *Word and Object* (Cambridge: MIT Press, 1960), 141 ff.
36. I owe this example to Nicholas Fotion.
37. For more on these much-debated matters, see John Martin Fischer, ed., *Moral Responsibility* (Ithaca: Cornel University Press, 1986), especially "Ability and Responsibility" and "The Incompatibility of Responsibility and Determinism," both by Peter Van Inwagen. Van Inwagen's essays are a potent rejoinder to Frankfurt's stimulating work.
38. See Aquinas, *On Evil*, trans. by Jean Oesterle (Notre Dame: University of Notre Dame Press, 1995), 506.
39. The language of "plane" or "axis" of causality, I borrow from Kathryn Tanner, "Human Freedom, Human Sin, and God the Creator," in *The God Who Acts*, ch. 4, 118. Tanner holds that "given the will of God, we never actually choose anything but what God wills us to

choose; what's more,...we never want to choose anything else" (128). In an all-too-brief response, I can only appeal to a familiar distinction and observe that it is one thing to say that the general human ability to choose is perpetually sustained by God's grace and thus is dependent upon God, it is another thing to say that one's specific choices, together with the concrete acts of choosing, are directly and ineluctably brought about by God. The latter view seems to be both Tanner's and Saint Thomas's, but the question then becomes: How do we make sense of human disobedience to God? Tanner's answer is the candid admission that "here I believe the theologian holding onto our picture must simply admit the limits the picture places on the intelligibility of sin" (132). Sin is, after all, an inexplicable "exception" to the universal efficaciousness of God's will (133-135). With this, however, Tanner surrenders a central premise of her otherwise determinist account of God as Creator.

40. Stump, "Aquinas on the Sufferings of Job," 348.

41. Authors as diverse as Terry Tilley and Judith Shklar suggest that we need to be weened from the theoretical gratifications of theodicy as tending cruelly to underestimate the scope and gravity of human suffering and injustice. There is no theodicy in this life, in the sense of proof of the *truth* of God's goodness given the reality of evil, even if there can be a defense of the *coherence* of religious faith that begins with the experience of *caritas*. See Tilley's *The Evils of Theodicy*, esp. ch. 9; and Shklar's *Ordinary Vices* (Cambridge: Harvard University Press, 1984), esp. ch. 1, and *The Faces of Injustice* (New Haven: Yale University Press, 1990), esp. ch. 2. Tilley frequently criticizes Austin Farrer as a dismissive theodicist who does not heed the warning of Job (e.g., pp. 89, 229, 233, and 245), but these judgments tend to be too harsh. Farrer is well aware of what he calls "Job's agony," and he explicitly acknowledges that "the value of speculative answers (to the riddle of providence and evil), however judicious, is limited... the substance of truth is grasped not by argument, but by faith." See Farrer, *Love Almighty and Ills Unlimited* (London and Glasgow: Wm. Collins Sons, 1962), 186-187.

42. This phrase, "since the good of human beings is charity," is from Thomas's "Commentary on Romans," quoted by Stump, p. 337.

43. This account does not leave Christianity with an impotent Deity incapable of acting in history, a *mere* fellow sufferer. There are two reasons for this: (1) God has acted decisively in time in the person of Jesus Christ, and (2) the inspiration of the Holy Spirit, when freely accepted, continues to empower individuals to do what would otherwise be impossible for them. It would not be compatible with true love, however, for God to compel particular actions by finite agents. In kenotic self-

limitation, God has created free creatures and thereby partially bound the divine will.

44. Stump, "Aquinas on the Sufferings of Job," 352 and 354.

45. Stump also embraces this broadly pedagogical view, albeit "with considerable diffidence;" see her "The Problem of Evil," in *Faith and Philosophy*, vol. 1, no. 2 (April 1983): 410.

46. I borrow the idea of pain "unmaking one's humanity" from Elaine Scarry, *The Body in Pain* (Oxford: Oxford University Press, 1985).

47. On these matters, see Thomas F. Tracy, "Victimization and the Problem of Evil: A Response to Ivan Karamazov," in *Faith and Philosophy*, vol. 9, no. 3 (July 1992): 301-319.

48. For more on the justice and mercy of God, see my "Is God Just?," in *Faith and Philosophy*, vol. 12, no. 3 (July 1996): 386-399.

49. Thomas writes: "Individuals...which undergo corruption, are not ordained as it were chiefly for the good of the universe, but in a secondary way, inasmuch as the good of the species is preserved through them" (ST, I, Q. 23, art. 7). This "not...chiefly" must be cold comfort for the reprobate. However biblical the language, to call some persons "vessels of wrath," created infallibly for destruction, is to deny that they are carriers of the *Imago*.

50. In *Providence and Predestination*, Questions 5 and 6 of *De Veritate*, trans. by Robert W. Mulligan, S.J. (South Bend: Gateway, 1961), Aquinas calls predestination one of providence's "parts" (100), even though it technically differs from both providence and election. "Providence...is concerned only with the ordering to the end. Consequently, by God's providence, all men are ordered to beatitude. But predestination is also concerned with the outcome or result of this ordering, and, therefore, it is related only to those who will attain heavenly glory" (101). Election, in turn, is a "prerequisite of predestination," "the choice (of God) by which he who is directed to the end infallibly is separated from others who are not ordained to it in the same manner" (102). I have mainly ignored these fine distinctions as irrelevant to my discussion of *Summa Theologiae* and *The Literal Exposition on Job*. Even in Question 5 of *De Veritate*, however, Thomas uses the familiar language of "permission:" "... since evil does not come from God, it does not fall under His providence of approval, but falls only under His providence of permission" (35). This language (and its critique) is not irrelevant to my purposes.

51. Aquinas, *The Literal Exposition on Job*, 146; emphasis added.

52. Ibid., 154; emphasis added.

53. Stump, "Aquinas on the Sufferings of Job," 350-351.

54. Aquinas, *The Literal Exposition on Job*, 149.

55. See, e.g., Ibid., 225-231.

56. Ibid., 228.

57. Good, "Job," in *Harper's Bible Commentary*, 415. See also *In Turns of Tempest* (206-207, 240-241), where Good argues that Job denies immortality and even longs for death in places, seeing it as freedom and rest, even as "liberation from the god" (207). It is worth noting, in passing, that the single place in the Old Testament where resurrection is clearly proclaimed is the "Book of Daniel" (12:2), which postdates "Job" by over 600 years, at a minimum.

58. Aquinas, *The Literal Exposition on Job*, 230.

59. Thomas even seems to flirt with the natural immortality of the soul: "Now the power of each corporeal creature is determined for finite effects, but the power of free will is directed toward infinite actions. Hence, this very fact attests to the power of the soul to last into infinity." See Aquinas, *Literal Exposition*, 231. He is truer to his deepest insights when he talks instead of "the *hope* of restoration" possible only "through *divine* power" (Ibid., 229-230; emphases added).

60. See Bernard Anderson, *Understanding the Old Testament* (Englewood Cliffs: Prentice-Hall, 1975), 548-560; Marvin Pope, *Anchor Bible Commentary on Job* (Garden City: Doubleday, 1973); and Gerhard von Rad, *Wisdom in Israel*, trans. by James D. Martin (New York: Abingdon, 1973).

61. What of original sin? The literature on this topic is immense, and I cannot begin to recapitulate Aquinas's views here. I would only suggest that even original sin is best understood as a universal disposition to evil, made all but irresistible by preexisting social structures, lest morality be exploded by fatalism. This is not to say that anyone is actually perfect in this life, only that "the fault lies not in our stars (or in our parents) but in ourselves."

62. The case of "Genie," the so-called "Wild Child" documented by PBS, may be a case in point. For her first ten years, Genie was so neglected and abused by her parents (locked in a room alone and tied to a potty-chair for weeks at a time, seldom spoken to, even less often held, etc.) that she never learned to speak or to interact with others on anything but a primitive level. See Nova, "Secret of a Wild Child" (WGBH/Boston, 1994).

63. For an excellent discussion of the "disinterestedness" of Job's religion, see Gustavo Gutierrez, *On Job*, 4-6 and 70-71.

64. Cf. Kant's moral argument for the immortality of the soul and the existence of God. Because duty requires perfection and we cannot become perfect in this brief physical life, Kant reasons, we must assume immortality as the realm of perpetual progress toward holiness. (If there were no immortality, then "ought" would not imply "can," and moral

perfection would be unintelligible.) Only an omnipotent and omnibenevolent Deity can guarantee an afterlife for creatures, however, thus we must also assume the existence of such a Being. This is a practical proof, Kant insists, not a matter of speculative knowledge; God and immortality are conceptual requirements of ethics, "postulates of pure practical reason," rather than inductive conclusions from empirical evidence. See Kant, *Critique of Practical Reason*, trans. by Lewis White Beck (Indiana and New York: Bobbs-Merrill, 1956), Pt. I, Book II, ch. IV and V, 126-136.

As I define it, strong agape treats God's love as the primary content of and criterion for moral uprightness, rather than as an external incentive for moral behavior. Practical rationality cannot be uncoupled from divine charity if we are to have an adequate picture of human goodness. Thus strong agape amounts to the sort of "theological morality" Kant rejects. Kant favors a "moral theology" that begins with "duties (man) finds grounded in his own nature" and derives religion from these alone. See Immanuel Kant, *Lectures on Philosophical Theology*, trans. by Allen W. Wood and Gertrude M. Clark (Ithaca: Cornel University Press, 1991), 31 and 40-42. Nevertheless, Christians may still have something to learn from the Master of Konigsbery about God, freedom, and immortality. Kantian insights help deliver us from determinism concerning the will and dogmatism concerning an afterlife, for example. Concerning the latter, Allen Wood has remarked that "in Reflection 8101, Kant describes faith in immortality as 'faith of the second rank' and suggests that it may not be necessary to the moral life after all (*Gesammelte Schriften*, vol. 19, 644)." See *Lectures on Philosophical Theology*, footnote #20, 131.

65. Portions of this and the following paragraph are drawn from my "The Disconsolation of Theology," 21 and 27.

66. Shklar, *The Faces of Injustice*, 32-33.

67. Austin Farrer presumes that God will "rescue" rational persons from "destruction," insisting that "(t)here is no getting round death...all we can hope for is resurrection." But Farrer also writes: "How God is to remake us is necessarily unimaginable to us...What God will do for us is God's secret; that he will do it is our faith. It is no part of our business in this book to prove that God raises the dead." Farrer, *Love Almighty and Ills Unlimited*, 182 and 110-111.

68. Quoted by Stump, "Aquinas on the Sufferings of Job," 352.

69. Gustavo Gutierrez allows that "the Christian profession of faith in a future life does not essentially alter the point the poet (who authored the "Book of Job") was trying to make." See Gutierrez, *On Job*, 89. I agree. I would add, nevertheless, that the "Book of Job," in turn, keeps Christians honest by forcing them to confront suffering and mortality.

Reductionist accounts of religion as centrally motivated by the fear or denial of death find their counterexample in Job. Love and gratitude are the wellsprings of his witness, not avoidance.

70. Tilley levels this charge specifically at Austin Farrer (see *The Evils of Theodicy*, 229). The accusation is unfair, however. Farrer repeatedly drives home the extent of human misery and the insidiousness of human sin, as the title of his relevant work suggests. See *Love Almighty and Ills Unlimited*, 114-120, 166-167, and 178-179, for instance.

71. This is not to say that one must self-consciously believe in God in order to be loving, though it seems to help in some cases. Obviously many atheists and agnostics display charity for their fellows, and this constitutes real moral worth. A theological version of strong agape does imply, however, that even putatively "humanistic" virtues are in fact causally sustained (though not necessitated) by divinity. Loving atheists just do not give credit where credit is due.

72. Shklar, *The Faces of Injustice*, 58-60.

73. The Wiesel quotations in this paragraph are from *Night*, trans. by Stella Rodway (New York: Bantam Books, 1982), 61-62 and 32. It once seemed possible to read the quoted passages as approximating a Jewish death of God theology, but Wiesel's recent "A Prayer for the Days of Awe" gainsays this reading after the fact. The silence and apparent absence of God during the Holocaust remain vexing—"Auschwitz must and will forever remain a question mark only"—but Wiesel writes: "What about my faith in you, Master of the Universe? I now realize I never lost it, not even over there, during the darkest hours of my life." See *The New York Times*, October 2, 1997, A15.

74. I wish to thank an anonymous reviewer for *The Thomist* for extremely helpful suggestions about how to improve this essay. My gratitude also goes to the following careful readers: Nicholas Fotion, James Gustafson, Eleonore Stump, and John Witte.

Chapter 12

Plato and Augustine on Doing Wrong Knowingly

Margaret Falls-Corbitt

How is it that we come to do wrong? What is it in us that goes wrong when we choose to do wrong? Plato maintains that anyone who does a wrong actually intended to do good and that what went wrong was a failure in knowledge. Had the person known what was actually good, she would not have done the wrong. On the other hand, Augustine speaks of stealing a pear out of a certain love for doing wrong. Had he *not* known it was wrong, he would not have done it.

Augustine never claims that all cases of wrongdoing are like this theft, but he opposes Plato by asserting that there are at least some cases of agents knowingly doing wrong. Wrongdoing is at least sometimes a problem of the will and not of knowledge; whereas Plato views all wrongdoing as a problem of knowledge. This essay is an attempt to be clearer about exactly what is at stake in asserting one position over the other, Plato's or Augustine's.

After offering an explanation of Plato's position, I turn to Augustine and show that he neither merely talks past Plato nor falls into a merely semantic debate with him. I then argue that the two conceptions of wrongdoing reflect differences in the two philosophers' understanding of both the soul and the nature of the Highest Good. These two general differences involve issues related to how we conceive the cognitive and practical faculties of the soul and whether we describe the Highest Good as personal or nonpersonal. Based on these differences, I end the essay with a brief remark about sin, a primarily theological understanding of wrongdoing.

Plato: *Wrongdoing as a Lack of Moral Knowledge*

There are, of course, a number of ways in which ignorance can lead to doing acts which are wrong, and even Augustine would grant that any one of these can, and sometimes does, occur. One class of wrongful acts would be those resulting from *unwillful ignorance about relevant particulars* such as when a junior high teacher, despite commendable efforts to get to the bottom of things, punishes an innocent bystander for the ill deed of another. A second class would be wrongful acts which result from *a misjudgment of consequences*, as when we harm loved ones though genuinely believing that we are helping them, based on reasonable evidence at hand. A third category of wrong acts would be those which result from a *failure of moral knowledge*. In such cases, the agents fail to grasp the wrongfulness of their acts, as when a citizen cannot see anything wrong with lying on income tax returns or when an adulterer cannot keep in mind persuasive moral reasons for not betraying the spouse.

As we shall see below, the controversy with Augustine arises because Plato reduces all wrongdoing to a combination of the second and third categories of wrong acts. That is, he blames all wrongdoing on a kind of failure to accurately judge the consequences of our acts but ultimately links this failure to a lack of moral knowledge.

In the *Apology* Socrates must defend himself against the charge that he is punishable for corrupting the young. He does so by arguing that even if he has corrupted the young, he must have done so unintentionally since no one does wrong willingly. In *Plato's Meno*, when the debate is over the proper definition of "virtue," Socrates is again found arguing that no one willing does wrong. The basic structure behind both arguments is as follows:

1. No one willingly harms himself.
2. Harming another harms oneself.
3. Therefore, no one willingly harms another.

We can glean from this argument a major mistake in reasoning which Socrates believes wrongdoers make. They think that they can harm someone else without harming themselves, and thus they mistakenly believe that harming others produces the good of taking care of oneself. The knowledge they lack is of premise 2, an ethico-metaphysical principle to which Socrates was firmly committed. For Socrates this is an article of knowledge, and thus he concludes that the problem with wrongdoers is that they lack relevant knowledge and in their ignorance about the real consequences of their acts cannot do what they truly will to do. On this reasoning, all wrongdoing is covered by the second category given above, i.e., the perpetrators of harm to others just do not understand the real consequences of their acts, namely misery and injury to self.

Filling out this Socratic understanding of wrongdoing with Plato's conception of the soul and the Good as found in the *Republic*, we shall see that this misjudgment of wrongdoing's consequences for the self results, according to Plato, from a failure to know the Good, the highest Good by virtue of which all other goods must be understood and evaluated.

Plato sees the world as rationally ordered, and he makes it clear in the *Republic* that this was tantamount to claiming two things: the diverse parts form a harmonious unity and they do so insofar as they are ordered in accordance with the Form of the Good. What holds for the world, holds for the soul; it is capable of rational ordering in accordance with its knowledge of the Good. The soul by nature seeks this knowledge and harmonious order. Speaking of the things that "really are good" as opposed to those that "merely seem to be so," Socrates says in the *Republic*, "This every soul pursues, and all its actions are done for its sake" (VI, 505e).

Without knowledge of the Good, the nature of true self-fulfillment and true self-harm go undetected. For without that knowledge, the innate desires for physical satisfaction, self-protection, honor, and glory are untempered by the appropriate sense of their place in the good life. The soul therefore seeks to achieve them in inappropriate ways to inordinate degrees.

This unknowledgeable and therefore misguided search for fulfillment of otherwise good desires is the only way the soul can harm itself. Since the cause of this harm is the soul's attempt to fulfill legitimate needs without knowledge of their true nature, this injury to self is not intentional. Furthermore, this state of disharmony and unfulfillment within the soul is both cause and effect of discordant relationships with other people (IV and VI, 500c). Any wrongful act, according to Plato, simply is an act that leaves the soul at odds with itself, disharmonious and less capable of achieving the knowledge and goodness it seeks. Hence, injury to another is harm that one unwillingly inflicts upon oneself due to false belief about the nature of the Good, i.e., to a failure of moral knowledge.

As this whirlwind tour of the *Republic* shows, what I find underpinning the argument from the *Meno* and the *Apology* is a conception of the relationship between rational activity and activity for the sake of the good. For Plato, denying that the soul desires the good would mean denying that it is capable of rational activity because he does not distinguish rational activity from activity in accordance with the Good.

This link upon which he insists is quite plausible. After all, activity that is not activity for the best conceivable reasons just is not rational activity. An agent incapable of acting for the sake of the greatest good she can conceive is an agent incapable of practical rational activity.

But this is not enough for the Platonic conception of wrongdoing to stand. Capacity is not necessity, and it would seem that Plato's notion that we always act for the sake of what we consider good holds only if it is the case that an agent who is capable of rational activity *necessarily* does what she conceives to be the greatest good at the time. Plato's fuller defense of this position lies in his depiction of reason and reason's nonrational competitors in the soul.

Reason and reason's competitors, the appetitive and spirited, are all desires, according to Plato, and it is their objects that distinguish them one from another. The appetitive is desire for physical fulfillment; the spirited, I would argue, is desire for due attention, protection, and honor. Both the *Republic* and the *Symposium* depict reason as the desire for truth and knowledge of the Good.[1] The reason for this, I believe, is that human behavior for Plato is fundamentally teleological.

The soul is fundamentally a "going after" this or that. Desire, variously called passion or eros, seems to be the ontological category which Plato has for this innate orientation toward ends. Having determined this, Plato further maintains that the natural end of each fundamental kind of innate desire is some good, something which in due proportion and in its proper place really is good—knowledge of the Good itself (reason's end), the proper respect and honor of the soul as a whole (spirited's end), and physical well-being (appetite's end; IV 436b to end and IX. 581b and 586d-e).

On this view, there is no such thing as not doing what one desires, since desire is the only motivational force in the soul, and there is no desire that does not aim at some kind of good. Therefore, the position Plato needs to defend is defended: a person always acts for the sake of the greatest good he can perceive at the time.

Someone might suggest that this line of reasoning does not successfully show that a wrongdoer did what she perceived to be the greatest good because it might be that the rational part of his soul knew better—conceived a greater good—but was simply overpowered by the appetitive or spirited part. However, Plato rejects this. Reason can be overpowered only because it lacks knowledge and has only opinions that are not "tied down" by knowledge of the Forms. Without sure knowledge, reason lacks the power of persuasion on the side of the true Good, while the other parts are certain and adamant about "the good" they seek. Thus, the person's highest conception of the good is rather low, and that is what she does.

If we join Plato in allowing into the soul only desires for things conceived to be good, then it seems we will have to grant that rational agents always do what they conceive to be the greatest good at the time. Why, however, should we so limit the makeup of the soul? Why does Plato so conceive it? I suggest two answers.

(1) Were Plato to acknowledge a desire that could be a desire for something intrinsically bad, then he would be positing a soul inherently at odds with itself—desiring both good and bad—and inherently incapable of unified rational order. For Plato, at least, this is inconceivable given the assumptions that reality is rationally ordered and that the true nature of each thing is established in accordance with the Good.

(2) That the soul, conceived as a set of desires, can still have only desires for perceived goods may also follow from the nature or structure of desire itself. Again in both the *Republic* and the *Symposium*, the soul's relationship to its objects is that of desiring to possess them, to be in their presence or to take them into itself. This wanting-for-oneself seems equivalent to a declaration that the object of desire is worth having, valuable for the purposes at hand, or in other words, good. I am suggesting that, on Plato's view, the very structure of desire is to declare its object good. To desire something is to think of that something as good. Of course, we can struggle over our desires and doubt that they are ultimately good, but this is because we also experience competing desires, and competing desires are alternate visions of what is good. Once we settle on following a particular desire, however, we necessarily are declaring the satisfaction of that desire more worthwhile than the conceived alternatives.

Augustine: Knowingly Doing Wrong

In Book II of his *Confessions* Augustine searches out a motive for his youthful theft of the pears. He initially claims to find no motive except the delight he took in wrongdoing:

> ...I was willing to steal, and steal I did, although I was not compelled by any lack, unless it were the lack of a sense of justice or a distaste for what was right and a greedy love of doing wrong. For of what I stole I already had plenty...I had no wish to enjoy the things I coveted by stealing, but only to enjoy the theft itself and the sin. (2. 4. 9)

In examining whether this could indeed be the best interpretation of his act he acknowledges the popularity of a Platonic interpretation of wrongdoing:

> When, then there is an inquiry to discover why a crime has been com-

mitted, normally no one is satisfied until it has been shown that the
motive might have been either the desire of gaining, or the fear of losing,
one of those good things which I said were of the lowest order...So even
Catiline did not love crime for crime's sake. (2. 5.11)

But in the final analysis Augustine is unwilling to give his own thievery
the more gracious Platonic interpretation typically granted even to
Catiline. He stands by his initial judgment that the theft of the pears was
an act of gratuitous evil: "I loved nothing in it except the thieving,
though I cannot truly speak of that as a 'thing'" (2.8.16).

From the above discussion of Plato we could imagine that Plato's
counsel to Augustine would take one of two routes. (1) Using Socrates'
argument from the *Meno*, Plato would suggest to Augustine that he
acted in ignorance of the harm he was bringing to himself. He must not
have known that wronging a neighbor harms oneself otherwise he could
not have done the act because he could not willingly harm himself. (2)
Plato would offer Augustine the comfort that he must not really have
known that stealing was wrong; he only thought he knew. What he mistook for knowledge was a mere belief not secured before the mind's eye
by sound reasoning and hence subject to dismissal by a soul vitally
interested in something else. But Augustine explicitly rejects both interpretations of his experience.

"It is certain, O Lord, that theft is punished by your law, the law that
is written in men's hearts and cannot be erased however sinful they are"
(II, 4, 47). Here Augustine accepts responsibility for knowing that stealing is wrong. Even our corrupted condition due to original sin does not
hide from us such basic truths about God's law. A lapse in moral knowledge shall not be his excuse.

As for his assessment of the consequences which his act held for his
own well-being, Augustine's writing suggests that he believed doing the
wrong meant toying with his own destruction and that this belief only
added to the wrongdoing's enticement:

> I loved my own perdition and my own faults, not the things for which I
> committed wrong, but the wrong itself. My soul was vicious and broke
> away from your safe keeping to seek its own destruction, looking for no
> profit in disgrace but only for disgrace itself. (II, 4, 47)

Had he not believed that stealing the pears was wrong and self-destructive, Augustine says, he would have been without motivation for com-
mitting the theft.

There remains the possibility that Augustine and Plato are only dif-
fering over words. Insofar as he desired and anticipated joy in wrong-

doing, Augustine at the time must have seen doing the wrong as the good he most wanted to pursue. Such is certainly the interpretation suggested by the Platonic theory of desire. In desiring the sin and his soul's disgrace, Augustine mistakenly judged these to be the highest good for him at the time. There appears, then, to be only a semantic difference between Plato's position that we do what we do because we think it is good and Augustine's claim that we can do wrong for the sake of doing wrong. It seems we do wrong for the sake of doing wrong because we think doing wrong is in and of itself good.

Augustine would not accept that only a semantic difference separates his depiction of wrongdoing from Plato's. What Augustine goes out of his way to explain is that he felt no desire for any of the possible benefits that stealing the pears might procure him; thus his thievery was not a case of the appetites demanding their goods over and against reason's predilections. On Plato's theory, when the nonrational parts of the soul misdirect reason into following their lead, they are pursuing what they think is their fulfillment and good. These nonrational desires have their sights on something that is good from their perspective. They are not singularly the desire to reject whatever reason would censor if left to its own opinions and power.

The immediate object of intention for the spirited or appetitive element in the Platonic soul is some good other than the mere rejection of reason's proposed good. But the immediate object of Augustine's desire is the rejection of the moral good his intellect proposes and knows. In other words, for Augustine but not Plato we can make the wrong itself the intentional object of our desire, the thing loved–and yes, our declared good. Between loving the sin and loving its perceived benefits there is a difference of substance, not just semantics.

The difference actually receives amplification in a passage which might easily be mistaken for a Platonic twist to Augustine's introspection upon this matter:

> What was it, then, that pleased me in that act of theft? Which of my Lord's powers did I imitate in a perverse and wicked way? Since I had no real power to break his law, was it that I enjoyed the pretense of doing so, like a prisoner who creates for himself the illusion of liberty by doing something wrong, when he has no fear of punishment, under a feeble hallucination of power? (II, 6, 50)

Here Augustine seems to light upon a conceivable good which he sought in doing wrong, namely participation in a freedom and power that are rightfully God's alone. But this perceived good is not a benefit of the sin; it is the sin. The creature's pitiable grasping after equality with God constitutes its sin against God. If this is what pleased him about the theft, then it is one and the same with loving the sin, but under this new description it accentuates what we said above. For here, Augustine discloses his love for the sin as the human capacity knowingly and willfully to defy God's power, moral righteousness, and authority. This knowledgeable defiance of what is known to be the Good is exactly what Plato found inconceivable.

Underlying Differences: The Makeup of the Soul and the Nature of the Good

In this section I shall argue that underlying Plato's and Augustine's opposing views of wrongdoing are disparate conceptions of the soul's faculties and of the nature of the Highest Good. What I intend to show is how Augustine's conception of the soul, of the Highest Good and of wrongdoing hang together and how Plato's conceptions of the same three things hang together. "Hang together" is an intentionally logically loose term.

I shall not be arguing that each man's view of wrongdoing is necessitated by his view of the soul and the Good. I only wish to show supporting connections among their conceptions and how shifts away from a Platonic conception of the soul and the Good open the door to Augustine's reasoning about our capacity to knowingly do wrong.

Let us begin with the two men's conceptions of the soul. I argued above that Plato represented the teleological function of all three parts of the soul as desire, such that even reason is a desire for truth. That is why for him, to know the good is to do the good. Reason loves wisdom such that its search for knowledge of the Good Itself is at one and the same time a passion for being in its presence. Thus we cannot know the Good Itself without desiring it; that is, we cannot know it yet deny it its rightful place in shaping our decisions.

Augustine makes really two shifts away from Plato's conception of the soul. First, the intellect for him is a faculty of perception separate from the soul's teleological or practical faculty, its faculty for "going after" and "bringing to oneself." Second, Augustine conceives the soul's practical faculty as "will" rather than desire. Both changes open the door to conceiving the possibility that we might know the good but refuse to follow it.

Since, on Augustine's interpretation, the intellect is a faculty of cognition but not of either desire or will, we can intellectually grasp our moral duty but not desire to do it or will it (Gilson, 77). Reason can be persuaded of the soul's moral duty and this not be sufficient to engage the will; whereas this option is not open to Plato since for him reason is a kind of desire, and indeed a wholly determinative desire when functioning properly.

The shift from "desire" to "will" as the soul's teleological function also allows a shift in interpretation of experience because, as I shall explain, the will has a sort of evaluative neutrality that desire does not. I argued above that, from Plato's perspective, we always do what we perceive to be good because we always do what we desire and whatever we desire we perceive as good. But the connection between "willing X" and "perceiving X to be good" is not as strong. This is suggested by ways which we would and would not feel comfortable speaking.

For example, I can will for or against something, but it is odd to speak of desiring against something. Admittedly, when one wills against something one is willing *for* its not coming to be or its not playing a role. The fact remains, however, that desiring is always most appropriately accompanied by "for;" whereas "willing" works equally well with "for" or "against," suggesting that will, more easily than desire, can be viewed as a capacity for going against, for rejecting. This being so, the connection between the soul's practical faculty being motivated and the soul perceiving something as good (as worthy of going after) is broken.

If the soul's practical faculty is conceived of as desire, then it rejects something as bad only relative to something else being perceived as good, or all things considered desirable; whereas a soul that is understood to have a will can simply reject without that which it rejects being measured against a perceived good. If the soul can simply will-against without declaring the object of its will good, then the door is open to thinking of the soul as capable of acting for the sake of something other than a thing's goodness. If I have been right to suggest that the linguistic connection between desiring X and declaring X good lends support to Plato's conception of wrongdoing, then the introduction of will, as opposed to desire, as the soul's practical faculty at least opens the door to—but does not necessitate—conceiving the possibility that the soul would simply will against any conceivable good.

In addition to Plato's conception of desire and of reason as desire, we above noted two further things about his reasoning concerning the soul. One was that Plato could not allow into the soul an outright desire for bad because that would leave the soul inherently at odds with itself, and hence incapable of ultimate unity and rational ordering. The second was that, for Plato, all human action succumbs to rational explanation and it is not rational to do what one thinks is bad. Augustine accepts the first but foregoes the second.

Augustine no more than Plato posits an evil will inherently opposed to a good will. A soul has only one will and it is inherently capable of ordered unity in blessed relationship with God. This one will nonetheless is mutable, can turn away from God, and in doing so makes itself bad. To the question "But what makes it turn if not an evil will?", Augustine responds simply that there is no efficient cause of a bad will (413/1950, 12, 6-8).

For Plato this turning away from the known good would require rational explanation and there can be no rational explanation for not willing the known good over the known bad. Thus, Plato's wrongdoer reasons ineffectively and yet still does something rationally explicable: he chooses the good as he understands it. For Augustine, the will just turns away. There is no positive or substantial cause which can be identified. There is only the will's lack and mutability, but this is no explanation since to point to the will's lack is simply to reaffirm its capacity to turn away from the known good.

Augustine is not being irresponsibly obscurantist. There just can be no rational explanation for not choosing the highest good we can conceive. It is in essence an irrational act, and Augustine, unlike Plato, is willing to live with the fact that the soul just does initiate irrational, inexplicable behavior.

Thus far in this section we have been discussing differences which underlie the two philosophers' views of wrongdoing and which are primarily related to how the two conceive the soul and its capacity for practical activity. A second major area of difference lies in how each conceives the nature of the highest good.

Plato conceives the highest good as an abstract formal principle. Augustine conceives it as God, a Divine Person. A relationship between persons is quite different from an individual's "relationship" to principles. Most important for a discussion of whether we can knowingly reject the good is the fact that what goes on when we reject a principle is quite different from what goes on when we reject a person.

Resentment is one form which our rejection of another person takes, but it would surely be odd to resent a principle. Principles are the sorts of things whose correctness and appropriateness for a given circumstance one either recognizes or fails to recognize. When a principle is seen to apply to a particular situation, even if the agent wished it did not, it makes no sense to cast ill feelings upon the principle. One does not resent *them* nor their "authority," since their only authority in themselves comes from one having recognized their validity. However, not only do we resent persons and their authority over us, we especially resent their having moral authority over us, and we can resent this authority even while agreeing with them about what our moral duty is.

In fact, it is cases of just this kind that seem to me to be primary candidates for falling under Augustine's category of knowingly doing wrong. For example, I firmly believe that we ought always to respect persons as ends in themselves. I believe that this is a beautiful and good principle, a correct guide for human conduct, even if sometimes difficult to understand and apply. My greatest temptations to violate this principle are occasions when I do not want the person whom I must in that particular instance respect to be the one who "holds me to it." In such cases I do not reject the validity of the principle but will that it shall not apply to my relationship with this person at this time. I take my duty to follow the principle as a case of this person having a kind of authority over me in that this very person is the one towards whom I must show respect. I do not so much turn intellectually against the principle as will not to do my duty towards this person.

Thinking about resentment, moral duty, and persons as we just have helps us see a major relevant difference between familiar attitudes toward principles and equally familiar attitudes toward persons. When we have good and sufficient reasons for believing that an abstract formal principle is true and applies to our situation, there is not much else that can be said about the principle; there is nothing in our "relationship" to the principle to motivate anything but acceptance of it. Thus, an agent is especially incomprehensible who would declare that a certain principle is an indubitably good and appropriate guide for him to follow in his circumstances yet at the very same time would refuse to follow it.

But not so incomprehensible, and in fact well within our experience, is the agent who acknowledges that another person asks of him only what is indubitably good and appropriate yet also declares that he will not have that person telling him how to behave. Indeed, we can have good and sufficient reasons for believing that a person loves us, cares only for our good and even knows our good, yet reject a relationship with that person. We can even resent that that person understands us so well; we can resent, oddly enough, their goodness and their desire to bring that goodness to bear upon who we are and what we do.

This is exactly what Augustine seems to have said about God and what Plato denies about the Good. We can have good and sufficient reasons for believing that God is, that God loves us, that God cares only for our good and knows what that good is, and yet we can turn from God and reject God's will for us. I am arguing that Augustine's having envisioned the highest good as a person opens a door that would have been harder for Plato to open so long as he retains the abstract formal nature of the Good.

I do not wish to maintain that anyone who believes that we can do wrong knowingly must also be a theist. I am arguing that a certain set of beliefs hold together well, mutually support one another, and serve as partial explanation as to why Augustine was willing to posit at the bottom of human wrongdoing the possibility of an inexplicable act, namely, turning from the highest conceivable good.

And do notice that shunning the authority of the Highest Good Person is still as rationally inexplicable as affirming that a given principle is undeniably the best to follow but not following it. What conceivably compelling reason can be given for refusing the dictates of One we firmly believe is all wise and all loving? There is no more rational justification for disobeying a perfectly good and loving ruler than there is for not following what our own reason tells us is unquestionably best. Thus, Augustine, unlike Plato, still leaves the "turning away" as an inexplicable event, as if to rationally explain it would be to justify it.

Although defying the will of an All Loving, All Knowing, Perfectly Good Person is technically just as irrational as violating the dictates of one's own reason, the former allows the interplay of a motive that the other does not. It does not threaten our autonomy to follow an abstract principle whose rightness our own reason can grasp. But obeying a Person who asks us, out of respect and love, to follow that principle can appear to threaten our autonomy. It gives us an Other whose authority we can resent, despite the irrationality of doing so. Plato's Form of the Good does not give us the will of an Other to oppose or to obey.

Conclusion

In this paper I have argued that four non-Platonic elements of Augustine's philosophy underlie and support his opposition to Plato on the question of whether we can knowingly do wrong. These four are: (1) Augustine's separation of the soul's cognitive and practical faculties; (2) his conception of the soul's practical function as will, as opposed to desire; (3) his willingness to accept that wrongdoing of a certain kind is at bottom inexplicable; (4) his envisioning of that highest good, whom we can know but defy, as a person rather than as an abstract principle.

Perhaps the difference between Plato and Augustine is the difference between doing wrong morally and the theological notion of "being in sin." Sin is more than the performance of wrongful acts; it is a condition we are in. And it is a particular kind of condition, namely, the condition of being in willful broken relationship to the Eternal Divine *Person*. This is what Augustine's configuration of beliefs affirms and Plato's cannot.

Notes

1. This is virtually the thesis of Socrates's speech in the *Symposium*. For a discussion of reason as desire in the *Republic* see V, 475e, 480 and VI, 485d, especially.

References

Saint Augustine. 413. *The City of God.* Trans. Marcus Dods. New York: Modern Library, 1950..

_____. 401. *Confessions.* Trans. R.S.Pine-Coffin. New York: Penguin Books, 1961.

Etienne Gilson. 1954. *History of Christian Philosophy in the Middle Ages.* New York:Random House.

Plato. 1961a. *Apology.* Trans. Hugh Tredennick. In *The Collected Dialogues*, ed. Edith Hamilton. New York: Pantheon Books.

_____. 1961b. *Plato's Symposium.* Trans. Michael Joyce. *The Collected Dialogues*, ed. Edith Hamilton. New York: Pantheon Books.

_____. 1974. *Plato's Republic.* Trans. G.M.A Grube. Indianapolis, Ind.: Hackett Publishing Co.

_____. 1976. *Plato's Meno.* Trans. G.M.A. Grube. Indianapolis, Ind.: Hackett Publishing Co.

Index

wrongdoing, 253, 258-59, 262, 263, 264

Banesians, 42

Bañez, Dominic, 1, 2, 20, 22, 25, 29, 36n.79

Behaviorism, 124, 127

Bellarmine, St. Robert, 44

Berkeley, George, 157

Burrell, David, 247n.32

Calvin, John

    predestination, 55,62-63n.2

    vs. antinomians, 57

causality, 153

Churchland, Paul, 125

compatibilism, v, ix, 3-4, 15, 18-19, 23-25, 27-30, 33-34n.49, 35n.67,

    39n.94, 41, 60, 76-77, 122, 170, 181, 221-22, 246n.19,

    247n.32

    See also Aquinas, Dennett, and Mackie

Conti, Charles, 108, 112, 114, 118n.17, 119n.23

Created effects, 20-24

    See also Aquinas and Lonergan

creation *ex nihilo*, 116

    See also Farrer

creative fidelity, 228

elicited motivational states, 171-75, 185-86n.9, n.10, n.12

eliminative materialism, 126

Erasmus, viii, 51, 71-72

  grace, 71-72

  See also Luther

eschatological freedom, 184

eschatological perfectionism, 221-22, 234, 240

evil, problem of, vi, ix, 25, 27-28, 35n.67, 217, 233

  defeasibility, 218, 243n.4

  evidential argument, 167

  logical argument, 167

  moral, 27, 170, 231

  natural, 168-69, 231

  See also Aquinas

Falls-Corbitt, Margaret, x

Farrer, Austin, vi-vii, 61, 85

  action-patterns, 128-29

  Aristotilian leaven, 99-100

  artistic creativity (author analogy), 91

  Assyrian aggression, 139

  connaturality, 134-35, 159

  creation *ex nihilo*, 103-104

  determinism, 157-58